PRODIGAL NATION

ANDREW R. MURPHY

PRODIGAL NATION

*Moral Decline and Divine
Punishment from
New England to 9/11*

OXFORD

UNIVERSITY PRESS

2009

OXFORD
UNIVERSITY PRESS

Oxford University Press, Inc., publishes works that further
Oxford University's objective of excellence
in research, scholarship, and education.

Oxford New York
Auckland Cape Town Dar es Salaam Hong Kong Karachi
Kuala Lumpur Madrid Melbourne Mexico City Nairobi
New Delhi Shanghai Taipei Toronto

With offices in
Argentina Austria Brazil Chile Czech Republic France Greece
Guatemala Hungary Italy Japan Poland Portugal Singapore
South Korea Switzerland Thailand Turkey Ukraine Vietnam

Published by Oxford University Press, Inc.
198 Madison Avenue, New York, New York 10016

www.oup.com

Oxford is a registered trademark of Oxford University Press

Library of Congress Cataloging-in-Publication Data
Murphy, Andrew R., [date]
Prodigal nation : moral decline and divine punishment
from New England to 9/11 / Andrew R. Murphy.
p. cm.
Includes bibliographical references and index.
ISBN 978-0-19-532128-9
1. Jeremiads—United States—History and criticism.
2. Christianity and politics—United States—History. I. Title.
BR517.M87 2009
973—dc22   2008026673

1 3 5 7 9 8 6 4 2
Printed in the United States of America
on acid-free paper

FOR BETH

Acknowledgments

I N SOME WAYS, *Prodigal Nation* looks quite different from the project—then entitled "Narratives of Decline in the History of Political Thought"—that the National Endowment for the Humanities awarded a Summer Stipend nearly ten years ago. Nonetheless, this book grew (more or less) organically out of those early inquiries. It began to assume its present form during a 2000–2002 visiting fellowship at the Martin Marty Center of the University of Chicago Divinity School. At the Marty Center, I was fortunate to participate in seminars coordinated by Professors Clark Gilpin, Frank Reynolds, and William Schweiker, and what had been a relatively wide-ranging series of explorations in the rhetoric of decline across time and place began to take shape as a more focused account of a specifically *American* way of talking about such issues. Needless to say, the events of September 11, 2001, which fell almost exactly at the halfway point of my time at Chicago, certainly influenced the casting of this project in American terms, and led me to focus more specifically on the jeremiad and its importance to the American experience.

More people than I can recall have offered help and advice, and it has been humbling to sit down and try to recount them all. (No doubt, despite my best efforts and intentions, I will leave some out here.) I have presented research from various parts of this book to the Annual Meetings of the American Political Association, the Midwest Political Science Association, the Western Political Science Association, the American Academy of Religion, and the Association for Political Theory. Especially helpful was a bracing roundtable discussion at the 2004 APT Conference in Colorado Springs, chaired by

Daniel Pellerin, where I was pushed quite hard, and quite constructively, by an engaged audience as well as by my interlocutors—Jim Block, Ann Davies, and Andrew Rehfeld—who simply refused to allow me to wiggle out of tight spots. The resulting book (four years later!) is immensely improved because of their careful attention to an early version of its argument on that day.

Other venues at which audiences helped me clarify my own thinking, and offered me the fruits of their own, have included "U.S. National Identity in the 21st Century," a 2006 conference at the Rothermere American Institute, University of Oxford; the "One Nation Under God?" conference in Aspen, sponsored by Res Publica, in the fall of 2002; Baylor University's 1999 Pruit Symposium on statecraft and soulcraft; and the 2002 Henry Institute Symposium on Religion and Politics at Calvin College. Audiences at a number of universities—Chicago, Willamette, Texas A&M, Notre Dame, Illinois, Rutgers, and North Carolina–Chapel Hill—also read, listened to, and eagerly responded to pieces of the argument. For the invitations to speak and help in arranging these visits, thanks go to Patchen Markell, David Gutterman, Cary Nederman, Michael and Catherine Zuckert, Jonathan Ebel, Dennis Bathory, and Michael Lienesch.

Eldon Eisenach, Mike Lienesch, Jim Morone, and Cary Nederman have provided a model of how senior scholars ought to behave toward their greener colleagues, and I hope that over the years I have expressed how meaningful their help and support has been to me. David Gutterman and I have been talking about jeremiads, and much more, for a number of years now; his friendship and critical insights remain invaluable. In addition, Alan Bloom, Mark Button, Joe Bowersox, John Carlson, Jerome Copulsky, Booth Fowler, Matt Hedstrom, Dan McAdams, Rob Martin, John Meyer, Sam Nelson, James Old, Haein Park, Jamie Skillen, Quentin Skinner, and Bernie Yack all offered insights at one point or another over the years, and I appreciate their willingness to help me think through issues related to the jeremiad and its important role in American history and politics. Just as this book was going to press, Mark Jendrysik of the University of North Dakota graciously sent me a copy of his *Modern Jeremiahs: Contemporary Visions of American Decline* (2008). I regret that, given the shortness of time, I was not able to incorporate his book's insights into *Prodigal Nation*.

I have benefited from the wisdom and good cheer of my colleagues Gretchen Buggeln, Marcia Bunge, Joe Creech, Scott Huelin, Kevin

Hoffman, Bill Olmsted, Mel Piehl, Jeni Prough, and Mark Schwehn in Christ College, the honors college of Valparaiso University, more than I can say. They tolerated my incessant talk of decline and destruction during my six years on the Christ College faculty, and cheerfully passed me jeremiads of all sorts whenever they ran across them. Far more importantly, they maintained a community of scholar-teachers as supportive and nurturing as it was intellectually rigorous. The writing of this book spanned two deanships of Christ College: Mark Schwehn and Mel Piehl unfailingly supported my work with intellectual, administrative, and (not least) financial resources, as did Valparaiso University's Committee on Creative Work and Research, which provided a Summer Research Grant during 2003 and a 2006–2007 University Research Professorship. I owe a special debt of gratitude to my Christ College colleague David Morgan, now at Duke University, who was never too busy with his own work to offer advice and keen critical insights on topics ranging from early American religion to the details of negotiating contracts. I was also extremely lucky to have the no-nonsense research and editing skills of Liz Hanson during 2006–2007. And there is simply no way to thank each of the countless students I talked to about the jeremiad during my time at Valparaiso; it is hard to imagine a more engaging undergraduate environment than the one I was fortunate to share while writing *Prodigal Nation*. This book's virtues, such as they are, owe much to Christ College; the book's shortcomings, alas, owe much to its author.

Writing a book like this requires access to lots of other books: *Prodigal Nation* could not have been completed without the resources of the Newberry Library, the Department of Special Collections at Regenstein Library (University of Chicago), the Library Company of Philadelphia, and the Interlibrary Loan Department at Valparaiso University's Christopher Center for Library and Information Services (who seem never to have met a book they can't obtain).

The gratefully appreciated assistance of all these people and institutions came together in its final form at the Rothermere American Institute (RAI) at the University of Oxford, where I spent Trinity Term 2007 making final revisions to the manuscript and receiving a final rigorous reading of chapter 5 from an interdisciplinary group of scholars in residence. Thanks to Paul Giles, director of the RAI, as well as Andrea Beighton, Laura Lauer, and Pauline Wyman, all of whom made my stay at the Rothermere a happy and productive one. The Rothermere is a gem of an institution, and it is a marvelous place to finish up this book, which had been so long in the making.

At Oxford University Press, Theo Calderara combined unflagging enthusiasm for the project with a razor-sharp editing pencil and the uncanny capacity to find ever more concise ways to make the same point. Leigh Schmidt and Randall Balmer read several early chapters as well as a complete draft of the manuscript, and their comments (not to mention their example of synthetic, deeply researched, and accessible scholarship on religion and American culture) improved the final product in ways too numerous to mention.

Finally, I thank the following publishers for permission to draw on my previously published work:

Equinox Publishing, for permission to use portions of "'One Nation Under God,' September 11, and the Chosen Nation: Moral Decline and Divine Punishment in American Public Discourse," which originally appeared in *Political Theology* 6: 1 (March 2005): 9–30.

Rowman and Littlefield Publishers, for permission to use portions of "The Enduring Power of the American Jeremiad" (coauthored with Jennifer Miller), which was originally published in *Religion, Politics, and American Identity: New Controversies, New Directions*, ed. David S. Gutterman and Andrew R. Murphy (Lanham, Md.: Lexington Books/Rowman and Littlefield, 2006).

Portions of Chapter 5 appeared originally in my article "Two American Jeremiads: Traditionalist and Progressive Stories of American Nationhood," *Politics and Religion* 1: 1 (2008): 85–112. I am grateful to Cambridge University Press for permission to reprint portions of that article.

My deepest gratitude of all goes to my family, who have awaited the completion of the book almost as eagerly as I have (though surely for different reasons!) and who have offered both personal support and their own substantive insights into American religion and politics. My sons Peter and Sam enrich each day just by getting up in the morning, and by asking questions like "What's a jeremiad?" I have been graced with Beth Angell's presence for twenty years now; each day is still a gift.

Contents

PRODIGAL NATION

ONE

The American Jeremiad

I thought how I would set you among my children, and give you a pleasant land, the most beautiful heritage of all the nations. And I thought you would call me, My Father, and would not turn from following me. Instead, as a faithless wife leaves her husband, so you have been faithless to me, O house of Israel, says the Lord. A voice on the bare heights is heard, the plaintive weeping of Israel's children, because they have perverted their way, they have forgotten the Lord their God: Return, O faithless children, I will heal your faithlessness....

They do not say to themselves, "Let us fear the LORD our God, who gives autumn and spring rains in season, who assures us of the regular weeks of harvest." Your wrongdoings have kept these away; your sins have deprived you of good. "Among my people are the wicked who lie in wait like those who snare birds and like those who set traps to catch people. Like cages full of birds, their houses are full of deceit; they have become rich and powerful, and have grown fat and sleek. Their evil deeds have no limit; they do not seek justice. They do not promote the case of the fatherless; they do not defend the just cause of the poor. Should I not punish them for this?" declares the LORD. "Should I not avenge myself on such a nation as this?"[1]

IN THE MIDST of calamities and momentous events of all sorts—hurricanes, floods, war—Americans have historically pulled together, emphasizing national unity and calling for a commitment to the common good. After September 11, Americans lined up to donate money, goods, and even blood far in excess of actual need. Several years later, the devastation of Hurricane Katrina prompted a similar outpouring of generosity, as did the South Asian tsunami halfway around the world.

But in the midst of these emphases on unity, Americans have also heard some rather different voices, seeking to assign responsibility for such events. Often, such voices use specifically religious language.

Just days after the September 11 attacks, appearing on Pat Robertson's television program *The 700 Club*, Jerry Falwell pointed out that "the Lord has protected us so wonderfully these 225 years," but that

> what we saw on [September 11], as terrible as it is, could be miniscule if, in fact—if, in fact—God continues to lift the curtain and allow the enemies of America to give us probably what we deserve.... The ACLU's got to take a lot of blame for this.... The abortionists have got to bear some burden for this because God will not be mocked.... [along with] the pagans... and the feminists, and the gays and the lesbians who are actively trying to make that an alternative lifestyle, the ACLU, People for the American Way...

Ever the agreeable host, Robertson added, "Well, I totally concur, and the problem is we have adopted that agenda at the highest levels of our government. And so we're responsible as a free society for what the top people do. And, the top people, of course, is the court system." Falwell concluded his remarks with a call for national repentance: "when the nation is on its knees, the only normal and natural and spiritual thing to do is what we ought to be doing all the time—calling upon God." In the following days, as he attempted to quell the furor that had resulted from his remarks, Falwell returned to the language of repentance and revival:

> I had no intention of being divisive. I was sharing my burden for revival in America on a Christian TV program, intending to speak to a Christian audience from a theological perspective about the need for national repentance.... [I] was asking a Christian audience on a Christian TV program to claim II Chronicles 7:14 and repent.... I was blaming no one but the terrorists for the terror, but I was chastising us, the Church, for a generation of departure from God. I was doing what I have done for nearly 50 years in the pulpit—confronting the culture and calling for national revival.[2]

Hurricane Katrina's destruction occasioned similar outcries, often from voices theologically, if not politically, allied with Robertson, Falwell, and the Christian Right. But the language of divine punishment can come from other, surprising sources as well. Six months after Katrina hit the Gulf Coast, New Orleans mayor Ray Nagin looked back at the recovery effort in his city:

> And as we think about rebuilding New Orleans, surely God is mad at America, he's sending hurricane after hurricane after hurricane and it's

destroying and putting stress on this country. Surely he's not approving of us being in Iraq under false pretense. But surely he's upset at black America, also. We're not taking care of ourselves. We're not taking care of our women. And we're not taking care of our children when you have a community where 70 percent of its children are being born to one parent.

Nagin went on to call for a unified reconstruction effort in keeping with the city's racial heritage: "It's time for us to rebuild New Orleans—the one that should be a chocolate New Orleans.... This city will be a majority African American city. It's the way God wants it to be."[3]

Like latter-day Louis Renaults, Americans from across the political spectrum professed themselves shocked—shocked!—when Falwell and Robertson interpreted the events of September 11 as evidence of divine displeasure at the growing ungodliness of American society; or when Mayor Nagin made his remarks about Hurricane Katrina. The response to Falwell and Robertson, not surprisingly, was swift, negative, and virtually unanimous. How could anyone—clergy, no less—hold such callous views, ascribing the deaths of thousands to God's socially conservative politics? What sort of theology saw catastrophe and barbarism as the punishment of a loving God upon innocent civilians? How could anyone conceivably connect the devastation of Katrina with the invasion of Iraq more than two years earlier, or the thirty-year tradition of legalized abortion in the United States, or the forty-year-old decision to remove prayer and Bible reading from the nation's public schools?

The standard response to such charges is to dismiss them as the histrionic outbursts of marginalized extremists, and in many cases such a response is probably appropriate. But when we look more closely, we see that there is much more to these sorts of narratives of American decline and punishment than the mere ranting of disaffected fringe groups. There is the long tradition of the American jeremiad, a far more mainstream and deeply American way of thinking about the nation's past, present, and future. In their appropriation of the language of divine punishment for national offenses, in their lament over a perceived decline from America's virtuous origins, and in their marshaling of claims about the past in search of an understanding of the present and future, the comments of Robertson, Falwell, and Nagin—not to mention Cotton Mather, Frederick Douglass, and countless others throughout American history—fit squarely within the tradition of the American jeremiad.

DEFINING TERMS: THE AMERICAN JEREMIAD

Although the *Oxford English Dictionary* traces the term *jeremiad* back only to the writer and philanthropist Hannah More in 1780, certainly the tendency to lament the present and admire a more virtuous past long predates the eighteenth century. Jeremiah was only one in a long line of prophets who, driven by a sense of crisis and a deep anxiety about their community, lamented Israel's violation of its covenant with God as a story of decline that invited God's punishment.[4] Although ruling elites often assumed that God would never forsake His chosen people, notes Walter Bruegemann, Jeremiah

> sound[ed] a counteropinion...that there is no such thing as "guaranteed shalom." *All shalom* is conditional, and Jerusalem has failed to qualify for Yahweh's *shalom* precisely because of ethical misconduct....Very often, the rhetoric moves in the direction of termination because this sovereign God will not be mocked.

Addressing the Jews after the destruction of Jerusalem and their subsequent exile in Babylon, Jeremiah's critique provided a rationale for the misfortunes that the community was experiencing. They had abandoned the covenant sworn at Sinai, and thus God had allowed or even recruited Babylon to serve as the instrument of His chastisement. But the prophet also held out the hope of restoration and forgiveness if the community repented and returned to obedience.[5] Though the time was late, a prodigal people might yet be redeemed.

Despite this connection with the Hebraic tradition, the jeremiad is not the unique property of any particular culture. Narratives of decline, chastisement, and renewal appear across time, culture, religion, and geography, from classical Asian and Western cultures to yesterday's news. The sacred texts of many religious traditions lament declining moral and spiritual standards, and hold out hope for renewal and revival, if only the community will see the error of its ways. The Protestant Reformation, for example, was driven in large part by the search for a lost pristine, uncorrupted church. And a variety of social movements depend upon sharp contrasts between a degenerate present and a glorious past.[6]

Yet this book is about America, where the jeremiad continues to cast a long shadow over American public debate, framing Americans' understanding of their past, present, and future.

So what makes a jeremiad?

1. *Jeremiads identify problems that show a decline vis-à-vis the past.* Jeremiads claim that their contemporaries have gone badly wrong, and offer vivid examples or statistics to back up these claims. After all, the Prodigal Son needed to acknowledge his lamentable state before he could even think of returning to his father's house. A prodigal nation is no different. Public figures on the right such as Pat Buchanan, Rush Limbaugh, and Bill O'Reilly propound a critique that is surely familiar to anyone who has followed American politics over the past forty years: due to an increasingly permissive and hedonistic public morality— exemplified by (but by no means limited to) Supreme Court rulings on public school prayer, displays of religious symbols on public property, and human sexuality—the nation has abandoned its moral and spiritual moorings. The consequences of this abandonment (divorce, abortion, violence, sagging public spirit, sexual promiscuity, the decline of individual responsibility) provide evidence of a moral and spiritual decline that threatens the very core of American life.[7]

And narratives of decline aren't limited to the political right. Progressives and liberals also see declines in social connectedness, and lament the perceived retreat from such American values as egalitarianism, community, and the common good due to an ever-increasing collusion of the American government with big business.[8] Perhaps the most prominent recent example of this type of jeremiad was Robert Putnam's best-selling book *Bowling Alone: The Decline and Renewal of American Community*, which marshaled an impressive body of statistical data to argue that late-twentieth-century Americans were not as civically engaged as their parents and grandparents had been. But Putnam's account, though statistically rich, was hardly new. Fifteen years before Putnam's book, another best seller, *Habits of the Heart*, put forward a similar argument about the rise of individualism in American culture and the consequent decline in biblical and republican languages of commitment and responsibility.[9]

2. *Jeremiads identify turning points.* Arresting portraits of a world sinking into decadence lie at the heart of the jeremiad, but they are only the beginning. In addition to explaining what is wrong, the jeremiad must also explain "Why *this* decline? Why *these* events? When and why did the nation begin to go so wrong?" Jeremiads usually propose a specific time in the past when the destructive ideas or practices first appeared, and trace their effects over subsequent years. Falwell's comments about September 11 offer a good example. His critique, and the Christian Right narrative of American decline more generally, ties together a series of legal decisions and political developments into a

narrative of growing departure from traditional Judeo-Christian public piety. Important components of this narrative include the Supreme Court decisions striking down public school prayer; the increasing social radicalism of the 1960s; the *Roe v. Wade* decision legalizing abortion; and the growth of feminism and gay rights since the 1970s. For example, during confirmation hearings in 2006, Focus on the Family asked its members to support Judge Samuel Alito's nomination to the Supreme Court as a way to "return to the Christian heritage upon which this nation was founded" in the hope that "prayer will be allowed in public schools and that the Ten Commandments will be displayed proudly on public property." "This," they wrote, "may be the year our country's secular trends will begin to be reversed."[10]

Many contemporary jeremiads point to the turbulent years of the 1960s as the key to understanding the civic, moral, and political decline that, in their view, afflicts the nation. Of course, different Jeremiahs interpret those years quite differently. Traditionalists like Pat Buchanan and Jerry Falwell blame twenty-first-century social ills on the rebellion against traditional authorities and the triumph of relativistic individualism, while progressives lament missed opportunities to overcome continuing large-scale social problems involving race, poverty, and gender.[11]

Of course, an account of what has gone wrong must be accompanied by an account of what previous generations did right. American Jeremiahs argue that our virtuous ancestors had it right; departure from their ways is the beginning of error. Since it anchors itself so deeply in founding virtues, the jeremiad can often claim, with good reason, to represent the most loyal patriotism even while engaging in the most strident dissent. Consider Martin Luther King's speech at the Lincoln Memorial in 1963. In King's telling of the American story, African-Americans

> have come to our nation's capital to cash a check. When the architects of our republic wrote the magnificent words of the Constitution and the Declaration of Independence, they were signing a promissory note to which every American was to fall heir. This note was a promise that all men, yes, black men as well as white men, would be guaranteed the unalienable rights of life, liberty, and the pursuit of happiness.

The civil rights movement, in King's account, had gathered in Washington in order to insist that Americans honor this check.

> It is obvious today that America has defaulted on this promissory note insofar as her citizens of color are concerned. Instead of honoring this

sacred obligation, America has given the Negro people a bad check, a check which has come back marked "insufficient funds." But we refuse to believe that the bank of justice is bankrupt. We refuse to believe that there are insufficient funds in the great vaults of opportunity of this nation. So we have come to cash this check—a check that will give us upon demand the riches of freedom and the security of justice.

King's imagery affirms the fundamental value of an original American promise regarding human liberty and equality; while his "refus[al] to believe that the bank of justice is bankrupt" skillfully blends an endorsement of fundamental American ideals with a lament over the realities of American life. King had no illusions about social realities at the time of the founding, but he located the power of the "check" in the American ideals of liberty and justice for all, in the radical potential of the American founding. Passing civil rights and voting rights legislation would represent a *vindication* of those founding promises. King's vision continues to animate many progressive political movements in America, but their political opponents display an equally fervent commitment to the founders. For example, David Barton's WallBuilders movement, dedicated to emphasizing the religious nature of the American founding and the dangerous shift in recent years to a secular public sphere, evokes the founding as well.

Thus, implicit in the American jeremiad is the nation's particular devotion to—one might say an obsession with—the founders. Be they first-generation New England Puritans or national figures like Washington, Jefferson, and Adams, these virtuous founders are crucial to the narrative power of the jeremiad. They provide concrete examples of individuals for whom religious or civic virtue trumped (or at least moderated) self-interest, and they represent a standing reproach to degenerate present-day Americans. This unfavorable contrast between the ills of times present and the glories of times past represents one of the keys to the jeremiad's rhetorical power.

3. *Jeremiads call for reform, repentance, or renewal.* Hand in hand with a narrative of decline and punishment come claims about what must be done—politically, right now—to set the nation on the right path. More was required of the Prodigal Son, of course, than simply a recognition of his folly: he had to take action, turn himself around, and approach his father's house once again. New England and Civil War jeremiads, often delivered in times of deep social conflict or distress, concluded with exhortations to their audiences to recapture the founding promise of their societies, and to do so with a specific set of political actions—

free the slaves, honor the Sabbath, refrain from ostentatious displays of wealth, and so on. The twenty-first century is no different. Today's jeremiads are almost always enmeshed in concrete political debates: about sexual morality, school prayer, protection of the environment, immigration, or the appropriate scope of government. In all of these cases, the jeremiad seeks to use political power to intervene on one side of a divisive cultural or political issue. And yet, given the long-term vision of the jeremiad, reform is never simply about a mundane set of policy proposals, but a vindication of the American past and the virtues of previous generations.

American Jeremiad

But there is much more to the American jeremiad than a simple narrative of decline from founding virtues and a call for political reform. What makes the American jeremiad American is its connection to a larger, sacred story tied intimately to the particularities of the nation's origins and development. In this sense, the jeremiad is part and parcel of what Robert Bellah and others call American "civil religion": "religious dimension, found . . . in the religious life of every people, through which it interprets its historical experience in light of transcendent reality." English Protestants, after all—many of whom saw themselves, and America, as "chosen," with a special relationship to the Creator— were responsible for much early American colonization. Such a view had its origins in John Winthrop's evocation of New England as a "city on a hill," and the more general Puritan tendency to draw parallels between themselves and the ancient Israelites. These presuppositions were deepened and strengthened by the events of the 1770s and 1780s, in which the notion of an American Israel throwing off oppression in order to take up its national mission settled ever more deeply into American public rhetoric. This link was only strengthened by the Revolutionary experience, the great evangelical revivals of the early nineteenth century, and the nation's first movements westward.[12]

If the people of this "Chosen Nation" have strayed from the path of rightly ordered politics and society, the consequences are not merely social and political but world-historical, even transcendent, in nature. In other words, the American jeremiad is not just a historical or political argument but a theological, even a cosmological, one. Images of American chosenness were reinforced by a widespread interest in millennialism, the notion that Christ will return for a thousand-year reign on Earth, and that America (later, the United States) had a special role to play in God's plans for the end times. Historian Terrie Dopp Aamodt explains that in nineteenth-century America, apocalypticism "had come to mean an imminent cosmic cataclysm in which God would destroy the ruling powers of evil and raise the righteous to life in a messianic kingdom.... Because the apocalypse is so closely tied to the concept of the Last Judgment, it is related to jeremiad rhetoric, with its tendency to call for repentance and to predict dire consequences if the warning is ignored."[13]

Thus the story of the jeremiad in America is the story of Americans' faith in God's providential oversight of human affairs, and more particularly of American affairs. Nicholas Guyatt has shown that although belief in providence is not uniquely American, it nonetheless played an important role in the formation of an American identity. As Guyatt notes—and as we shall see throughout this book—providential claims are "*arguments:* efforts to explain God's purpose in the world that were harnessed to political goals in the present."[14]

So although the American jeremiad so often laments a perceived decline from founding ideals, we should not view it as inherently pessimistic. The nation may be prodigal, to be sure, but even the Prodigal Son had a forgiving father. Current decline notwithstanding, adherents of the narrative of America as Chosen Nation generally saw a crucial role for the United States in preparing the way for God's reign on earth. Indeed, such a role explained both the promise of the American nation *and* the bitter trials through which it was currently passing. In the words of historian James Moorhead, "The millennium...was viewed simultaneously as a promise and a threat: a specific mission awaited the redeemer nation, but it would suffer wrath if it proved false to its vocation."[15] The rhetorical power of the American jeremiad lies in this perennial and dynamic tension between perceived national decline and enduring national promise.

Of course, not every jeremiad presented in this book will present a clear and overt example of each of these elements. Some jeremiads lean heavily on imagery of chosenness and sinfulness; others offer a detailed time line of the nation's descent into moral and spiritual decline. In the real world of politics and social conflict, we are dealing with variations on this theme, as critics present their diagnoses of the contemporary scene in particular ways for particular audiences and occasions.

Prodigal Nation offers an exploration of the American jeremiad as it has appeared across American history, from seventeenth-century New England to the events of September 11. I focus most closely on early

New England, the Civil War, and the rise of the Christian Right. Of course these examples do not *exhaust* the many ways in which such rhetoric has appeared throughout American history, and I touch on others as I proceed. But if the jeremiad is as ubiquitous as I have claimed, why focus on these three?

The three episodes most closely examined in this book are singularly important if we want to understand the development of religious and political discourse in American life. New England Puritans, who raised the political sermon to an art form, viewed their colonizing endeavor as part of the westward progress of the Gospel, and they placed each crop failure, calamity, or Indian attack—as well as their good fortunes—firmly into this providentialist context. More than 200 years after the first settlements in Massachusetts Bay, the great national tragedy that took over 600,000 lives produced an explosion of national soul-searching. Civil War Jeremiahs repeatedly looked to the founders for ways to understand what was happening all around them. Lincoln's Second Inaugural—a tentative jeremiad if there ever was one—phrased the issue of God's judgments on American slavery rather obliquely, but many of his contemporaries were not so shy and linked the war's carnage (and the ultimate Union victory) directly to God's purposes. And the notion that the United States has a unique historical mission to uphold Judeo-Christian values and to combat godless communism fired the Christian Right's entry into American electoral politics during the 1970s and 1980s. Though often perceived as a "conservative" trope, especially when used by the Christian Right, the idea of American messianism has never been the sole possession of one political party. Robert Kennedy was as comfortable using the jeremiad as was Jerry Falwell.[16]

THE JEREMIAD'S RHETORICAL POWER: HOPE AND DESPAIR IN TENSION

The jeremiad's political and rhetorical power, its ability to move Americans to social and political action, lies in its ability to evoke a dynamic tension between despair and hope. Not simply a lament over American decline, nor merely a celebration of the Chosen Nation, the jeremiad combines these two fundamental American ideas into a powerful narrative of imperiled national promise and a yearning for national renewal. This weaving together of these two strands of rhetoric distinguishes the jeremiad from both the doom-and-gloom rantings of nostalgics and the self-righteous proclamations of those whose faith in national blessing never wavers.

True, the American jeremiad contrasts the virtues of the past with the degeneracy of the present and warns of divine punishment for these offenses. But to focus exclusively on America's declining trajectory is to miss the *hope* so crucial to the jeremiad. America's decline in ordinary (historical) time is linked to an equally strongly held conviction that the United States is part of a larger, transcendent purpose. At the grandest level, we find interpretations of American history that root themselves in myths of the nation's origin and view its rise to world power as part of a divine blessing bestowed on the earliest settlers and national founders. This inheritance, furthermore, shapes, or ought to shape, the political decisions of subsequent generations.[17]

This tension between despair and hope is the critical feature separating jeremiads from other types of political narratives. Perhaps most obviously, as a story of crisis and decline the jeremiad arrays itself against narratives of American progress that either insist that all is well in America or invoke ideas like "Manifest Destiny" and American triumphalism. On the other hand, as a form of rhetoric that seeks to call its audience to repentance, the jeremiad is never cynical or without hope. Martin Luther King's jeremiad of 1963, with its refusal to believe that the bank of American justice was empty, was aimed at several groups, not only those in Washington that day but also mainstream whites who would have to get behind civil rights legislation if it were to have any chance of passage. But just as importantly, King directed his remarks to many in the African-American community who viewed the American experiment as irredeemably flawed by its denial of justice to citizens of color since its earliest days. (Malcolm X had famously referred to the 1963 March as the "Farce on Washington.") King made a direct appeal to black Americans *not* to resort to separation and violence, but to claim the American founding as their own. As David Howard-Pitney put it,

> Unlike separatist forms of black nationalism such as those voiced by Marcus Garvey and Malcolm X, the dominant black jeremiad tradition conceives of blacks as a chosen people *within* a chosen people. The African American jeremiad tradition...characteristically addresses *two* American chosen peoples—black and white—whose millennial destinies, while distinct, are also inextricably entwined.[18]

Of course, narratives that deny any American national promise, that dismiss the ideals of life, liberty, and the pursuit of happiness as just so much window dressing, are nothing new. As early as 1837, in his noted address "Fourth of July in Providence," William Lloyd Garrison spoke of "the first settlement of this country by the 'pilgrim fathers' and found them laying its foundation in blood and violence—in slavery and the slave trade—in a war of extermination with the proprietors of the soil..." Since nations cannot be punished in a future life, the consequences would be dealt in this world: "This nation is destined to perish, because in wading through blood and carnage to independence, *it at the outset discarded the Prince of Peace, and elected George Washington to be its Savior...*" Later that same year, he referred to the nation as "diseased beyond the power of recovery."[19] We might contrast Garrison here with a figure like Frederick Douglass, for whom abolitionism was always rooted in a broad faith in American ideals. Though often deeply concerned about the present—note the arresting title of Robert Bellah's important book on the jeremiad and American civil religion, *The Broken Covenant*—the jeremiad always views the foundations of American life as fundamentally sound and worth preserving.

If the prophetic tradition is about anything, it is about calling a community back to faithfulness, and from the earliest New England sermons to the resurgence of the Christian Right in the 1980s—indeed, to September 11 and Katrina's destruction in our own day—we see the nation called to repentance time and time again. The story of these calls, and the responses they have evoked, is the story of this book.

PART I

THREE AMERICAN JEREMIADS

TWO

Puritan New England and the Foundations of the American Jeremiad

This people of New-England are a people whom God hath signally owned and blessed in our first and former times; our fathers coming into these ends of the earth not upon any worldly design but merely on the account of religion; they had much of the gracious presence of God with them in their planting and building work, and in laying the foundations in church and common-wealth, and in the additional blessings of heaven and earth, and sea and land; So that from a day of small things New-England in a few years was grown up to be a thriving and flourishing plantation: But alas, we their successors have not answered the Lord's expectation, or our own profession, but as we have been multiplied and encreased, so have we sinned, and provoked the Lord to anger against us, so that of late years he hath severely witnessed against us by the variety of his judgments in a successive way, and for a long time; So that we are at present an afflicted and poor people, greatly diminished, impoverished and brought very low...[1]

I N 1674, WHEN Increase Mather delivered *The Day of Trouble Is Near*—a sermon that his biographer calls "the first of the great sermons that were to make him famous," and one that placed him "among the first rank of his generation of Puritan preachers"—it is unlikely that even he could have guessed just how near the trouble would turn out to be. That December saw the outbreak of sustained conflict with the natives, known to later generations as King Philip's War, a conflict that one historian has called "the great crisis of the early period of New England history." Between the spring of 1675 and the summer of 1676, fully half the towns in New England would be damaged; twelve completely laid waste; the economy left in shambles; colonial treasuries near bankruptcy; and hundreds killed, wounded, or carried away in captivity. For the natives, of course, the toll was even more bitter: to the enormous loss of life would be added disease-ridden captivity and death, loss of land, and the misery of seeing many of their number sold into slavery. The war may have claimed as many as 68 percent of the Indians in southern New England.[2]

Of course, these grim details lay well in the future on the day Mather preached in Boston. And yet, as his title indicates, he did not rise to offer congratulations to his fellow New Englanders. What Mather saw all around him were the horrendous sins of a once-godly people. He lamented "a great decay as to the power of godliness amongst us"; neglect of religious duties; spiritual and carnal pride "in apparel, fashions, and the like"; disobedience within families, churches, and the commonwealth; insensitivity to the poor; and growing contentiousness and disunity. And the younger generation was even worse![3]

Mather drew parallels between New England and the ancient Israelites—"Without doubt, the Lord Jesus hath a peculiar respect unto this place, and for this people," he preached, "here the Lord hath caused as it were New Jerusalem to come down from Heaven"—and connected the sins of the Israelites with those of his fellow colonists. Taking his sermon text that day from the seventh chapter of Ezekiel, Mather noted that although in Scripture the *Chaldeans* had inflicted judgment on Israel, the ultimate cause of these events had been God Himself, who sent the Chaldeans as punishment for Israel's sins. Yet he assured those in attendance that God's punishments of His chosen people are not merely punitive but corrective, intended for a specific purpose: "that which the Lord intends by bringing his people into the furnace of affliction, is that he may make pure metal of them, yea, that they may be purged and sanctified, and become vessels meet for the master's use."[4]

But more than present sin ailed the New England settlements. Tying together Mather's catalog of sins was a larger and more troubling *historical* development: what had begun as a religiously based settlement populated by godly folk had degenerated, and become infected with the poison of worldliness. "Alas! We have changed our interest. The interest of New England was religion, which did distinguish us from other English plantations...whereas now we begin to espouse a worldly interest, and so to chase a new God, therefore no wonder that war is like to be in the gates." Still, despite the signs of trouble all around, Mather expressed faith in God's promises to New England, reverence for the founding generation, and hope for the colony's relationship with its God: "Our fathers have built sanctuaries for his name therein, and therefore he will not destroy us."[5]

Not destroy, perhaps, but Mather felt sure that God was preparing to *afflict* New England. And afflicted they were: armed hostilities broke out in 1675, and by the spring of 1676 the Wampanoags and their allies were within ten miles of Boston. Churches throughout New England lamented the colonies' sins and regularly called the faithful to repentance, attempting to regain God's favor—with decidedly mixed results. On April 20, 1676, for example, as churches in Boston observed a day of humiliation and fasting, the natives attacked the town of Sudbury, less than twenty miles away, took several hostages, and later that night "stripped them naked, and caused them to run the gauntlet, whipping them after a cruel and bloody manner, and then threw hot ashes upon them, cut out the flesh of their legs, and put fire into their wounds, delighting to see the miserable torments of wretched creatures."[6]

"King Philip"[7] was killed in August 1676, and hostilities came to a speedy end after his death. Shortly thereafter, New Englanders began to produce histories of the war, trying to understand what had happened and why. All told, more than twenty such accounts would appear.[8] One of the first was authored by none other than Increase Mather: not surprisingly, his *Brief History of the Warr with the Indians* viewed the conflict as God's chastisement of a wayward New England for its religious backsliding. (Like the Chaldeans examined in his earlier sermon, Philip and his allies were important to Mather's narrative only insofar as they served God's purposes.) Bound along with the *Brief History* was a piece that Mather entitled *An Earnest Exhortation to the Inhabitants of New-England*. In it, Mather lamented the fact that New England continued in its sin even after nearly two years of war and destruction, and despite God's continual warnings in the form of epidemics, Indian attacks, and other extraordinary portents. His list of sins was as sweeping, if not more so, than the one he had laid out in *The Day of Trouble* two years earlier: contention, sensuality, drunkenness, pride in appearances, luxurious apparel, meager support for ministers of the gospel, religious formality (the letter without the spirit), covetousness and land speculation, mistreatment of the natives, swearing, disregard of the Sabbath, dishonor to parents and magistrates, oppression, and a lack of zeal to convert the Indians.[9]

Each of these sins, in Mather's view, represented a departure from the high moral and religious standards set by the colony's founders.

> When as our fathers were models of sobriety, they would not drink a cup of wine nor strong drink, more than should suffice nature, and conduce to their health, men of latter time could transact no business nor hardly engage in any discourses, but it must be over a pint of wine or a pot of beer, yea so as that drunkenness in the sight of man is become a common sin.

Those founders—the generation of Mather's parents—had ventured to America for religious reasons, to convert the natives and erect a biblical community, not only for their own sakes but for their children's, "that so their children might not see evil examples, and be in danger of being corrupted thereby, as tis in other parts of the world."[10] How far things had fallen since those days!

As do all jeremiads, Mather's *Exhortation* called for "a sincere reformation of those evils which have provoked the eyes of God's glory," and especially endorsed the practice of church covenant renewal, in which church members publicly and collectively repented of their sins and reaffirmed their allegiance to each other and to the religious foundations of the New England settlements. The ritualistic similarities between church covenant *renewals* and the founding generation's original church covenants clearly appealed to Mather as he sought to evoke the virtues of the colonists' godly predecessors, in sharp contrast to his contemporaries' degeneracy. He counseled against giving in to despair and assuming that New England was already too far gone to receive God's mercy. And yet if New England was God's land, and the Puritans God's people—as so many of their rulers and leading citizens seemed to think—they seemed singularly unable (or perhaps just unwilling?) to act that way. Just three years later, the churches of Massachusetts Bay convened a general synod devoted to discovering why God was *continuing* to send evils upon the land.[11]

THE SOCIAL AND POLITICAL CONTEXT OF THE NEW ENGLAND JEREMIAD

The rhetorical form that Increase Mather employed with such vigor laid the foundation for a much larger genre of American public rhetoric. Yet like so many other aspects of the nation's development, the American jeremiad has English roots. The notion that calamities of various sorts represented "outward signs of God's displeasure and [were] indicative of the spiritual sickness of the community" reached back into the sixteenth-century English Puritan movement.[12] English Parliaments had long proclaimed public fasts in response to auspicious public events, as well as to localized disasters of various sorts. Such proclamations involved treating a designated day as a Sabbath (i.e., refraining from work and sexual activity, wearing plain clothing, attending religious services) in an attempt to focus the community's attention on its spiritual shortcomings, in hopes of spurring repentance and thus turning aside any further displays of divine wrath.

The seventeenth-century migration to New England, dominated symbolically (if not numerically) by Puritans, was motivated by many factors, from individual spiritual strivings to the search for a better economic future. Among the more influential colonizers, though, the notion that God was preparing to punish England for its people's sins played an important role in their thinking about, and planning for, their colonial endeavor. Spurred on by narratives of England as God's chosen nation (such as those advanced by sixteenth-century martyrologist John Foxe), English Puritans like Thomas Hooker suggested that their land was provoking God's wrath by its failure to reform its church fully, as well as by its broader corruption in social life and mores.

> As sure as God is God, God is going from England...God begins to ship away his Noahs...and God makes account that New England shall be a refuge for his Noahs and his Lots, a rock and a shelter for his righteous ones to run unto.... Tell me, are there not as great sins amongst us as were in Jerusalem...? Are we better than other brethren and neighbor nations, that have drunk so deeply of God's wrath?[13]

America would be a refuge from God's impending wrath on England, but it might also serve as a model for those Puritans who stayed in England and attempted further reformation. The outbreak of the English Civil Wars—armed conflict between Parliament and King Charles I, which broke out in 1642 after years of growing tension—and the prominent role played by English Puritans in the Parliamentary opposition to Charles fed this hope. The sense of connection between New Englanders and their English brethren was articulated by many early leaders, including Richard Hooke, who exhorted his New England listeners in 1641 not to forget England in its time of trouble. Indeed, Perry Miller interpreted the Puritans' "errand into the wilderness" not as a retreat, but rather as an undertaking imbued with a positive sense of mission. Given the importance early Puritans like Winthrop attached to the notion of an *audience* for their undertaking ("The eyes of all people are upon us," he preached on board the *Arbella* in 1630, whether it was true or not), maintaining ties with their compatriots in England assumed supreme importance.[14]

But what if England turned out to be uninterested in learning the lessons New England wanted to teach? Or—worse yet—what if English Puritans took a radically different road, politically speaking, than their American counterparts? As Harry Stout puts it, "The founders' meticulously constructed laboratory had produced a workable, even thriving, operation, but they now realized that no one in Europe would imitate them, or even cared about their creation." By the mid-seventeenth century, the idea of New England as model was fading fast. Ironically, perhaps, the divergence between English and American Puritanism became most clear in the wake of the Puritan-Parliamentarian *victory* over the King: Oliver Cromwell, a theological fellow-traveler but committed tolerationist who ruled England during the 1650s, perplexed New England Puritans with his willingness to permit a wide range of Protestant dissent. The fact that many New Englanders (including two of Increase Mather's brothers) forsook the colonies to return "home" and participate in these conflicts only added to the disbelief and frustration among New England elites. After Cromwell's death in 1658 and the restoration of the Stuart monarchy in 1660, Puritans lost even the theological sympathies of English ruling elites, and faced the prospect of dealing once again with their old ecclesiastical and political enemies at the highest levels of power.[15] Rather than preaching across the ocean to an England watching their every move, then, New England Puritan elites instead were forced to understand their experience on its own terms.

While an English jeremiad helped spur migration to New England, the language of decline reappeared almost immediately in the new settlements, as elites there began to exhibit a great deal of concern over a perceived lack of religious zeal, especially among the young. As a recognizable social and literary form, the jeremiad came into its own in second-generation New England, and most scholars emphasize the years between 1660 and 1685 as the period in which it attained its most highly developed form.[16] The 1660s were the early Restoration years in England, and as mentioned above gave rise to the realization by settlers that their community would *not* be serving as a model for a fully reformed England; increasingly vocal concerns about the younger generation suggest that New Englanders were beginning to realize that they did not merely circle in a holding pattern, always ready to return to the mother country. Domestic controversies during these years included the 1662 Halfway Covenant (which provided a conditional form of church membership for the children of church members who could not attest to a conversion experience, yet lived respectably); King Philip's War during the mid-1670s; and the increasing practice of church covenant renewal. The accession of the openly Catholic King James II in 1685 set in motion a series of events that would lead to James's ouster in the Glorious Revolution three years later, an event with significant ramifications for New England. Fewer jeremiads would appear as the 1680s wore on, perhaps reflecting increased tensions between the colonies and England: as Harry Stout has observed,

> Those sermons that addressed internal problems like leadership turnover, materialism, instability, and contention invoked the rhetoric of failure and impending doom for New England's native-born generation. Other sermons directed against external enemies celebrated the superior piety and unconquerable faith of the same generation.[17]

But where, in concrete, social terms, would an early New England settler have encountered a jeremiad? The jeremiad most often appeared in the form of an "occasional sermon," delivered at a public event authorized by the civil government and thus joining piety and politics in one event. Such occasions were "solidarity rituals," in Richard Gildrie's words, designed "to celebrate and rectify society's relationship with God, to define and legitimate their social and political order, and to control internal conflict." By restricting public expression on election days, or fast days, to clergy selected by civil magistrates, New England elites ensured that the sermon would occupy a prominent, virtually unchallenged, status on that day. In addition, by authorizing the publication of sermons delivered on such special occasions, and through their tight control of the press in early New England, colonial elites attempted to reinforce the spoken word's emphasis on order, public piety, and social hierarchy. While not necessarily "representative" (most sermons in early New England were preached on Sundays, and dealt with issues of personal salvation and spiritual discipline), occasional sermons played a vital role at the moment the people were choosing their leaders, or collectively exhorted God to show mercy on them in times of strife or uncertainty. Such official "occasions" (fast days, thanksgivings, elections) were more common in New England than in the mother country; and being asked to deliver such an address provided evidence of a minister's public stature.[18]

The occasional sermon was intended, then, to remind audiences of the religious roots of their colonizing enterprise, to assess the current status of the settlements and their inhabitants, and to call the community to repentance. The speaker aimed "not to be innovative or entertaining, but to recall for his audience the vision that first impelled New England's mission." With some variations, clergy inveighed against a society that had fallen away from its religious roots and was reaping the consequences in faction, pride, vanity, Indian wars, and natural disasters. In sharp contrast to "the supposed spiritual temperature of a past generation," Stephen Foster writes, "New Englanders could know they had fallen into a state requiring immediate repentance mainly because in the election sermons the minister regularly told them so." T. H. Breen describes the aims of the jeremiad thus: "The speaker would observe that his contemporaries had deserted the ways of their fathers, succumbing to a myriad of worldly temptations. Lest their audiences be discouraged, however, Jeremiahs explained that, if the colonists reformed and returned to the pristine manners of the founders, New England might still be saved from God's wrath."[19]

THE INTERNAL NARRATIVE: PIETY AND DECLINE IN EARLY NEW ENGLAND

The language of decline fills New England jeremiad sermons, as clergy traced a process of falling away from the unity and godliness of the founding generation to the fragmented and degenerate status of the community as they perceived it. "In spite of full churches and growing prosperity they envisioned the society as one in decay: a society that was losing the strength and zeal of the founders, was rapidly being passed to a weak and degenerate generation, was threatened on all sides by the forces of evil and from above by the hand of an angry God, and was therefore doomed to likely destruction."[20] But what, specifically, did these clergy say when they faced the assembled electors, clergy, and magistrates on their communities' election or fast days? How did New England elites lay out their view of the community's past glory, present danger, and future promise? I suggested in chapter 1 that the jeremiad proceeds by identifying symptoms of decline, contrasting the degenerate present with a virtuous past, and calling for reform and repentance; all within a scheme in which America plays a key role in God's plans for human history and the progress of the gospel. Let us consider each of these elements as they appeared in early New England.

Lamenting the Present: God's Chastisements and
New England's Sins

Central to every jeremiad in early New England was a catalog of misfortunes and calamities, along with the sins considered responsible for them. For New Englanders, real-world events like crop failures or Indian attacks could not be explained solely by reference to natural or political causes, but provided evidence of God's providential sovereignty and covenantal concern with their behavior.[21]

Perhaps the most alarming signs of divine wrath during these years were found in the destruction of King Philip's War. Increase Mather was only one of a number of New England divines who used the war's devastation to further their jeremiads. In his introduction to Samuel Hooker's 1677 election sermon in Hartford, John Whiting lamented "an adversary stirred up against us; the sword gone through the land, and thereby wasting and terror, desolation and death, carried up and down." One year earlier, William Hubbard, pointing to "the rage of the heathen so far let loose against us," had given voice to long-standing Puritan fears of barbarism and "wilderness" when he referred to "one of the forest...come upon us, the sword, and that of a cruel enemy." King Philip's War reminded New Englanders, if they needed to be reminded, that the wilderness just beyond their borders represented a significant threat to their very existence. "Coming after ministerial prophecies of doom," Harry Stout writes, "the devastation of King Philip's War strengthened the sermon's place in New England society....Such destruction was, after all, exactly what the ministers had predicted in their fast day sermons."[22]

The Native Americans had long represented a clear threat to the project of erecting a godly commonwealth in the American wilderness. It was a threat that (to New England minds, providentially) had been minimized by a smallpox epidemic that emptied the area around Boston just before the Winthrop fleet landed in 1630. Nonetheless, the natives not only posed military threats, but also cultural and psychological ones. The wilderness was not only all around the English settlers; it was, potentially, *within them* as well, and the natives represented an especially visible reminder of what would happen if wilderness was allowed to triumph over the forces of Christianity and civilization. As the seventeenth century drew to a close, Increase Mather's son Cotton was still worrying, in his own jeremiads, about "Indianizing" New Englanders.[23]

Close behind the Indian war and concerns about the natives' more subtle effects on New England piety came a series of natural disasters and catastrophes that provided clear evidence of God's disapproval of New England's religious backsliding. In a colony so dependent upon agriculture, crop failure was an ever-present concern: Samuel Danforth asked, "Why hath the Lord smitten us with blasting and mildew now seven years together, superadding sometimes severe drought, sometimes great tempests, floods, and sweeping rains, that leave no food behind them? Is it not because the Lord's house lyeth waste?" Increase Mather considered the explosion of a ship's cache of gunpowder in Boston Harbor as "itself a loud sermon . . . a warning piece from heaven," and interpreted a comet over New England as one more attempt by God to effect the colony's repentance, after war, fire, disease, and death had proven unsuccessful. Samuel Wakeman highlighted the increasing prevalence of disease, caterpillars, worms, and floods. Noting barren fields, sickness, scarcity, and war, Nicholas Noyes speculated, "Might not much of this have been prevented, if we had considered what was like to follow upon the degeneration of God's covenant-people?"[24]

But regardless of how severe any of these punishments might be, New England Jeremiahs considered them merely *signs* or symptoms of God's wrath over the community's betrayal of its covenant, evidence of deeper ills. How had such a promising colonizing project—one that evoked the Israelite passage into the Promised Land, that sought to re-create in the American wilderness the pristine virtues of the primitive church, if not the unspoiled Eden[25]—gone so wrong?

One word lay at the root of all the explanations on offer: *sin*. To explain decline from the high standards set by the first generation and the colony's eminent founders, clergy placed the blame for New England's moral decline on the sins—individual and collective—of its people: "the blame belongs to and must be laid upon our sins, and our selves for them . . . tis sin pushes God from a people." To Samuel Hooker, "Sins more than enough have been found with us to deserve all our sufferings, that we sin no more lest a worse thing come to us is the duty incumbent . . ." Although he offered a variety of possible reasons for New England's decline—the vagaries of human psychology, the human attraction toward novelty, the rarity of powerful preachers, and the always present concern for worldly advantage—Samuel Danforth admitted that "[t]he ground and principal cause [of forgetting our errand into the wilderness] is our unbelief."[26]

But *how* had sin brought about this decline? Insisting that one should not view sin simply as an action, or a series of discrete actions, but should also consider its cumulative *effects* on an individual or a community, John Davenport envisioned a "chain of evils, whereof sin is the first link, and draws on all the rest..." This idea of sin as an expansive and growing presence in New England society was also suggested by John Higginson, who observed that "This people of New-England are a people whom God hath signally owned and blessed in our first and former times...but as we have been multiplied and increased, so we have sinned, and provoked the Lord to anger against us." So the narrative of New England decline did not require a sudden or radical breaking-point with the founders' vision; given the nature of sin, such decline could result from a series of gradual deviations from proper belief and conduct. However its particulars were communicated, though, the jeremiad presented New England's dilemma as a dangerous falling away from original communal, spiritual virtue: "To begin well, but not hold out, not to maintain our integrity, purity, fellowship, faithfulness unto death, this is breach of covenant, and to belie the Lord and his ways."[27]

"Sin," though, remains a rather general term. Which sins, more specifically, or what sorts of sinning, lay at the root of New England decline? When we descend further into the specifics of how New England Jeremiahs described the sins they saw all around them, we encounter a list that will become more and more familiar as this book proceeds: worldliness, profanity, covetousness, swearing, luxury, apostasy, libertinism, Sabbath-breaking, sensuality, drunkenness, and hypocrisy were often rolled together into a potent rhetorical mixture that decried the fallen nature of New England society. Identifying the precise meaning of each of these terms is not always easy, as many of them shade into others on the list, and at times preachers simply let fly a string of vices and assumed that their meanings would be self-evident to their listeners.[28]

Take some more particular examples. The New England jeremiad tended to equate division and disagreement with irreligion. Urian Oakes lamented "those bitter contentions, and un-Christian distances and divisions among us"; Thomas Shepard included "wrangling and contention" as one of the fruits of "spiritual drunkenness"; and Increase Mather condemned the ways in which personal rivalries had gotten in the way of the community's responsibility to guard itself against sin. Introducing Samuel Arnold's 1674 election day sermon, Thomas Walley and Thomas Thatcher claimed that "the ensuing discourse is fitly spoken...considering...that we are fallen into a self-seeking generation...there is so much of a selfish private spirit prevailing, and so little of the contrary..."[29] (This concern about private interest and contentiousness was hardly new in New

England: Thomas Shepard, father of the second-generation clergyman, had identified private interest as a growing threat as far back as his election sermon in 1638, just eight years after the Winthrop fleet landed.[30])

Critics also decried increasing "worldliness" in New England. Defining worldliness as "an insatiable desire after perishing things," William Stoughton included it as the first in a long line of specific sins that he saw besetting the colony. This criticism was meant to sting New England audiences especially, since colonial leaders were adamant in their claims that religious and not economic impulses had driven their colonization effort. (Worldliness might not be such a concern in a colony like Virginia, but New Englanders felt that *their* settlements were a different story, with a different colonizing impulse, and thus a different set of expectations for religious and social life.) Decrying "that worldliness that is among us," Urian Oakes argued to his audience, "Surely there were other and better things the people of God came hither for, than the best spot of ground, the richest soil in the world..." "The first design of New England was purely religious," wrote Increase Mather, "but now we begin to espouse, and are eagerly pursuing another, even a worldly interest." Prosperity brings apostasy, Mather claimed, especially among the young, and in recent years "the interest of New-England is now changed from a religious to a worldly interest."[31] Closely connected to denunciations of worldliness were criticisms of New England colonists as addicted to luxury, sensuality, and economic prosperity.

Of course, an increasing emphasis on worldliness, sensuality, or luxurious apparel might be framed, alternately, as a cooling of the religious zeal that had characterized the colony's earlier days. Even without specific sins of commission to point to, New England Jeremiahs lamented a general falling off of religious intensity or fervor among the populace.

> Now let us sadly consider whether our ancient and primitive affections to the Lord Jesus, his glorious Gospel, his pure and spiritual worship, the order of his house, remain, abide, and continue firm, constant, entire, and inviolable....Doth not a careless, remiss, flat, dry, cold, dead frame of spirit grow in upon us secretly, strongly, prodigiously?

Temperature metaphors were widespread. Oakes lamented the "great decay of the power and practice of godliness that is too visible among us...are they not grown customary, formal...lukewarm, neither hot nor cold?" Thomas Walley put it most succinctly: "Faith is dead, and love is cold, and zeal is gone."[32]

Critics often saw all of these troubling developments as illustrating the more fundamental sin of pride. Pride could explain both "active" sinning as well as neglect of the covenant. "God would rather have his children poor and humble, than rich and proud," preached William Hubbard, while Oakes complained about the increasing effort many put into fine apparel and rich garments; because of this spirit of pride "we are in a tottering, ruinous, falling condition." Hubbard distinguished between spiritual pride and a more general pride in appearances, locating the former at the root of division, contention, and envy. "Worldliness," sensuality, the appeal of fine clothing and luxuries, and covetousness in New England society: all were rooted in pride.[33]

Not surprisingly, the ills and shortcomings of the present caused New England Jeremiahs to look to their collective past. There they found the settlements' founders, who had made such strides in the pursuit of a godly society and whose example continued to serve as a moral, spiritual, and political rebuke to their wayward progeny.

Looking to the Past: Praise for Virtuous Founders

New England Jeremiahs drew forceful narrative contrasts between the virtue of New England's founders and their children's degeneracy. "Puritan writers of the 1670s tended to see New England as having left its best and brightest days behind.... In the praise of the past we are to read a critique of the present..." The historical dimension of the jeremiad narrative is key here: rather than an abstract critique, jeremiads claimed that piety and godly order had once existed and had subsequently been lost. In the midst of calamity and decline, clergy repeatedly exhorted their audiences to remember their "first works" and "first love." Lamenting declining moral conduct, Increase Mather claimed simply that "[I]f [John] Winthrop, [Thomas] Dudley, [and John] Endicot were upon the bench such profaneness as this would soon be suppressed." Clergy repeatedly hearkened back to these larger-than-life personalities—"Winthrop, Dudley, [John] Cotton, [Thomas] Hooker...the instruments, under God, of laying the foundation of both our civil and ecclesiastical state"—who dominated the colony's public life during its early years, nurturing the young settlements through their difficult and vulnerable early years. Living up to the example of such illustrious parents was no mean feat, and speakers at times noted the unenviable position of the second New England generation. Heirs of a perhaps unprecedented "progress in Reformation," children of the founders almost inevitably faced "gradual declinings till that light hath almost been extinguished..."[34]

The biblical imagery of the vine—which brought together Jeremiah and the Christian Gospels—appeared frequently in descriptions of these founders. Nicholas Noyes called them "a noble vine...holiness to the Lord...men eminent in piety and virtue," and William Stoughton wondered, "Were our fathers as a noble vine, and shall we be as the degenerate plant of a strange vine?" Samuel Wakeman made clear that continued religious backsliding carried the threat of even further divine punishment: "Tis the noble vine that God planted so lately that hath brought forth such degenerate fruits.... Can this be but greatly provoking [to God]?" Samuel Hooker exhorted his Hartford audience to take heed of God's lesson, "that the vine brought from far and planted here, may still retain its ancient nobility."[35]

What made these founders so worthy of imitation? Why did jeremiads try so hard to "create an image of earliest New England radiant with qualities of the primitive"? For second-generation Jeremiahs, New England's founders had envisioned, created, and presided over a society that acknowledged its covenant with God in all aspects of its social life. In these early days, the jeremiad went, New England society had walked rightly with God. Speakers often explicitly compared New England's founders to Biblical heroes, and especially those of the Hebrew Scriptures:

> As for...the present generation in New-England...your fathers were such as did serve the Lord...they were Abrahams...Davids...there never was a generation that did so perfectly shake off the dust of Babylon...as the first generation of Christians that came into this land for the gospel's sake.[36]

Of course, these founders could not have done such great deeds on their own: God aided them by clearing the Pequots just prior to the Winthrop fleet's arrival, and by blessing their undertakings as a reward for their faithfulness. But such comparisons with Biblical heroes only served to emphasize further the view of New Englanders as latter-day Israelites. Addressing "New-England Israel" in 1673, Urian Oakes pointed to the founders: "You have had Moses, I mean, [men] of the same spirit, to lead and go before you.... They were wise and sober, and industrious and good men that laid our foundations, and did what men could do...toward the settling of us upon a lasting foundation of righteousness and holiness."[37]

Continued blessings, to be sure, depended on the continued willingness of the people and their leaders to remain steadfast in God's ways, a continuance that seemed sorely tested with the passage of time. Generational turnover evoked anxieties about the future of New England's covenantal status. As the 1670s progressed, and the first generation's leading citizens began gradually to die off, such anxieties appeared in jeremiads more frequently. Samuel Hooker's lament—"Is not the old generation almost gone?"—drew its rhetorical power from the fear of loosening social control similar to the scriptural account of Israel after Joshua's death.[38]

This fulsome praise was directed toward the founders not merely for what they *did* (found and nourish the young settlements), but for the religious impulse that drove them. In this account of the early settlement of New England, God effected his purposes through the efforts of "wise master-builders" who "laid the foundation of the building." "Our fathers neither sought for, nor thought of great things for themselves, but did seek first the kingdom of God and its righteousness, and all these things were added unto them." In John Higginson's words, "[T]his is never to be forgotten, that New-England is originally a plantation of religion, not a plantation of trade," and the first planters toiled to administer their society according to God's requirements. Having laid those foundations, the founders "left the carrying on of the superstructure unto [us, their successors and children]." The metaphor of building also appealed to William Stoughton, who viewed the task of his generation as "foundation work; not to lay a new foundation, but to continue and strengthen, and beautify, and build upon that which hath been laid."[39] Perhaps even more importantly, such *religious* attributes led to *social* virtues, and for second-generation Jeremiahs the founders embodied a vanishing commitment to social unity. Contention and disunity appeared prominently on nearly every catalog of the community's sins.

Whether actively rebelling against the government of God and good magistrates or merely drifting away from the requirements of a godly society, then, New England society was presented by its Jeremiahs as falling short of the piety necessary to sustain Winthrop's "city on a hill." Eleazar Mather looked back to a time characterized by "less trading, buying, selling, but more praying, more watching over our own hearts..."[40]

The Call to Reform and Renewal

Perched precariously between a glorious past and an uncertain but threatening future, New England Jeremiahs emphasized that their communities' prospects depended on the degree to which the present generation repented of its sins and reformed its behavior. This call for repentance, reform, and renewal drew its power not only from the rhetorical buildup within each sermon—as the clergy proceeded in straightforward Puritan fashion through the "Doctrine" and "Application" sections and toward the final teaching on "Use"—but also from the narrative elements laid out above: the litany of sins, the fetishism of founders, and the ongoing fear that true religion was imperiled both in America and in England. The jeremiad was always intended as a call to action, an exhortation to reform the community back into the image of its founders and godly ancestors, and *never* as an invitation to pessimism and resignation.[41] Reformation was always presented as a returning to the earlier covenantal relationship between God and the community. "Certainly we need reformation. Where is the old New-England spirit, that once was amongst us? Where is our first love? Where is our zeal for God, especially in matters respecting the first Table, which was once our glory? What is become of that life and power of godliness, that hath been in this place?" For Samuel Torrey,

> Reformation hath been the design of New England, and therefore Reformation it is the profession of New England. This work of reform, it hath been (especially by this generation) (not only) much neglected, but even (almost) utterly deserted, by a general defection and declension, which we are fallen into.... The first ministry of these churches, it was evidently a reforming ministry...God made them great reformers, and wrought a great work of reformation by them...[42]

But what did reformation *mean*? Recall that many a jeremiad was delivered on election day, when clergy reminded their fellow colonists that their civic and religious duties supported each other. A key element of these duties involved the wise casting of ballots for government officials. Of course, seriously contested elections were rare in early New England, and these events were not really "elections" in the way that contemporary readers might initially think of them. Nonetheless, the connection between civic and religious duty was always a theme of the election sermon. Jeremiads delivered on other occasions—public fasts and humiliation days, for example—served similar civic functions.

But if religious and civic affairs were clearly linked, what exactly did Puritans consider "good government"? Which qualities did they deem most important for a governor to possess? Here again the standard, explicitly or implicitly, was the first generation of New England settlers. When James Fitch advised the freemen to cast their votes for candidates most able to uphold New England's glory, he had already, just prior to this advice, spelled out what he had in mind: "The first rule is, Let us call to mind the first glory of the first planting in New England, and of the churches here... grace ruling and ordering both rulers and people under the glorious banner of true gospel holy love." Jonathan Mitchell and William Hubbard exhorted their listeners to eschew division on lesser matters of church practice; such an achievement, James Allen reiterated, would represent a worthy emulation of the founders, who did not let minor differences distract them from their common colonial undertaking. Not only was division contrary to the Christian charity urged on the company by John Winthrop on board the *Arbella*, it set a poor example for the younger generation.[43]

When divines told their audiences to choose carefully on election day, to choose godly men to rule over them, they drew on long-standing themes in Puritan social thought. The work of electing magistrates was crucial, since "a small error in the foundation will prove very destructive to the building." William Hubbard specifically insisted that electors not use their liberty "as an occasion to the flesh, but by love to serve one another"—eschew worldliness, in other words—by looking for fear of the Lord, learning, constancy, moderation, and humility among those who would be their rulers. The civil magistrate, on this understanding, was to serve as "nursing father" to the church, to defend God's ordinances, and to promote virtue and true religion, while suppressing vice; in brief, to ensure that the community lived up to the terms of its covenant with God. Indeed, the 1679 Reforming Synod claimed that "[w]e do not read in the Scripture, nor in history, of any notable general reformation amongst a people, except the magistrate did help forward the work."[44] All such sermons were predicated upon the view that magistrates would be held responsible for their community's sins.

But if the people had the solemn duty to choose godly rulers, clergy also reminded rulers of the solemn trust being bestowed upon them. Jonathan Mitchell exhorted Massachusetts leaders to look after the populace's spiritual welfare: "the concernments of a people framed into a body politic, are put into your hands, and of such a people as are the people of God... a part of God's Israel... This part of Israel do under God confide in you, and betrust you with their welfare..."[45] Both excessive severity and excessive leniency toward religious dissenters were equally liable to criticism, and clergy uniformly endorsed the civil magistrate's regulation of the colony's religious life.

Along with standard exhortations to repent for their worldliness and support godly rulers, audiences might hear calls for curtailing celebrations of Christmas (a Puritan staple from Old England), for suppression of alcohol trading with the Indians, against frequent visits to taverns, or any number of other specific sins for which the community ought to repent. Michael G. Hall argues that during the 1670s—the heyday of the New England jeremiad—"the attempt to legislate morality reached its high water mark," and Increase Mather played an instrumental role in helping the General Court formulate its laws against "Provoking Evils" during King Philip's War. In addition, Jeremiahs sometimes turned the tables, taking the older generations to task for failing to serve as strong role models. While Increase Mather noted that "the rising generation have many of them broken the covenant themselves," his brother Eleazar had earlier pointed out that parents had a responsibility for the formation of their children.[46]

In sum, if decline represented New Englanders' greatest fear, then repentance and reformation represented the best answers to those fears. New England's future moral-spiritual-political health, Jeremiahs insisted, could only be assured by recapturing some measure of the qualities of New England's godly and glorious past. Samuel Danforth reminded his audience that the reason for colonization in New England was "the expectation of the pure and faithful dispensation of the Gospel and the Kingdom of God." As they moved forward from a declining present into an uncertain future, Danforth mixed the present tense and the future tense: "Attend we our errand, upon which Christ sent us into the wilderness, and he will provide bread for us."[47]

THE EXTERNAL NARRATIVE: THE NEW ISRAEL AND THE MILLENNIUM

But the narrative of decline from godly foundations was only ever half the story. The "ordinary time" account of New England's history— including the ocean crossing, the building up of a holy commonwealth, and its subsequent decline and call to repentance—always appeared alongside (and nested within) a far grander story, a "sacred story" that viewed New England's history in theological and cosmological terms.

Explicit parallels between the Israelites—God's chosen people, led from captivity in Egypt through the wilderness to freedom—and New England settlers fill these sermons, and the almost exclusive selection of Old Testament passages as sermon texts further reinforced the analogy.[48]

Such parallels were fostered by typological readings of Scripture, in which people and events in the Old Testament were taken to pre-figure ones in later times. John Bishop called New England "a parallel people" with the Israelites. "They were highly favoured of God, so have we been; they deeply revolted from God, so have we done." In his explication of 1 Chronicles 12:32, William Hubbard made clear that although "Israel" in the particular text referred to "the posterity of Jacob," "we are by another trope (as often elsewhere) to understand, the holy people in covenant with God." Just like the Israelites, who journeyed into the wilderness to worship God purely, the first New England generation migrated "three thousand miles into this wilder-ness, that they might serve God with pure worship according to his own institution…"[49]

In clarifying that the cause of God's people was to live holy lives, John Higginson drew the parallel explicitly: "This was the cause of God and Israel then, the same is the cause of God and his people now…. This is the cause of God and his people in New-England…" Others identified the two peoples so strongly as to run them almost completely together: "Jerusalem was, New England is, they were, you are God's own, God's covenant people, and what concerned them in that their day, no less concerns you in this your day, this word that the Lord sent to Jacob, and it lighted on Israel, comes now to be applied to you…. never were any people more nearly parallel with them."[50]

The consequences of this New England–Israel parallel could be both comforting and deeply troubling, often at the same time. The belief that God has entered into a particular and protective relation-ship with one's community is certainly heartening and imbues com-munal life with a sense of chosenness and exceptionalism. At the same time, the nature of the covenant was clear: God requires fidelity or else there will be dire consequences. (The Israelites, after all, had had their golden calf.) Anthony D. Smith has written with regard to "chosen peoples" more generally, and offers these comments.

God's favour…is conditional on the fulfillment by the chosen of detailed moral and ritual codes…. God uses Israel's enemies, the Assyr-ians and the Babylonians, to redeem a purified Israel and thereby the world; while the Exodus from Egypt and the Covenant at Sinai are part of God's redemptive plan for humanity as a whole. Such a conception imposes a heavy burden upon the chosen. They are continually required to live up to strict moral standards. Backslidings are liable to severe punishment. This affords great scope to prophets, judges, sages and other moral crusaders to warn their kinsmen and thereby periodically to reaffirm the distinctive qualities and unique destiny of the community.[51]

For all the self-congratulatory rhetoric about Israel and their parallel status as God's chosen people, New England jeremiads were filled with anxiety and unease. How secure, after all, was the "chosen" status of this chosen people? For Sacvan Bercovitch, the jeremiad attests to New Englanders' unswerving faith in their status as God's people, and to their belief that God had already chosen them and thus would never forsake them. No matter how dire the outlook, Bercovitch argues, New England Jeremiahs echoed their prophetic precursor and sought to convince their audience that "their punishments confirmed their promise" and that, despite the persistent rhetoric of disaster, "restoration is already a foregone conclusion in God's mind." We should not, in Bercovitch's view, confuse the jeremiad's rhetorical structure of lament with a real crisis of confidence. The New England jeremiad, although laden with ambivalence, possessed a "stubborn optimism," and it served a *consensual* function in New England society, attempting to rally colonists around a notion of communal chosenness. More generally, in Bercovitch's view, the jeremiad infused American culture with confidence in its own destiny, and helped form commercial, middle-class American values. "America was consecrated from eternity for the New England Way."[52]

Certainly there is evidence for such a view.[53] At the same time, Bercovitch's interpretation understates the real mood of dark despair present in so many of these jeremiads, the fear that the community's sins, if not corrected, would indeed drive God to forsake New England entirely. As Perry Miller put it,

France and Spain are unlucky, or they miscalculate, or smallpox ravages them, and that is that. But a nation in covenant is systematically punished, the degree of affliction being exquisitely proportioned to the amount of depravity. While thus being chastised it is still in covenant—or, at least, as long as it has not committed the unpardonable sin which conclusively severs the covenant. Until that moment, no matter how bleak the prospect, there is always hope: if it reforms, it will recover the blessing. But where is that point of no return?"[54]

William Stoughton, for example, pointed out that God *could* cut New England off and use other communities to accomplish his purposes if the people did not reform. John Bishop provided a stark warning. "The ensuing discourse shows the great danger of a peoples departing from God by sin; it will cause God to depart from them, as here we find threatened," he wrote, and his readers would do well to remember that God's relationship with New England "is under condition (not absolute)." Wakeman told his audience that if people refuse to reform after God sends warnings, pleadings, and exhortations, "God will leave and give over such a people, though his own people…God's free promise and covenant is conditional."[55]

The introduction to Joseph Rowlandson's provocatively titled *The Possibility of Gods Forsaking a People* argued that the sermon's printing was highly valuable to "a land that have in some measure forsook their God, and are in danger of being forsaken." Rowlandson explained his title clearly to his listeners: of course God is everywhere, and thus can never fully withdraw his presence from any place, but what is meant here is "his especial presence, his favourable and gracious presence" with a people. Rowlandson was clear that just because a people had once been near to God, God could nonetheless forsake them if they continued in sin, a point echoed by Eleazar Mather: "If we forsake him, he will forsake us, notwithstanding all former engagements." The New England–Israel analogy, then, cut both ways—invocations of chosenness provided a comforting notion that God was especially concerned with New England's welfare, while such a close relationship also carried significant responsibilities for New Englanders and the threat of corrective punishments if they failed to live up to their covenant—and presented a stark dilemma to a people wanting to claim God's special protection. Far from a foregone conclusion, New England chosenness had to be reasserted each day. Perry Miller saw jeremiads as "necessary releases…[that] played a vital part in the social evolution because they ministered to a psychological grief and a sickness of the soul that otherwise could find no relief."[56]

THE JEREMIAD IN EARLY NEW ENGLAND: NARRATIVE, COMMUNAL IDENTITY, AND SOCIAL CONTROL

My goal in this chapter has not been to assess whether or not New England *was* in fact declining during the 1670s and 1680s, and if so in which ways; nor whether New England's Jeremiahs sincerely believed that they were declining or were rather using decline rhetoric to achieve other purposes. Evidence on these questions is sketchy, and often contradictory: some scholars claim that there was never any primitive unity, others that it did not outlive the settlements' first decades, and others that the first fifty years of New England settlement provide a remarkable example of relative social peace in the early modern world. What seems beyond dispute is that, among other things, generational pressures (including the clamor for land among the rising generation) and a rising merchant class served to heighten fears among the colonies' religious elites that the collective sense of mission they inherited from their parents was increasingly endangered. The jeremiad arose as a "ritual response" to such fears.[57] Far more important to the purposes of this book are a series of different questions: Which purposes or functions did the story of New England's decline accomplish for second-generation speakers and audiences? What do these stories tell us about the dynamics of New England society, and about the American society that it helped to bring into existence?

The jeremiad is a form of political rhetoric, a narrative deeply involved in the formation and maintenance of communal identity. As a response to perceptions of disorder and degeneracy, the jeremiad evokes a past characterized by unity and piety as well as a future in which such unity and piety might be recaptured. In other words, the New England jeremiad served as an instrument of social cohesion and control, an attempt to "prod an oft-quarreling and ever-diversifying citizenry into a more unified whole" and to direct that whole toward a specific political vision of New England's future.

It would be easy to view this sort of social control function as primarily a negative or repressive undertaking, some kind of ideological smokescreen or trickery perpetrated by educated clergy on a gullible populace. To do so, however, would be a mistake, and would oversimplify a complex social process: the jeremiad's role in creating and constructing early New England was a *creative* process as well. New England clergy sought simultaneously to bolster social bonds among the populace and to hold on to their own power, which they feared was slipping from their hands into those of rivals with very different (and less pious) visions of New England society. Much of this evocation of earlier times reflected a frustration with the clergy's loss of prestige and influence—whether due to increased immigration of non-Puritans, the internal rise of commercial interests, external pressures from England, or some combination of all these factors. By identifying New England's sins—worldliness, drunkenness, selfishness, private interest—and offering new hope for the future, the jeremiad made an appeal for a degree of control over its wayward and prodigal audience, but control in the service of a larger moral, religious, and social vision. One scholar of the period notes that "Puritans found themselves in a situation defined by the curious intermingling of three elements: the crumbling of their design, the waning of their piety, and the waxing of their prosperity."[58]

The power of the jeremiad always lay, in part, in the way it expressed *both* a sense of chosenness *and* a deep anxiety about the prospects of continued blessings, and tied the hope as well as the anxiety directly to the American experience. Certainly the notion of hope and collective renewal lies as much at the heart of the American jeremiad as does the notion of a brooding God watching for the nation's missteps. Taking only the (ordinary time) story of decline would miss the crucial element of hope and assurance that the jeremiad communicates; seeing only the "Chosen Nation" in sacred time would miss the moral drama at the heart of the jeremiad. This moral drama will become clearer as this book proceeds, and we will return to these questions about the role and function of the jeremiad in American life frequently in the chapters to come.

TOWARD THE REVOLUTION, AND BEYOND

New England *did* survive King Philip's War, despite Increase Mather's fears—and, apparently, without heeding his earnest exhortation. But by then, having triumphed over American enemies, New England faced foes in England. Massachusetts Bay's charter was revoked in 1684, and New England found itself under the thumb of (Anglican) royal governor Edmund Andros until he was removed in the fallout from the Glorious Revolution of 1688–89. (Increase Mather played no small part in defending Massachusetts Bay's interests as its colonial agent in London during and just after the Glorious Revolution. Mather secured a new charter, one that—to his initial chagrin—granted the franchise to all freeholders, rather than limiting the vote to church members as had been the practice.) Looking forward from the concerns of seventeenth-century Puritanism, we can see the gradual emergence of a self-consciously *American* identity over the course of the eighteenth century. Scholars continue to dispute the timing, or the pace, of such an emergent American identity, but over the course of the eighteenth century American elites and, more gradually, ordinary Americans—not only in New England, but also their middle Atlantic and Southern neighbors—began, if only haltingly and tentatively, to think of themselves as Americans. While Bercovitch certainly overstates his case when he states that "[t]he myth of America is the creation of the New England Way"—this myth has many sources, and no single region can claim exclusive responsibility for such a complex creation—he does highlight the jeremiad's centrality in American rhetoric and literature. It remains essential to national self-understandings down to our own day.[59]

Increase Mather's son Cotton stands as a crucial transitional figure in the jeremiad's history. In his 1702 masterwork, *Magnalia Christi Americana*, Cotton Mather sketched out a grand narrative of New England's history as central to the progress of the Reformation. The *Magnalia* told the story of the "wonders of the Christian religion, flying from the depravations of Europe to the American strand," and the "change in the tenor of divine dispensations" toward New England due to the backsliding of a generation who came to forget the reasons for their errand into the wilderness. Still, Cotton Mather argues (from his vantage point in the early eighteenth century) that through individual self-reformation, the renewal of church covenants, and the firm action of civil magistrates, it became evident that "the people of God in this land were not gone so far in degeneracy...and there was proportionally still more of true religion, and a larger number of the strictest saints in this country, than in any other on the face of the earth." With all the ambivalence we might expect from a descendant of such hallowed founders, Mather acknowledged "the increased frowns of Heaven upon the country, since [the Reforming Synod of 1679]"; despite the many saints who properly ordered their spiritual lives, "yet the number of them that so strictly 'walk with God' has been woefully decaying." Echoing so many of the jeremiads discussed in this chapter, Mather concluded that "[t]he old spirit of New England hath sensibly been going out of the world, as the old saints in whom it was have gone; and instead the spirit of the world, with a lamentable neglect of strict piety, has crept in upon the rising generation."[60] Eight decades into New England colonization, and still the concern with worldliness.

Of course, as Mather's *Magnalia* so clearly shows, the New England jeremiad did not vanish after its heyday in the second half of the seventeenth century. Fast and election day sermons continued, and clergy continued to lament perceived spiritual decline. "There was once a very distinguishing work of God's grace in the midst of us," preached John Webb in 1734, but "[t]his work of divine grace...is fallen into a languishing state for the present." Nor did natural disasters go unnoticed: the New England earthquake of 1727 spurred a variety of theological and social commentaries, and although most commentators admitted that earthquakes and other such calamities had natural causes, Thomas Prince exhorted his listeners to remember also that "the Lord has placed us over great and hideous vaults...ready to open when he feels it time to bury us in them...and execute his most righteous judgments."[61]

As the eighteenth century progressed, the jeremiad continued to play a prominent role in the life of New England communities. In 1740, Joseph Sewall took the example of the Ninevites in Jonah 3:10 as a fast day sermon text, listing a familiar litany of sins (disrespect of the Sabbath, oppression, the abuse of taverns) and calling on his compatriots to "seek...God with prayer and fasting...with true repentance, and sincere endeavours after reformation." "[I]f we refuse to repent and reform," he continued, "we shall be condemned out of our own mouths." And the title of Samuel Wales's 1785 *The Dangers of Our National Prosperity; and the Ways to Avoid Them* illustrates that concerns over worldliness and wealth did not die with Cotton Mather. The tradition of public fasts continued as well, providing further occasions for jeremiadic warnings to the people of the young nation.[62]

Nor did eighteenth-century Jeremiahs speak only of decline. The idea of America as New Israel continued to echo down through the Great Awakening and into the Revolutionary period. Parallels with Israel provided powerful rhetorical support for the struggle for independence: in 1777, Nicholas Street compared George III with Pharaoh, but reminded his listeners that God humbled the Israelites in the wilderness in punishment for their sins. True to the jeremiadic tradition, Street pointed to Americans' greed, selfishness, disregard for the Sabbath, profaneness, and corruption, and assured them that such judgments will increase "till we are brought to a repentance and reformation." In the same year, Abraham Keteltas preached that the American Revolution was a godly cause, that the Americans were "contending for the rights of mankind, for the welfare of millions now living, and for the happiness of millions yet unborn."[63]

As hostilities neared an end, Ezra Stiles preached a sermon in which he hastily dispatched the Scriptural text before him and launched into a commentary on current events. After a cursory look at the passages in which Moses glimpses the Promised Land, Stiles admitted, with disarming sincerity, that "I have assumed the text only as introductory to a discourse upon the political welfare of God's American Israel, and as allusively prophetic of the future prosperity and splendour of the United States." Some years later, Samuel Langdon boldly proposed that "[i]f I am not mistaken, instead of the twelve tribes of Israel, we may substitute the thirteen states of the American union..." And finally—at least, with regard to the nation's founding period—William Gribbin has pointed out that jeremiads played an important role during the War of 1812, emphasizing the ways in which a jeremiad taking issue with *elected* American leaders had to be more delicately managed than those that targeted a distant and tyrannical monarch:

> For several more terms, deists would foul the presidential chair, while New England remained within the unrepentant Union, tied to slave states ever bolder in their infamy. Mail would still be delivered on the Sabbath, in spite of Christian protest. The Constitution would not be amended to recognize the Trinity, nor would religious tests for public officials be accepted. And yet—a great puzzle—Heaven's justice would not overtake America.[64]

Edmund S. Morgan famously identified a "Puritan Ethic" as instrumental in guiding the colonies' resistance to British control, and their eventual establishment of a national government of their own.[65] This is not to say that Puritanism per se, as an explicit theological commitment, long outlasted the second generation of New Englanders.[66] In fact, the nation's founders and early presidents (so heavily drawn from the American South) were in many ways the antithesis—religiously, socially, philosophically—of the Puritans. Yet the Puritan ethic continued to exercise a strong cultural and rhetorical pull on the new nation, serving as a model for the American Whig movement in the 1820s. Such prominent Americans as Timothy Dwight, Ralph Waldo Emerson, and George Bancroft (not to mention that observant Frenchman, Alexis de Tocqueville) located the roots of the American spirit in early New England Puritanism. Indeed, these later authors put the Puritans to some distinctly un-Puritan uses, such as trying to justify the young commercial republic and its fundamental values:

> [I]n the hands of Whig orators, the Puritans...were made into a founding legend that demonstrated how the commercialization of the economy and the central role of government in promoting this development could invigorate a sense of community and restore order to a fragmented American population.[67]

The continued presence of American slavery would make this rhetoric increasingly untenable. Indeed, the eighteenth-century revolutionaries—less sectarian, more willing to compromise in the interest of political agreement—would vie with first-generation New Englanders for the status of American founders, a status central to the jeremiad's rhetorical power. In the next chapter, we turn to antebellum and Civil War narratives to understand more fully the continuity and change in the history of the American jeremiad.

THREE

Decline, Slavery, and War

The Jeremiad in Antebellum and Civil War America

For the sake of a principle our fathers dared to defy the proudest nation on the globe. They suffered. They conquered. We are never tired of praising them. But when we are called on to stand firm for principle, we tremble, we whine, we evade duty, and shuffle up a compromise, by which we may sell out conscience, and save our pocket.... Our past greatness sprung from our obedience to God's natural and moral law.... The Southern states and the North alike found poisonous seed sown in colonial days. The North chose to weed it out. The South determined to cultivate it, and see what it would bear. The harvest-time has now come. We are reaping what we sowed.

Not only are these calamities upon us, but they are sent, as we verily believe, in retribution of our sins. The hand of God is in them. He is visiting upon us the threatenings he denounced against his ancient people—and for a similar reason. We have, as a nation, forsaken God's law, and broken his statutes; we have resisted his authority and abused his forbearance; we have sinned against him so long and so audaciously, that his patience was exhausted:—and he is now visiting our transgression with the rod, and our iniquity with stripes.

A whole nation may thus indulge its sins, may proudly and daringly rush onward in a career of oppression, and maintain that such wickedness is the indefeasible right of popular sovereignty, till all the veins, arteries, and vital organs of the social system and the state are filled and poisoned with the mischief; and then the spontaneous combustion ensues, and the repulsive, smoking, worm-eaten carcass of an empire is cast forth into God's providential Gehenna, an offence and a warning to the nations.[1]

THE JEREMIADS OF JANUARY 4

Horatio Nelson Taft, an examiner in the United States Patent Office in Washington, D.C., confided to his diary that although January 4, 1861, was a "mild and pleasant day…people feel much like wearing sackcloth."[2] Outgoing President James Buchanan, whose recent State of the Union Address had blamed the crisis facing the nation largely on Northern abolitionist agitators, had designated January 4 a Day of Prayer and Fasting for the imperiled Union. Just two months earlier, Illinois Republican Abraham Lincoln had been elected president from among a field of four candidates. Although he garnered just under 40 percent of the popular vote (and was left off the ballot entirely in most Southern states), Lincoln received more than twice the electoral votes of his nearest rival. In the months since the election, Lincoln had made no public comment on the issues dividing the nation; during the campaign he had done little more than refer inquirers to the Republican Party platform, which opposed the spread, but not the existence, of slavery. Despite (or perhaps because of) Lincoln's silence, Southern states spent November and December 1860 charting their own, separate, political futures. The Mississippi legislature passed resolutions in favor of secession less than a month after Lincoln's election; South Carolina passed a secession ordinance on December 20.

Americans took President Buchanan's call to heart. From Kentucky to Maine, from Virginia to Iowa, clergy laid out for their congregations the litany of misfortunes—"national sins"—afflicting the American polity. Not surprisingly, interpretations of who was to blame and what was to be done differed radically. Taken as a group, however, the clergy's offerings that day illustrate some of the American jeremiad's central features: a lament over the nation's sins; reflection on the past, and especially on the example of founders and founding principles; a call to repentance and renewal; and an overarching sense that God's hand was active in the course of American political life.

Of course much of the discussion that day had to do with slavery, "the root of all this bitterness," according to one preacher; and "not only a sin, but…a fountain from which have flown so many sins," according to another. Critics denounced slavery not only for its incompatibility with American ideals of liberty—it contradicted "every principle and sentiment in our Declaration of Independence, and revers[es], in its spirit, operation, and tendencies, the theory, objects, and working of our Constitution and National inspiration," said Henry W. Bellows—but also for the way it had given rise to polarization and extremism across the nation. Not all Jeremiahs identified slavery itself as such a singular national sin: abolitionists also came in for harsh criticisms (from both Northerners and Southerners) for their confrontational and provocative behavior. Henry J. van Dyke connected abolitionism with infidelity and irreligion, while Thomas Guion and Carlton Chase noted how abolitionists ignored the culpability of the North in the origin and perpetuation of American slavery. (In Baltimore, George Cummins emphasized the responsibilities that slavery placed on the Christian South, including the spiritual and physical care of an inferior race and the oversight of a practice that had existed since Biblical times.[3]) All such critiques, however, identified slavery as the clear nexus of political, social, economic, and religious conflicts facing the nation.

And yet the nation was concerned about a great deal more than slavery. Southern as well as Northern clergy emphasized American profanity, greed, luxury, pride, and a more general disrespect for authority as evidence of grave moral defects in the public character. In Massachusetts, G. W. Hervey ranged across a host of sins—badly behaved children, church dissensions, ostentatious philanthropists, failure to observe the Sabbath, arrogance, and pride—as symptoms of a deep crisis in national life. Henry Ward Beecher, perhaps the nation's most famous preacher, offered a list that, in addition to slavery, included rising crime and vice in the nation's cities, corruption bred by economic prosperity, and the spread of avarice, bribery, vanity, and boasting. What greater national sin could exist, still others wondered, than the lack of an explicit recognition of God in the United States Constitution? "Why should we expect God's blessing on our Union as one nation? There is one constitutional defect in our organic law. It contains no acknowledgment of God; no recognition of Jesus Christ." After all, a nation that failed to honor the Sabbath—that delivered mail, or drilled soldiers, on the Lord's Day—could hardly fail to arouse God's wrath.[4]

Identifying national sins, though, was only the first step. Placing them into a historically meaningful context was equally if not more significant. In true jeremiadic fashion, speakers argued that the nation's political crisis was a direct consequence of abandoning the legacy of the nation's founders. "If our nation has attained its present greatness," preached Cornelius Swope, "it has been in spite of our departure from the purity of principle and practice of the patriots who first framed the charter of our independence." Both North and South shared a deep rhetorical commitment to the founders. For many in the North—especially newly emerging Republicans and less strident antislavery audiences—the founders had scrupulously avoided mentioning slavery in the text of the Constitution, expecting that the South's "peculiar institution" would die a gradual death. (Abraham Lincoln's Cooper Union speech is a powerful example of this view of the founders' intentions.) "And now the question is to be decided," preached John Abbott, "whether we will adhere to the constitution which our fathers formed, or, intimidated by these [Southern] threats, abandon this constitution, and establish another, modeled in accordance with the demands of slavery?" But Southern clergy valorized the nation's founders as well, and present-day Americans suffered by comparison: in Richmond, Virginia, C. H. Read likened the "time of Washington" to "our *golden age*" and lamented the present as an "age of brass, now running its rapid course." Seven hundred miles away, in Bath, Maine, John Flavell Mines similarly lamented the fading of revolutionary brotherhood and the growth of rancor among the children of the founding patriots.[5]

Finally, like all jeremiads, the sermons of January 4 concluded with calls for reform. If national sins imperiled the moral and spiritual health of the nation, then national repentance seemed the obvious solution. Robert Breckinridge, whose nephew, the vice president, had just lost to Lincoln in the 1860 election, asked his Lexington, Kentucky, audience to remember that

> [n]ational judgments never come except by reason of national sins; nor are they ever turned aside except upon condition of repentance for the sins which produced them...[R]epentance for sin...is the infallible condition of divine pardon and acceptance, not only in the case of individuals, but more obviously still and more immediately in the case of nations, since nations, as such, have no existence in a future life.

Don't expect political solutions, Breckinridge counseled, before changing individuals' hearts and minds.[6]

As a *political* narrative, however, the jeremiad is never simply about individual responses; it is about collective action as well. Breckinridge, loyal to the South but convinced that secession was neither wise nor constitutional, advised Kentuckians to resist joining the secessionist movement, which he saw as dominated by cotton interests not concerned with the welfare of their state. Other Southern voices, of course, such as Florida's "rebel bishop" Augustin Verot, saw things quite differently. Those who worried about the absence of God from the federal constitution, not surprisingly, called for a constitutional solution to rectify that omission. A few Northern speakers recommended simply letting the Southern states leave, confident that God would look after the North.[7]

The confident assumption that God was providentially interested in the American political experience, which we encountered earlier in the New England jeremiad, continued to play an important role in the nineteenth century, and January 4 showed just how central the notion of American chosenness remained. After casting an eye over the history of the Jews—chosen by God, but seen as having ultimately been given over to ruin because of their disobedience and rejection of Christ—Benjamin Dorr asked,

> Is there anything in those portions of Scripture which we have been considering, that does not meet our own case?...Look back over all the past in our history, our rapid increase, our multiplied blessings, our numerous deliverances, and our ungrateful returns for all God's mercies; and tell me if the Psalmist does not describe these as truly and clearly, as if he intended the description for us alone?

Even if the connection between America and Israel was not so direct, the nation was clearly central to God's purposes. Orlando Hutton discerned the hand of God in the origins of the American political system, and Alexander McGill saw God using both England *and* America as instruments in the progress of the gospel and the redemption of the world.[8]

The January 4 national fast proved about as successful as Buchanan's subsequent attempts at holding the Union together. That very day, on orders from Alabama governor Andrew Moore, four companies of the state's militia seized the federal munitions depot near Mount Vernon, near Mobile. Meanwhile, back in Washington, Senator Jefferson Davis wrote to Mississippi governor J. J. Pettis, discussing the most advantageous timing for Southern secession. Davis advocated the resignation of Southern senators as soon as the "Black Republican" administration of Abraham Lincoln took power.[9] Less than two months later, Davis would be sworn in as president of the Confederate States of America. Seizures of federal property throughout the South continued, as did the secessions of Southern states: Mississippi seceded just five days after the national fast; Florida, on January 10; Alabama, the following day; Georgia on the nineteenth; Louisiana, a week after that. The first half of February 1861 saw the secession of Texas and the adoption of a provisional Confederate Constitution. A month later the official Confederate Constitution was ratified and the Confederacy inaugurated.

The journey from the national fast of January 4, 1861 to the attack on Fort Sumter on April 12 of that year, and ultimately to Lee's surrender at Appomattox Courthouse four years later, was set in motion, and the resulting carnage spurred on, in part, by the rhetorical power of the American jeremiad. But the tensions and anxieties to which the jeremiad gave voice did not spring forth out of thin air on that day, nor did they cease on January 5.[10]

CONTEXT: EARLY AMERICAN POLITICS, RELIGION, AND SOCIETY

The first half of the nineteenth century saw remarkable growth in the complexity of American political and economic life, as the young nation spread inland from the eastern seaboard and further developed its internal markets. Thomas Jefferson's Louisiana Purchase of 1803 doubled the nation's area and provided a host of new territory to explore and map; further expansion came four decades later, in the decidedly less peaceful Mexican War. By 1850, the Union had grown to thirty-one states. Hand in hand with the nation's political expansion went debates over the nation's economic development, as such figures as John Quincy Adams, Henry Clay, and the nascent Whig party sought to use the national government to facilitate internal improvements and the emergence of a commercial economy, while Democrats viewed such developments with suspicion and championed the interests of rural and lower-class Americans.[11]

Political and economic developments went hand in hand with religious ones such as the Second Great Awakening, ongoing revivalism, and the heavy involvement of evangelical Protestants in movements for moral and political reform (e.g., temperance, women's rights, antipoverty, abolition). Despite the variety of religious movements present during the early national period—and pluralism had characterized the American religious landscape since its earliest days—Anne C. Rose has rightly pointed out that "Protestant Christianity was the original language through which most Americans understood their purposes as individuals and as a people." Of course American Protestantism was a multifaceted and complex entity; as we saw in the January 4 jeremiads, clergy of all stripes managed to criticize mainstream materialism, selfishness, and dishonor of the Sabbath.[12] The war, when it finally came, represented not only a devastating armed conflict but also a crisis of meaning, of theological understanding, of biblical interpretation.[13]

All of these developments ensured that battles over slavery would continue. Yet we should take care not to read the war back into every piece of political rhetoric produced during the first half of the nineteenth century. Eugene D. Genovese has rightly argued that regional and cultural differences between North and South should neither be overestimated (making the Civil War seem inevitable) nor underestimated (making the war seem merely a result of political indecision and bungling). Certainly the American political system had managed on several occasions to pacify the various parties to these debates, at least temporarily.[14] So although slavery remained a cause of great concern to many, and schemes for gradual or compensated emancipation were widespread (promoted, not least, by Henry Clay and Abraham Lincoln), it is by no means certain that Americans saw the nation moving inexorably toward civil war. Even many of the January 4 Jeremiahs found it hard to believe that North and South would actually come to blows.

Politics, economics, culture, and religion represent intertwined elements of a developing national self-image. By the 1850s a powerful conception of American chosenness—which David Blight calls "a central unifying myth of nineteenth-century America"—had firmly entrenched itself in American public discourse. In the words of Ernest Tuveson, "Confidence in the ideal of America as the new chosen people reached a peak of enthusiasm in the years immediately preceding 1860." Mark Noll points to a powerful "Christian republican synthesis" in antebellum America, which involved a skepticism of received authority, a focus on the Bible alone, an emphasis on the need for grace, a deep suspicion of Roman Catholicism, and a confidence in the ordinary powers of "common sense" human reasoning. Such a synthesis, in Noll's view, made possible the simultaneous development of American capitalism and American evangelicalism. Robert P. Forbes has coined the phrase "evangelical Enlightenment" to denote this confluence of evangelical fervor and Enlightenment self-interest, a confluence that promoted a commitment to social and material progress, reform, and intimations that a new age was just around the corner.[15]

Nor was this language of chosenness the exclusive property of white evangelicals. Not only did it undergird an emerging sense of African-American nationhood, as Eddie Glaude has shown, but African-Americans would turn much of the vocabulary and imagery of evangelical Protestantism back on itself by constructing a jeremiad of their own, in which white Protestants were not so much Israelites as Egyptians, holding God's long-suffering chosen people captive and threatening to bring God's judgment down upon their own heads. In addition, even many New England Transcendentalists and Unitarians, who had long left behind the Puritan orthodoxy of their ancestors, would find it difficult to avoid speaking of sin, salvation, millennium, and apocalypse when seeking to understand the Civil War.[16]

The perpetuation of this national self-image required, and in turn fostered, new forms of communication. David Walker Howe identifies a "communication revolution" in which over the course of thirty-odd years "there would be greater strides in the improvement of communication than had taken place in all previous centuries" as one of the defining features of the early national period. The years between 1800 and 1850 saw a revolution in the production, distribution, and consumption of printed materials, much of it spurred on by evangelical Protestantism's missionary impulses. (In 1825, for example, the Executive Committee of the American Tract Society declared the printing press to be "the grand medium of communication in all parts of the missionary world."[17]) Westward expansion left many Americans without a direct relationship to a pastor or a Christian community, despite the best efforts of revivalists and traveling preachers, a fact that only reinforced the determination of evangelical Protestants to place religious materials into the hands of as many Americans as possible, as quickly as possible. Advances in printing technologies and an emerging national economy (with its attendant transportation and monetary systems) facilitated exchange on an ever-larger scale and made the increased circulation of printed materials possible. By the mid-nineteenth century an expansive system for national distribution was firmly in place.

American society had come a long way, then, since the dreams of godly community that had animated early New England divines. Clergy in early New England had possessed, if not a monopoly on religious speech, certainly a near monopoly on institutional resources to promote that speech, as well as control over educational and social institutions. Having such speakers selected and invited by the civil magistrates—and having their sermons subsequently reprinted and distributed by order of the General Court—was an effective way to shape public discourse and to present a unified set of guidelines for acceptable public behavior. Social critique, when it arose, came largely from within the colony's ruling elite. The attempt was clearly to harness both the spoken and printed word to the task of social control.[18]

As in New England, during the antebellum and Civil War years jeremiads often appeared first in the form of fast, thanksgiving, or election sermons, which were then republished and circulated to a wider audience. But the American *nation* had disestablished churches and ensured freedom of the press, association, and peaceful assembly. State establishments of religion were not outlawed, but clearly on the decline; the final one, in Massachusetts, fell in 1833. By the nineteenth century, increases in clerical professionalism, mobility, and the congregational role in hiring and firing had changed the public role of American clergy in important ways. There is no denying, of course, that many Protestant leaders occupied powerful public positions during the antebellum period, but they were leading players in a lively religious marketplace rather than an elite marked off from the people by distinctions of education and literacy. Religious discourse during the early national period came from increasingly diverse corners: not just in annual or occasional public events solemnized by civil magistrates, but through revivals, lecture tours, newspapers, and a host of other opportunities for religious and political leaders to weigh in on public issues.[19]

All in all, then, despite the radical transformations of American society from the early eighteenth through the mid-nineteenth century, the United States remained in many important ways a deeply Christian nation throughout the Civil War years. Of course, no cultural norms go entirely unchallenged, and many American clergy expressed deep reservations about the moral health of the nation's citizens (and its churches), who often seemed only too eager to offer their blessings to the nation's commercial and expansionist westward conquest. These moral concerns, articulated against the backdrop of the nation's transition from a rural, agriculturally based economy to one more dependent on manufacturing and markets, often mirrored republican objections to luxury and the political-moral degeneracy it brought, and dovetailed with the concerns of Jeremiahs of various sorts.

THE INTERNAL CRITIQUE: STORIES OF AMERICAN SINFULNESS ON THE EVE OF THE CIVIL WAR

Symptoms of Decline: The Nation's Sins

The nineteenth-century jeremiad, like its New England predecessor, catalogued a litany of sins that threatened to bring God's judgment on the land. With the outbreak of war in 1861, the notion of divine judgments became painfully real, but the sense of urgency about the nation's moral and spiritual state long predated the attack on Fort Sumter. The January 4 fast day offered a microcosm of arguments that had been circulating in the United States for years, but the complete picture is much more complex.

At the broadest level, American Jeremiahs lamented the nation's collective sins. Recall that all jeremiads presume a God who attends providentially to human history and who acts in history through the distribution of rewards and punishments, victories and setbacks for communities that (respectively) do or do not follow God's laws. In the words of Southern Presbyterian bishop Benjamin Palmer, "The nation is in a clear sense a sort of *person* before God—girded with responsibilities which draw it within his comprehensive government." Such sentiments were echoed by his Northern counterparts as well, who also viewed earthly communities as moral agents, collectively responsible to God for their actions. The Puritan idea that rulers would be held responsible for tolerating the misdeeds of their people continued to cast a long shadow.[20]

Of such national sins, the debate over slavery clearly loomed largest over the national landscape, and had done so for many years. Variously described—by opponents and supporters, respectively—as "a moral cancer that is eating at the vitals of our piety" or "a trust providentially committed to us," slavery ultimately proved beyond the ability (or will) of American politicians to settle. Abolitionist jeremiads viewed the institution as an affront to Christian and American ideas of equality, and the thundering voice of Frederick Douglass had been on the scene since the early 1840s, seeking to hold white Americans' feet to the fire of reform and abolition. By continuing to condone this cardinal political sin, said Gilbert Haven, the nation essentially forgot its own founding principles. But Northern clergy, even those hostile to abolitionist extremism, often stressed that the North was far from innocent. According to S. A. Hodgman, "[T]he nation is responsible for the existence of the system of slavery… [therefore] the expiation of the guilt thereof, is justly required from the whole nation." At least in theory, such attempts at evenhandedness might avoid the sorts of recriminations that polarized and poisoned antebellum political debates: Haven, for example, claimed that he sought "not [to array] the North against the South, but the whole nation, North and South, against [slavery]."[21]

Calling slavery a sin was rhetorically effective when speaking to certain Northern audiences, of course, but radically complicated any hopes of achieving a political settlement. In the words of Eugene Genovese, "To declare slavery a sin meant to reject all proposals for gradual emancipation, to say nothing of amelioration, for it condemned every slaveholder as a wanton sinner. It was a call to holy war." For their part, proslavery preachers presented a powerful and coherent biblical defense of slavery that appealed to Americans' widespread sympathy for literalist approaches to Scripture. Even many of those who opposed slavery valued the Union more, and were unwilling to sacrifice almost 100 years of American progress for the freedom of blacks.[22]

Other sins besides slavery deserved the nation's consideration as well. The religious character of the nation and the importance of its Protestant heritage were common themes. Clergy often pointed to the lack of any mention of God or Christianity (let alone Protestantism) in the Constitution. This point became an especially sensitive one after the establishment of the Confederacy, whose Constitution, while closely mirroring that of the Union, invoked "the favor and guidance of Almighty God." George Duffield pointed to the nation's toleration of polygamy among Mormons, while Beecher reminded his listeners of the experiences of Native Americans: "A heathen people have experienced at the side of a Christian nation, almost every evil which one people can commit against another." Mexicans have cause to lament their sufferings at the hands of the United States as well, Beecher insisted, evoking a larger religious concern about the values that underlay American expansionism into the West.[23]

These sins were collective ones, and cast the longest shadow over the American political landscape; yet they were hardly the *only* vices for which God might be angry at the nation. An almost interminable litany of more individually based spiritual transgressions, many of which evoked earlier New England jeremiads—"worldliness," profanity, boastfulness, avarice, pride, declining respect for authority or the Sabbath, loss of public-spiritedness, intemperance, badly behaved children, gambling—poured forth from clergy, public figures, and social critics of all stripes. Greed and love of material gain appear prominently, as increasing threats to public virtue. "In our prosperity we have forgotten our dependence [upon God]," preached Henry Boardman on Thanksgiving Day in 1860. Just several weeks earlier, Robert L. Dabney had lamented the "general worldliness" and "selfish profusion and luxury" he saw all around him, along with profanity, blasphemy, and the violent defense of personal honor so common among his compatriots in the South. Issues like drunkenness had long animated evangelical social critics and temperance reformers, and straddled the line between individual and social pathology.[24]

The coming of the war muted some of these moralistic critiques, but concerns about individual moral standards remained on preachers' minds, and reappeared especially in the wake of military defeats. Steven Woodworth's comprehensive account of the religious lives of Civil War soldiers documents both the revivalist piety widespread in each army's camps *and* the vice and licentiousness that led so many to fear divine judgment. As George Freeman looked back at the war's outbreak from the vantage point of 1865, he recalled how focused Americans had been on moneymaking, when they should have been focused on averting the impending crisis. While expressing confidence that the war's outcome was in God's hands (and that God would ultimately favor the Union), Ezra S. Gannett spoke bluntly of Americans' irreligion, worldliness, selfishness, and passionate and prejudiced political behavior, and implied that the war's trauma might be good for the nation's soul. Southerners, for their part, saw similar moral failings throughout the war years. Many noted troubling symptoms of moral decay both early on—just after the war's outbreak, Benjamin Palmer lamented that "the greed of gain has rusted into the hearts of our people"—and especially as the tide turned against them after 1863.[25]

Eventually, of course, the war itself became the most obvious evidence of moral, spiritual, and political decline—both punishment for, and evidence of, the nation's continuing sinfulness. The grandchildren of the revolutionary generation taking up arms against each other was itself a sign that something had gone terribly wrong with the American "experiment." As in New England, then, so in the nineteenth-century United States: Jeremiahs found no shortage of sins to decry as they examined the perilous moral state of the nation.

Virtuous Founders

Like their New England predecessors, virtually all nineteenth-century Jeremiahs engaged in hagiography—we might almost say fetishism—of the founders. Imagery of decline filled jeremiads during the years leading up to the Civil War. Since the founders had covenanted with God, proclaimed Israel Dwinell, God was, through the war, pleading with the country to repent and change its ways.[26]

Most antislavery critics saw a stark contrast between the political values of the nineteenth-century United States and those of the founding generation. George Boardman feared that patriotism was "rapidly becoming a virtue only historical," and others mentioned the fading memories of revolutionary brotherhood. Frederick Douglass's noted July 4, 1852, address displays this rhetorical contrast with utmost clarity:

"I scarcely need say, fellow-citizens, that my opinion…fully accords with your fathers.…How circumspect, exact, and proportionate were all their movements! How unlike the politicians of an hour!" Just two years after Douglass made his remarks, Theodore Parker opined that "since '76 our success was never so doubtful as at this time." Douglass's caustic response to Lincoln's 1861 Inaugural Address contrasted the new president's political timidity with an earlier generation of national figures:

> How sadly have the times changed, not only since the days of Madison—the days of the Constitution—but since the days even of Daniel Webster. Cold and dead as that great bad man was to the claims of humanity, he was not sufficiently removed from the better days of the Republic to claim, as Mr. Lincoln does, that the surrender of fugitive slaves is a plain requirement of the Constitution.[27]

Of course, such invocations of the founders were often intensely partisan. Henry Ward Beecher justified growing antislavery sentiment in the North, and (later) armed conflict, as a revolution "back to the doctrines of the fathers…in favor of our institutions. We have simply taken the old American principles," he claimed. "We stand for the doctrines and instruments that our fathers gave us." Others tied antislavery politics directly to the founders by name. Charles Elliot proclaimed that "[i]t is impossible…to vindicate slavery without condemning the political government of the nation. It throws odium on the authors of our revolutionary independence, and brands the name of Franklin, Washington, Jay, Adams, Hancock, and their associates, with the opprobrious names of robbers, murderers, and rebels." Frederick Douglass lamented that the American people "have forgotten their own heroic age," claiming that John Brown "imitated the heroes of Lexington, Concord, and Bunker Hill," while Gilbert Haven suggested that Americans place December 2, 1859—the date of Brown's raid at Harper's Ferry—alongside July 4, 1776, the battles of Lexington and Concord, and October 1492 and December 1620 as landmarks in the history of human freedom.[28]

Southerners praised the founders as well, and with no less vigor. Preaching at an 1861 South Carolina state fast, J. H. Thornwell lamented that "in less than a century we have spoiled the legacy of our fathers," arguing that the *North* had broken faith with the South and thus that *it* was withdrawing from the Union. Just after Lincoln's election, Benjamin Palmer lamented that "the Union of our forefathers is already gone." Two years later, Palmer again tied the Confederate cause to that of American Revolution, viewing the Republican electoral victory in 1860 as foreshadowing the sort of tyranny repudiated by the

Declaration of Independence. Stephen Elliot also used the term "our forefathers" to refer to the American founding, noting that Southerners had always asked only for literal enforcement of the Constitution. Indeed, claims about *Northern* apostasy from the virtues and practices of the founders formed a large part of the Southern argument for secession, and the Declaration's tenets of self-government and self-determination were central to many Southerners' defenses of their actions during 1860 and 1861. If the Yankee Horace Bushnell criticized the lack of religion in the nation's founding document, so too did Southern partisans like Benjamin Palmer.[29]

Reverence for the founders took several additional forms, other than invoking them by name. The Declaration of Independence, with its triumphant rhetoric of human equality, served as a touchstone for many opponents of slavery. W. H. Furness ended his fast day sermon in 1861 with a call for a *new* Declaration of Independence, which would recognize the self-evident conflict between slavery and the basic principles of American political identity. Countless nineteenth-century Jeremiahs—from noted preachers like Gilbert Haven and Henry Ward Beecher to antislavery activists like Frederick Douglass—drew a stark contrast between the language of human equality in the Declaration and the willingness of nineteenth-century Americans to evade its political implications. Lincoln famously valorized Jefferson as

> the man who, in the concrete pressure of a struggle for national independence by a single people, had the coolness, forecast, and capacity to introduce into a merely revolutionary document, an abstract truth, applicable to all men and all times, and so to embalm it there, that today, and in all coming days, it shall be a rebuke and a stumbling-block to the very harbingers of re-appearing tyranny and oppression.

Shortly after the war's outbreak, Henry Ward Beecher argued against those who sought national unity at the expense of the Declaration's principles.[30]

But it was not only the Declaration that animated antislavery activists; they showed reverence for the Constitution as well, though in a more complex fashion. Certainly William Lloyd Garrison's position—that the Constitution represented a "covenant with death" and "an agreement with hell"—resonated with only a tiny fraction of Americans. The Constitution might be less inspiring and idealistic than Jefferson's soaring prose, but it merited admiration for its endurance and its commitment to the nation's unity. Lincoln's dedication to the Union and all it represented, though grounded philosophically in the

Declaration above all else, granted the Constitution a place of high honor and framed his position on slavery for much of his career. As he put it in 1861:

> Without the *Constitution* and the *Union*, we could not have attained the result; but even these, are not the primary cause of our great prosperity. There is something back of these, entwining itself more closely about the human heart. That something, is the principle of "Liberty to all"—the principle that clears the *path* for all—gives *hope* to all—and, by consequence, *enterprize*, and *industry* to all....
>
> The assertion of that *principle*, at *that time*, was *the* word, "*fitly spoken*" which has proved an "apple of gold" to us. The *Union*, and the *Constitution*, are the *picture* of *silver*, subsequently framed around it. The picture was made, not to *conceal*, or *destroy* the apple; but to *adorn*, and *preserve* it. The *picture* was made *for* the apple—*not* the apple for the picture.
>
> So let us act, that neither *picture*, or *apple* shall ever be blurred, or bruised or broken.

Only when he became convinced that slavery was incompatible with the preservation of the Union—in other words, until the war changed his understanding of the dynamics of American politics—did he take decisive action that struck at the very existence of slavery, including the Emancipation Proclamation and plans for the amendments that would do away with slavery once and for all.[31]

Part of the wisdom of the founders, according to the jeremiad prominent in the North, lay in their attempt to allow slavery to die a gradual and natural death (it seemed to be headed that way late in the eighteenth century), and thus effectively to balance their commitments to liberty with the progress and prosperity that the American Union promised. Henry Ward Beecher noted the "temporary refuge" that the founders had allowed for slavery in their system devoted to liberty; that system, he insisted, still commanded the loyalty of a vast majority of Americans, who supported American institutions "according to their original intent."[32]

What those founders did not foresee—could not have foreseen—was the rise of an organized "slave power" and the ways in which the slave system would so effectively come to control the mechanisms of the federal government. Many Northern critics saw clear evidence of the betrayal—the hijacking—of founding principles in a growing conspiracy by Southern elites to *nationalize* their peculiar institution.

Lincoln taunted Stephen Douglas with this charge during their 1858 debates, accusing Douglas and his political allies of seeking to nationalize slavery. According to this interpretation, the slave power's gradual but inexorable grasp—squeezing the nation in its deathly grip—could be seen in a series of political developments, from the passage of the Fugitive Slave Act to the Kansas-Nebraska Act, the vicious beating of Senator Charles Sumner by a Southern colleague on the Senate floor in 1856, and the Supreme Court's decision in *Dred Scott*. It culminated in the host of Southern secessions before Lincoln was even inaugurated and in the attack on Fort Sumter. As with so many potent political narratives, evidence that such a conspiracy actually existed is secondary in importance to the very real fears it stoked in Northern audiences. The idea of a slave power was sobering to many Northerners: as Thomas Wentworth Higginson put it in 1854, "We talk of the Anti-Slavery sentiment as being stronger; but in spite of your Free Soil votes, your Uncle Tom's Cabin, and your New York Tribunes, here is the simple fact: *the South beats us more and more easily every time.*"[33]

Beecher, Haven, and Frederick Douglass hammered this theory home with all the vituperation they could muster, and throughout his debates with Douglas, Lincoln reiterated his position that the founders had set slavery on a course of ultimate extinction, and that his solution would be to "plac[e it] upon the basis that our fathers placed it upon."[34] Such an approach sought to do justice to the founders' vision (for the eventual demise of slavery) while respecting the constitutional procedures they had put into place (restricting slavery to those places where it was currently intact). Attacking the "slave power" provided a political explanation of events that went a long way toward freeing the founders from responsibility for the Union's increasingly fragile bonds, and allowed opponents of slavery to claim fidelity to founding intentions.

Reversing Decline: Reform, Renewal, and War

Few on either side thought that the war was unavoidable, and in the months and years leading up to its outbreak almost everyone had a proposal for avoiding further conflict. Most of these solutions involved recapturing lost individual or collective virtue: restoring individual self-discipline and Christian morality, reaffirming the rule of law, honoring the intentions of the founders, and so on. None explicitly framed their prescription as purely backward-looking, but all sought to recapture something that had been lost in the pursuit of a brighter American future. Of course many of these proposals were incompatible with each other, many betrayed a hazy nostalgia, and none proved ultimately viable in an atmosphere of such distrust and disaffection. Abraham Lincoln, surveying the difficult political landscape early in 1860, noted how every scheme for national reconciliation seemed to underestimate the difficulties before the nation, and the ways in which property considerations influenced people's perceptions of each proposed settlement.[35]

Many public figures drew on the language of reform and repentance: Gilbert Haven counseled "[p]enitential abasement before a just and holy and good God, whose justice, goodness, and holiness we have nationally rejected."[36] Calls for individual repentance, as we have seen, figured heavily in the January 4 jeremiads, and exhortations to general reformation, a rededication to the principles of true Christianity, and moderation and humility continued throughout the war years. Of course, precisely *what* was to be repented of, and *how*, divided the nation deeply.

If one of the nation's sins involved the lack of any religious basis in the Constitution, then rectifying that absence ought to be a high priority. Although such an argument had been made at various points since the Constitution's ratification, it received further support in the wake of the Confederacy's explicit recognition of God in the Confederate Constitution of 1861 and subsequent Union difficulties on the battlefield. Southerners were quick to point out the Christian roots of their society, and counseled fidelity to Christian teachings and perseverance in the struggle before them as their military situation worsened.[37]

Since slavery had become *the* political issue throughout the 1850s and 1860s, most reform programs had to address it. For abolitionists, the solution had always been rather straightforward: abolish slavery, and thus remove the moral blot on the nation's conscience. (Often, given the thorny constitutional and political questions raised by antislavery advocates, calls to work against American slavery sought to begin by abolishing slavery in the District of Columbia.) As early as 1854, in the wake of the Kansas-Nebraska Bill, Frederick Douglass had called for a new political party dedicated to the principles of liberty. Born out of opposition to the Bill, the Republican Party nonetheless proved to be more restrained in its aims than Douglass had hoped, content to call for the restriction of slavery and a reclamation of the founders' original vision that slavery should die a gradual, lawful death.[38]

In taking action against slavery, American Jeremiahs proclaimed, the nation could avert the coming judgment of God, foreseen since Thomas Jefferson's famous admission that he "trembled...when

[he] consider[ed] that God is just." "God is pouring down his spirit," George B. Cheever observed in 1858, "trying us with the last argument of mercy he ever uses, and is throwing in the mightiest of all elements for the conquest of this tremendous evil, this terrific sin." Frederick Douglass warned his fellow Americans:

> The American people have been called upon...to abolish and put away forever the system of slavery....The cries of the slave have gone forth to the world, and up to the throne of God. [The *Dred Scott*] decision, in my view, is a means of keeping the nation awake on the subject. It is another proof that God does not mean that we shall go to sleep, and forget that we are a slaveholding nation....If these [warnings] shall fail, judgment, more fierce or terrible, may come.

Abolishing slavery would not only avert the anger of God, but make possible the reclaiming of the American republic's original promise. But not everyone stopped at abolition: Gilbert Haven proposed an even more radical social agenda to reclaim the promise of American public life by eliminating racial prejudice more generally.[39]

Perhaps things seemed relatively simple (in theory, if not in practice) from the abolitionist perspective. But for most of the nation, the sectional crisis presented far more complex and daunting problems. Furthermore, strong arguments from providence weakened the case for radical changes in the American social system. The idea that God's providence ruled over all frustrated reformers, as traditionalists could argue that agitators of various sorts were objecting, not merely to unjust social structures or political practices, but to God's government of the world.[40]

Of course the specific intentions of the founders, and the ways in which they might inform political debate nearly a century later, were hotly debated by the parties. As we have seen, many Southerners understood their attempts at secession as wholly consistent with the American tradition of self-government and the principles of the Declaration of Independence, and thus many prominent Southern clergy gave their blessing to secession. Southerners, and many Northern Democrats, often preached a devotion to the rule of law (especially in the wake of *Dred Scott* and the Fugitive Slave Act) and a restriction of federal intervention in state decisions regarding slavery, as the true legacy of the founders.[41]

As the war went on, discussions of national repentance were intertwined with practical disputes over the terms upon which armed conflict might cease. Abolitionists continued to prod a reluctant Lincoln administration on behalf of their cause, seeking an explicit recognition of emancipation as a war aim.[42] Preaching on the one-year anniversary of the attack on Fort Sumter, Henry Ward Beecher cited a growing understanding that "the North, for its own sake, must exert every proper constitutional influence, and every moral influence, to cleanse the South of the contamination of slavery." Thus the goal of reform was clear: "to repent of past days, to break away from the past and to call God to witness that in time to come we will consecrate, individually and nationally, every energy to repair the mischief of slavery, to do it away utterly, and to establish the reign of universal liberty." By doing so, and bringing back the Union as it was meant to be, Beecher averred, "We shall see a glorious Union. We shall see a restored Constitution.…We shall live to see a better day."[43] Lincoln continued to believe, apparently, in the possibility of colonization, as well as in the potential viability of a compensated emancipation program. But as the war dragged on, he arrived where so many others had already: a commitment to emancipation as the only real way to defeat the Confederacy, and as a guiding principle for amending the Constitution and for postwar reconstruction of the Union.[44]

EXTERNAL CONTEXT: THE MILLENNIAL NARRATIVE OF AMERICAN REDEMPTIVE PROMISE

Almost as soon as the first guns had fired, Protestants set about reevaluating their conception of the historical process and of national destiny. Drawing on the Puritan tradition of pulpit jeremiads, the clergy suggested that the nation's hope had gone awry because the people had sinned. Since their virtue and piety had declined from the glorious example of their reverend ancestors, God demanded expiation in blood. Simultaneously Protestants concluded that the woes of the Apocalypse applied even to the United States.[45]

Providentialism, the Chosen Nation, and the Millennium

Preaching on George Washington's birthday, in 1863, William Adams called for a reinfusion of "religious patriotism," asserting that at this trying time in the nation's history, "We need to be lifted up to loftier conceptions of our nationality, as related to the Providence of God in the progress of His eternal kingdom."[46] Notwithstanding Abraham Lincoln's pointed demurral—his reference to the United States as an "almost-chosen people," a construction that grants a special status with one hand while not-too-subtly undermining it with the other— themes of chosenness and national mission were widespread during the nineteenth century, and more particularly during the war years.

The view of America as critical to the progress of God's kingdom traced its American origins, as we have seen, to John Winthrop's evocation of New England as a "city on a hill" and a light to the nations. This understanding survived through the Revolutionary era and into the early national period. In the words of J. F. Maclear:

> The destiny of the American Republic to lead the world to millennial glory was claimed immediately on the birth of the new nation.... With independence, the establishment of the Republic, and victory, the conviction became irresistible that a final and American stage preparatory to the millennium had now commenced.... Probably the most successful years of postmillennialism in the concept of national mission were those between 1815 and the Civil War.[47]

Providentialist interpretations of early American history bolstered such claims about national chosenness: "Under the divine providence our fathers were led to these shores," preached Orlando Hutton in 1861. S. A. Hodgman referred explicitly to the "city on a hill" imagery of Matthew 5, and connected it with both America's mission and God's terrible judgments on the nation:

> It was not because the Lord abhorred us as a people, but because of his great favor towards us, that he hath purged us, as gold is purified in a furnace. We have a great mission to perform, and there is a bright destiny before us, in the future; and it was necessary that we should receive a discipline to prepare us for both.... Our mission is to give the nations of the earth, a practical demonstration of the great problem, never before solved, that, *man is capable of self-government*. It is to be our destiny, to teach all tyrants and oppressors, that their days are numbered. We are to be a city set on a hill, whose light can not be hid.[48]

Providentialism was a powerful background assumption in such accounts, which stressed the nation's role as a model for movements for freedom and self-rule around the world.[49]

With the outbreak of war, the violent and apocalyptic imagery of Revelation could, without much difficulty, be seen all around. Within this millennial scheme, those who saw the United States as a chosen nation believed that it could prepare the way for God's reign on earth by purging the land of the sin of slavery. James T. Moorhead has noted the "sheer intensity and virtual unanimity of the Northern conviction that the Union armies were hastening the day of the Lord—that the war was not merely one sacred battle among many but was the climactic test of the redeemer nation and its millennial role." This shift in tone and emphasis appears powerfully in the words of Julia Ward Howe's "Battle Hymn of the Republic," in which "[t]he advent of the Union armies represents...the coming of the Lord, and their cause is the cause of God's truth." God's truth may be marching on, as the song intones, but the most immediate marches in everyone's mind were those of the opposing armies. Such an understanding embraced a *progressive* historical trajectory, presenting an understanding of "history bounding forward...illuminat[ing] an essential element in the apocalyptic mentality: God was the engine of history, and his interventions kept it on a course of progress."[50]

As the ultimate overseer of human history, God determined the outcome of battles to show his assessment of each side's spiritual state: victory, of course, provided evidence of God's favor, while defeat represented a sign of the lingering presence of sin. Reading these divine judgments into specific developments was made more difficult by the ebb and flow of each side's fortunes. Expressing confidence in the outcome of the war, Ezra S. Gannett proclaimed that "every event is included within the Divine providence; and...therefore the issue of the present struggle, and all the steps to that issue, and all the means by which it may be accelerated or determined, are under the control of an almighty and righteous power." Of course, such a view had also been voiced by Confederate supporter J. W. Tucker, who, preaching in 1862, also "recognize[d] the hand of God in the origin and process of this conflict," and affirmed providential assumptions similar to those of his Northern counterparts. Tucker argued that

> God is on our side—is with us in this conflict—because we have had reverses. 'Whom the Lord loveth he chasteneth, and scourgeth every son whom he receiveth....' God sent our reverses for our good. They were necessary to humble our pride; to stop our foolish and absurd boasting, and to make us feel the importance of the conflict in which we are engaged.

Jeremiahs on both sides alternated between elation and deflation with each report from the battlefield.[51]

In such a polarized political atmosphere, the potential for the idea of chosenness to lead to a kind of patriotic frenzy was nearly irresistible. Take, for example, the career of Gilbert Haven. In a remarkable set of sermons preached between 1850 and 1868, published in 1869 as *National Sermons*, Haven responded to the series of public events that eventually led to war. Preaching in 1862, Haven referred to "the coming of the kingdom of God in the work of emancipation in America...us, who were less than a century ago no people, the people of God." Although midway through the war Haven warned against the "favorite conceit of all famous peoples, that they have a mission," later in the very same sermon he stated that "I feel that America is at the center of the history of the world today. For good or evil, in wrath or mercy, God has lifted her up before all men..." As Grant approached Richmond, Haven argued that God was aiding the Union effort, "not for the welfare of America, as an especial and peculiar nation....He contends for us, because He has certain ends to be consummated on earth, that can only be effected through the overthrow of the doctrines and usages of the rebellious confederacy." Haven's millennial patriotism reached its apex, not surprisingly, on July 4, 1864, when he declared, "Upon us the ends of the world have come. We are the depository of the civil principles of the millennium." This millennial vision pointed toward something far grander than American liberty: "[The spread of democratic ideas from America to Europe] started from Independence Hall. It will not cease to march until it has subdued the world.... [The elections of 1860 and 1864] are steps of God in His march through the earth."[52]

God in American History

But with chosenness came responsibility. Within the mid-nineteenth-century jeremiad lay a persistent fear that the American mission in the world was imperiled. Not only had the American nation forsaken its abundant promise—by tolerating slavery, or by departing from the Constitution as written—but in doing so it had endangered its own relationship with the God who had marked the nation for a central role in world history. In 1839, Horace Bushnell predicted that the controversy over slavery would not abate "till the decree of an irreversible Providence was accomplished in the downfall of this hideous institution." Harriet Beecher Stowe's 1852 best seller *Uncle Tom's Cabin* evoked the specter of God's thundering hand. If the church does not come to the aid of the despised slaves, "the country will have reason to tremble, when it remembers that the fate of nations is in the hands of One who is very pitiful, and of tender compassion." Not only orthodox Protestants, but a wide spectrum of Northern critics and commentators, viewed the danger of divine punishment as a chief reason to support emancipation.[53]

The case of Gilbert Haven is again instructive. Reacting to the passage of the Kansas-Nebraska Act in 1854, Haven proclaimed that "the judgment of Heaven is upon us. Let us imitate the elders of Jerusalem, the godly Daniel, and Nehemiah, and pour out tears and prayers before their God and ours, who alone casts down, who alone can build up." Later, after the outbreak of hostilities, Haven repeatedly linked political and military developments to God's purposes: "[God] has poured out upon us the plague of war and its abounding miseries, because His Church would not testify and toil for the salvation of their brethren; because it arrayed itself by indifference or by open violence against its brethren." As the war entered its fourth year, Haven noted the curious parallel between the number of men engaged in the war and the number of American slaves (roughly three and a half million, he estimated): "Strange coincidence! Nay, a marvelous providence, rather—a revelation of the righteous judgment of God."[54]

Haven was hardly alone; clerics on both sides of the political divide, no less than political activists like Douglass and Garrison, endorsed the idea of a providential God who saw injustice and acted accordingly. Searching for an explanation for Confederate setbacks during the war, Stephen Elliot voiced certainty that "[i]t is the aggregate of sinfulness that is working our ruin," although he was uncertain precisely which sins, and called for humble prayer so that God would make this clear. "It is evident," claimed J. W. Tucker, "that God has a plan and a purpose in reference to all nations, revolutions, and wars…He has a providence in all national revolutions. He directs, controls, governs and regulates them."[55]

Yet again, as with Mather in New England, such punishments were not viewed as merely punitive or retributive, but medicinal and even therapeutic, directly related to claims about America's millennial role. Alonzo Quint phrased it most succinctly—"National sin must have its expiation in national suffering"[56]—and his use of the term "expiation" clearly evokes a model in which healing is the goal. God did not merely punish, but healed, purged, reconciled, and strengthened, and the nation that emerged from the Civil War would not be the same one that had entered it. Haven likened God to the "Great Surgeon and Physician…[whose] wounds…probe deeper and deeper. Our cries break forth more sharply…" And yet divine justice coexisted with mercy: "God has chastened us very sore, yet far less than our desert."[57]

COMPETING NARRATIVES: THE AFRICAN-AMERICAN JEREMIAD AND THE LOST CAUSE

The African-American jeremiad was in many ways a genre all its own and, though closely paralleling the rhetoric we have examined thus far in this chapter, confronted claims about American chosenness directly and on their own terms. David Walker's *Appeal to the Coloured Citizens of the World*, first published in 1829, is probably the best-known example of this genre in the years prior to the Civil War. Eddie Glaude notes how the *Appeal* "illustrates the inseparable linkage between black religious life and black political activity." Walker held the language of the Declaration of Independence up to the nation, judging its practice in light of its ideals:

> Hear your language, proclaimed to the world, July 4th, 1776—"We hold these truths to be self evident—that ALL MEN ARE CREATED EQUAL!! that they *are endowed by their Creator with certain unalienable rights;* that among these are life, *liberty,* and the pursuit of happiness!!" Compare your own language above, extracted from your Declaration of Independence, with your cruelties and murders inflicted by your cruel and unmerciful fathers and yourselves on our fathers and on us—men who have never given your fathers or you the least provocation!

Slaveholders, Walker submits, "forget that God rules in the armies of heaven and among the inhabitants of the earth, having his ears continually open to the cries, tears, and groans of his oppressed people; and being a just and holy Being will one day appear fully on behalf of the oppressed, and arrest the progress of the avaricious oppressors..." Walker drew on the stories and characters so familiar to a biblically literate populace—Lot, Noah, Moses, a providential God—and skillfully used them to rebuke a nation that proclaimed ideals of liberty while tolerating such a sinful practice.

> I know that thousands will doubt—they think they have us so well secured in wretchedness, to them and their children, that it is impossible for such things to occur. So did the antideluvians doubt Noah, until the day in which the flood came and swept them away. So did the Sodomites doubt, until Lot got out of the city, and God rained down fire and brimstone from Heaven upon them, and burnt them up. So did the king of Egypt doubt the very existence of a God.... Did he not find to his sorrow, who the Lord was, when he and all his mighty men of war, were smothered to death in the Red Sea?

Walker assured American slaves that "God...will give you a Hannibal...will deliver you through him from your deplorable and wretched condition under the Christians of America."[58]

Walker's contemporary Maria Stewart looked forward to divine deliverance for slaves after God humbled the nation that had oppressed them for so long, and corrupted them so.

It appears to me that America has become like the great city of Babylon.... She is, indeed, a seller of slaves and the souls of men.... But many powerful sons and daughters of Africa will shortly arise, who will put down vice and immorality among us, and declare that by Him that sitteth upon the throne that they will have their rights...I believe that the oppression of the injured African has come up before the majesty of Heaven; and when our cries shall have reached the ears of the Most High, it will be a tremendous day for the people of this land; for strong is the hand of the Almighty.[59]

Similar invocations of God's providential and particular concern for American slaves were voiced by James W. C. Pennington in 1841, when he observed that "God is continuously working with men, among them, and over them.... It is even so with nations.... If God has over-turned strong nations for sin, he is doubtless doing the same now, and will do it again."[60]

If any thinker bridged the African-American and white jeremiads, it was certainly Frederick Douglass. Despite his blistering attacks on timid Northerners, hypocritical Southerners, and pandering politicians, Douglass never questioned the chosenness of the American nation, nor the fundamental value of its most basic principles. As he put it in his noted speech of July 4, 1852: "[t]he principles contained in [the Declaration of Independence] are saving principles. Stand by those principles, be true to them on all occasions, in all places, against all foes, and at whatever cost."[61]

Indeed, Douglass intimated that the war's result—the death of an "old Union" and the birth of the new—had, in fact, brought about a millennium of sorts. Such a view appeared repeatedly in Douglass's work, which articulated this notion of collective national responsibility to American whites from the beginning:

Before high heaven and the world...you are responsible for the blood of the slave. You may shut your eyes to the fact...but as sure as there is a God of justice and an unerring providence, just so sure will the blood of the bondman be required at your hands.... Do you really think to circumvent God?—Do you suppose that you can go on in your present career of injustice and political profligacy undisturbed? Has the law of righteous retribution been repealed from the statutes of the Almighty?"

Two years after penning these words, Douglass argued that true patriotism placed the law of God above the law of country, and that "strong, proud, and prosperous though we be, there is a power above us that can 'bring down high looks...' and who can tell how soon the avenging angel may pass over our land...." Before the American Anti-Slavery Society in 1857, Douglass called the *Dred Scott* decision "another proof that God does not mean that we shall go to sleep, and forget that we are a slaveholding nation.... If these [warnings] fail, judgment, more fierce or terrible, may come." Douglass's rhetoric did not change with the onset of war. He told a Philadelphia audience in 1862 that "nations, not less than individuals, are subjects of the moral government of the universe, and... flagrant, long continued, and persistent transgressions of the laws of Divine government will certainly bring national sorrow, shame, suffering, and death." Looking back on his long career, Douglass maintained that the Civil War "was an instrument of a higher power than itself."[62]

The African-American jeremiad employed images of chosenness and covenant, but emphasized the experience of slavery in Egypt as foundational to the formation of the Israelites' nationhood. At least in its current state, the United States certainly did *not* appear in the African-American jeremiad as the Promised Land, but rather as Egypt; African-Americans were called to identify *not* with the Jews in the wilderness, making their way toward the Promised Land (Exodus 15–40), but with the enslaved Jews awaiting God's mighty and liberating work in history (Exodus 1–12). In addition to providing a sense of "chosenness" for a people who had suffered unspeakably in America, the African-American jeremiad "offered the terms to imagine a national community—to constitute a collective identity." Freed from the debasing nature of slave society, such exemplars as Douglass and Walker suggested, African-Americans might take their rightful place within an America destined for great things. Such sentiments, drawing on notions of *black* Americans as a chosen and oppressed people *within* the American nation, only increased in stridency with the passage of the Fugitive Slave Act, the Kansas-Nebraska Act, and John Brown's abortive raid at Harper's Ferry. Emancipation and the eventual Union victory added a singular dimension to this narrative of trial and deliverance.[63]

The Exodus story played a crucial role for African-Americans in the nineteenth century. And yet the remarkable malleability of this narrative is evident in the fact that even *apologists* for slavery drew upon it as illustrative of their situation. On the eve of war, Benjamin Palmer likened Abraham Lincoln to the hard-hearted Pharaoh who would not let the Israelites go. Stephen Elliot counseled his listeners to recall that the Israelites, God's chosen people, also encountered doubts and setbacks along the way. "Those whom God is intending to make a nation to do his work upon earth, are precisely those whom he tries most severely."[64]

So Southern whites had a jeremiad of their own, one based on their understandings of Southern society as a Christian culture with its own collective mission. Charles Reagan Wilson has documented the persistence of this "Lost Cause" narrative—the story of "a Redeemer Nation that died"—as a fundamental element of Southern mythology and especially post–Civil War culture, a rhetorical means by which Southern elites sought to preserve "Southern values" and honor the memory of Confederate heroes. Wilson has likened this "Southern jeremiad" to the New England version in its expression of collective identity and meaning, its valorization of founders and denunciation of the loss of foundational values, and its interpretation of military and political defeat as evidence of divine displeasure.[65]

Like their Northern rivals, Southerners had their own analogies to the chosen Israelites (who after all had built the Temple and served God, not coincidentally, with slave labor). Given the predominance of biblical literalism in nineteenth-century America, such a narrative could ground slavery, not only in expediency or in the particularities of Southern economic development, but in God's direct command. Early Confederate successes on the battlefield—most dramatically, at First Manassas/Bull Run—encouraged this sense of a "chosen" Confederacy, although clergy continued to warn that sinfulness threatened to bring God's judgment on the South, and fast days and calls for repentance were common throughout the Civil War South. (Stonewall Jackson reportedly told his troops that Confederate sinfulness posed an even greater threat than the Union army.[66])

After the tide of the war turned against the Confederacy, many Southerners continued to hope that God would intervene in dramatic fashion to ensure them a victory. In the aftermath of the Union victory, Southern thinkers struggled to make sense—practically, politically, theologically—of the war's outcome.

> When the Confederacy fell, bereaved white Southerners experienced the destruction of their cherished "Christian" slave society. As they struggled to read aright the signs of the times, they could hardly escape the thought that, once again, a wrathful and inscrutable God had called upon the heathen to punish His disobedient chosen people.

As political and economic contact between the victorious North and subjugated South increased in post–Civil War America, and those seeking national reunion stressed the mutual sacrifices that both sides had offered in the crucible of war, Southern Jeremiahs "warned their brethren of the dangers in abandoning traditional Southern values and failing to meet the high standards of the Confederate past."[67]

The Lost Cause narrative replicated the traditional features of the jeremiad from its earliest days in America. It understood the community's misfortunes to be derived from its disobedience to God, with the corollary being that had that community remained faithful to God's commands, victory and prosperity would have followed. A clear generational dimension drove the narrative, and even the lists of sins were relatively unsurprising: worldliness, greed (often attributed to the influence of the capitalist and atheistic North), intemperance, gambling, and decreasing political deference to traditional centers of authority. Some even argued that moral decline had infected the Southern *black* population as they were freed from the benevolent discipline of the slave system and faced with an unprecedented and dangerous freedom. Although clergy had often advocated on behalf of improved conditions for American slaves in order to ensure that American slavery lived up to the standards laid down in the Bible, it was far more controversial—as Georgia Methodist John H. Caldwell would discover, just two months after the war's end—to suggest that slavery itself was the cause of the Confederacy's defeat.[68]

LINCOLN'S UNCONVENTIONAL JEREMIAD: PROVIDENCE AND THE WAR'S CARNAGE

Certainly Henry Ward Beecher and those like him might be forgiven a bit of crowing as the Union emerged victorious from such a long, divisive, and bloody confrontation. Beecher certainly had no doubts about the mind or intentions of God when he looked out from Fort Sumter in 1865, across the harbor to Charleston: "We exult...not that *our* will is done, but that God's will hath been done!" The wreckage of that city, said Beecher, is a sign that "God hath set such a mark upon treason that all ages shall dread and abhor it....God does not stretch out his hand, as he has for four dreadful years, that men may easily forget the might of his terrible acts." Harriet Beecher Stowe, writing in the *Atlantic Monthly*, noted how "the land where the family of the slave was first annihilated…has been made a desolation so signal…that the blindest passer-by can not but ask for what sin so awful a doom has been meted out."[69]

But although voices of vengeance and retribution were the most numerous, and the most insistent, they were not the only ones. The most politically and historically significant of these dissenting voices, of course, was that of President Abraham Lincoln. Lincoln had alluded to providence in his First Inaugural, using it to counsel patience and a cooling of tempers, and linked God's will with the will of the American people: "If the Almighty Ruler of nations, with his eternal truth and justice, be on your side of the North, or on yours of the South, that truth, and that justice, will surely prevail, by the judgment of this great tribunal, the American people."[70] But of course the story of Lincoln and his uneasy relationship with the religious rhetoric of his day is far more complicated.

Given Lincoln's known aversion to creeds and his coolness toward the evangelical piety of his contemporaries, the members of the president's cabinet who gathered for the September 22, 1862, cabinet meeting were shocked, not by his decision to issue an emancipation proclamation—such a step was one of many being considered by the president, and had been debated at previous cabinet meetings—but by his explanation of the *timing* behind his decision. Lincoln claimed that, based on a vow made to himself and God, he interpreted the Union victory at Antietam as indicative of a divine will in favor of emancipation. Allen Guelzo writes:

> No one who knew Lincoln could have ever predicted that he would pop familiar references to the Ancient of Days into a cabinet discussion, and Chase was so amazed that he asked Lincoln to repeat himself just to be sure he had heard him aright. Much less could the members of the cabinet have believed that Lincoln was going to commit them, and the nation, to outright emancipation on the strength of a sign he had asked from God, as though it were the Emperor Constantine or Oliver Cromwell rather than Abraham Lincoln sitting at the head of the cabinet table. The idea of making policy on the basis of communications from the heavens was so foreign to Lincoln, not to mention old political warriors like Seward, Blair, Bates, Chase, and Welles, that Lincoln himself, "in a manner half-apologetic," conceded that "this might seem strange."[71]

Certainly this sort of one-to-one correspondence between battlefield results and political action seems anything but typical of the sort of mystical providentialism that Lincoln eventually came to profess in the Second Inaugural. Mark Noll has analyzed the evolving nature of Lincoln's understanding of providence—calling him a "holdout" from the prevailing opinions all around him—and claims that this Antietam–Emancipation Proclamation episode represents "a specific reading of providence to guide a course of action, evidently something [Lincoln] had not done before and would not do again."[72]

Indeed, Lincoln struck a different chord that same month in the so-called Meditation on the Divine Will, a private document apparently written for private purposes. This remarkable document is well worth quoting in its entirety.

> The will of God prevails. In great contests each party claims to act in accordance with the will of God. Both *may* be, and one *must* be wrong. God can not be *for*, and *against* the same thing at the same time. In the present civil war it is quite possible that God's purpose is something different from the purpose of either party—and yet the human instrumentalities, working just as they do, are of the best adaptation to effect His purpose. I am almost ready to say this is probably true—that God wills this contest, and wills that it shall not end yet. By his mere quiet power, on the minds of the now contestants, He could have either *saved* or *destroyed* the Union without a human contest. Yet the contest began. And having begun He could give the final victory to either side any day. Yet the contest proceeds.[73]

The "Meditation" is shot through with Lincoln's peculiarly conditional and tentative statements, the kind that would later make their way into the Second Inaugural: he is "almost" ready to say that it is "probably" the case that God's will differs from that of the combatants. The first and last sentences of the "Meditation" convey this ambiguity: "The will of God prevails…And yet the contest proceeds." In its hesitancy to pronounce on God's designs, its willingness to consider the possibility that *neither* side in the war might represent God's purposes, Lincoln's "Meditation" moves away from the confident reading of the signs of the times that so often characterized the American jeremiad, and which he himself seemed to have followed in linking Antietam with the Emancipation Proclamation. The almost breezy invocation of providence from the First Inaugural is clearly being replaced by an acknowledgment that God's purposes may be far more difficult, and well-nigh impossible, for humans to fathom.

In many ways the "Meditation" lays out, in a private document, what Lincoln would say very publicly two and a half years later. In the

Second Inaugural, Lincoln dwells on the ways in which things had gone quite differently than expected:

> Neither party expected for the war, the magnitude, or the duration, which it has already attained. Neither anticipated that the *cause* of the conflict might cease with, or even before, the conflict itself should cease. Each looked for an easier triumph, and a result less fundamental and astounding. Both read the same Bible, and pray to the same God; and each invokes His aid against the other.... The prayers of both could not be answered; that of neither has been answered fully.[74]

The only real explanation for this state of affairs must be, as Lincoln speculated in the "Meditation," that God's purposes are not reducible to North versus South. As he puts it in the Second Inaugural, "The Almighty has His own purposes." This sort of fatalism has attracted the attention of most Lincoln scholars, and the Second Inaugural shows a mature Lincoln "propound[ing] a thick, complex view of God's rule over the world and a morally nuanced picture of America's destiny." Lincoln concludes the Second Inaugural with the call to action: "let us strive on to finish the work we are in; to bind up the nation's wounds; to care for him who shall have borne the battle, and for his widow, and his orphan—to do all which may achieve and cherish a just, and a lasting peace, among ourselves, and with all nations."[75]

Alfred Kazin describes the wording here—in a bit of an understatement—as "religiously tentative." Lincoln raises the possibility that the war represented a punishment for American slavery, yet he was never so concrete and confident regarding the ability of humans to know God's purposes to make such a claim in more than tentative ways. After all, he posed his famous remark regarding the Civil War as God's punishment for American slavery as a *hypothetical:* "If we shall suppose that American slavery is one of those offenses which, in the providence of God, must needs come, but which, having continued through his appointed time, he now wills to remove...shall we discern therein any departure from those divine attributes which the believers in a living God ascribe to Him?" Lincoln's detachment, framing God's purposes in the war in hypothetical or mystical ways, combined his penchant for understanding God as Judge with his essentially mystical understanding of providence as *not* perceptible by human reason. Compared with his more triumphalist fellow Americans, eager to see divine blessing in the Union's military triumph, writes Harry Stout, "Lincoln...bowed to a different God."[76] The Second Inaugural may be a jeremiad, of sorts, but it is an oddly hesitant one.

THE JEREMIAD BEYOND THE WAR

Lincoln's Second Inaugural notwithstanding, vengeance was the reigning Northern sentiment in the spring of 1865 (and after), and most Northerners were uninterested in the more complex ideas about causality and providence expressed by their president. Indeed, a number of sermons delivered on the occasion of Lincoln's funeral suggested that God, in his providence, had taken the sixteenth president from the political scene just at the moment of victory precisely because he lacked the severity to punish the South in the manner it really deserved.[77]

I argued in the previous chapter that, among other functions, the jeremiad served as an instrument of social control in early New England. Such is certainly the case with the Civil War jeremiad, although the democratizing and pluralizing trends laid out in the opening sections of this chapter show how much more difficult such efforts at social control were in the nineteenth century than in the seventeenth. Northern spokespersons continued to weave together ideas about chosenness, suffering, expiation, and shared sacrifice to sanctify the war's carnage. The jeremiad assists this process by drawing on the past, on images of founders and wise ancestors, to enhance the prestige of its agenda for the future. But which aspects of the past? In Civil War jeremiads, the particular notion of the national past is more contested than it was in New England, with its relatively concise list of founders and relatively narrow understanding of the past (which had only existed, in New England, for about forty years).

Gilbert Haven's identification of founding *principles*, noted above, is important in this regard. Decline, on this view, was conceived as a steady retreat from the radical *promise* of American founding documents and a betrayal of Americans' birthright. Nineteenth-century antislavery Jeremiahs were more likely to point to founding principles, or, if they did refer to the founders' intentions, to locate them not so much in the social reality of their time (which obviously included the toleration of slavery) but in more general expectations the founders held regarding the gradual withering away of slavery. Lincoln's early views, seen especially clearly in the Cooper Union speech, provide an example. He evoked the intention of the founders that slavery gradually wither away and die; thus, faithfulness to those founders' intentions meant working to eradicate a practice that was a widely accepted part of their world. On this understanding of founding intentions, plans to nationalize the peculiar institution flew in the face of the liberationist political *potential* inherent in the nation's founding documents.

The political agenda, then, was not to *imitate* the actions of the founders in all respects, but rather to discern the promise carried in the *spirit* of the nation's founding documents—and to make it a reality. Without this interpretation, Frederick Douglass could not have charged slavery-tolerant America with being "false to its past."[78]

One prominent American arguing the opposite was Stephen Douglas, who denied, in his debates with Lincoln, that America's founding documents implied any further "promise" or "birthright" than what was written, and who interpreted the Declaration of Independence as speaking only of the rights of white Englishmen.[79] Not only did such a view fit with widespread American ideas of white supremacy, its textual literalism was also deeply sympathetic to the biblical literalism that characterized nineteenth-century America. (Similarly, Southerners often framed their political demands as seeking enforcement of the Constitution as written.) The goal of the present and future, on this view, ought to be the close approximation of the past in terms of institutions and practices. Since slavery was a widespread practice in early America, tolerated and even protected by the founders, it simply made no sense to claim that slavery violated the spirit of the United States Constitution, just as the practice of slavery throughout the Old Testament provides its own rebuke to those who would claim that it somehow violates the "spirit" of Christianity.

Antebellum and Civil War jeremiads, then, show us both change and continuity: change, in that they illustrate a growing disjuncture between religious and political elites in American society, a gradually increasing distance between prominent clergy and the larger culture they sought to castigate and reform; and continuity, in that the language of evangelical Protestantism continued to serve as a common American vernacular on questions of national purpose and meaning. The notion of a national mission certainly survived the war, and was likely even strengthened by it. "An American civil religion," argues Harry S. Stout, "incarnated in the war has continued to sacralize for its citizens the idea of American freedom." Continuing through the nineteenth century, with the push westward, into the early twentieth century and beyond, Americans took for granted that the United States was not just another nation but, in some way, acted on God's behalf. This sense of national mission was rooted in the blood sacrifice of a half million young Americans—in Stout's apt phrase, "a sort of massive sacrifice on the national altar."[80]

FOUR

Taking America Back

The Christian Right Jeremiad

Sin has permeated our land...The strength of America has always been in her righteousness, in her walk with God. Now we see national sins that are permeating our nation, and we find that our citizens are without remorse, without regret or repentance, and we are not far from the judgment of God upon this great nation of ours. With our erosion from the faith of our fathers, we are seeing an erosion in our stability as a nation.

No nation in history has survived that legitimized sodomy and gross sexual excess. No nation in history has survived whose leaders plundered future generations to ensure their continuance in power. No nation can survive that refuses to pass on its history, traditions, and moral standards to its youth. No nation can survive that cannibalizes its unborn for its own convenience....If the past is any guide, we know that a righteous God will not hold back His judgment forever. A great nation can slowly be destroyed by pervasive moral decay. We sow the seeds of our own destruction, or God Himself can strike sudden devastating blows—violent earthquakes, hurricanes and tornadoes, massive flooding, extended drought, widespread disease, even the impact of an asteroid. Or God can raise up fierce enemies who delight only in destruction and death.[1]

MORAL DECLINE AND MURPHY BROWN

When Vice President Dan Quayle rose to address the Commonwealth Club of California on May 19, 1992, it had been less than a month since the Los Angeles riots—sparked by the acquittal of four white policemen of the charge of beating African-American motorist Rodney King. Quayle's address that day would become known as the "Murphy Brown" speech, although he referred to the popular television character only once and in passing. In fact, Quayle's remarks were more specifically devoted to the recent riots, and to a consideration of the factors that best explained them. In the course of doing so, however, the vice president articulated a jeremiad that looked beyond economics or politics, and identified a deep spiritual and cultural crisis facing the American nation.[2]

As we have seen in previous chapters, all jeremiads begin by lamenting a present crisis, and Quayle's was no exception. Certainly the riots provided observers with much to lament. In the days following the officers' acquittal, violence and looting engulfed parts of Los Angeles. Images of mayhem and destruction were broadcast around the world. Four thousand National Guard troops patrolled the streets of the city, fires raged, schools and businesses closed, and crowds attacked bystanders. Not until May 4—just two weeks before Quayle's speech—did life regain some semblance of normalcy for those in the affected neighborhoods. And the toll was staggering: more than fifty people killed, 4,000 injured, 12,000 arrested, and damage to property approaching $1 billion.

But as we have seen, the jeremiad does more than simply report bad news; it contrasts the dire present with a more virtuous past. Denying that the riots were an inevitable outcome of an ethnically and racially diverse society, Quayle argued that "the lawless social anarchy that we saw is directly related to the breakdown of the family structure, personal responsibility, and social order in too many areas of our society." Of course, the riots themselves were evidence of desperate social pathologies, but Quayle also presented a number of alarming statistics, most of which involved contrasts between the state of black America in the 1960s and the 1990s: the rise of gangs to take the place of absent black fathers, ghettos filled with children having children, rising unemployment and poverty among young blacks, and so on. The 1960s had seen great progress in combating racism and removing legal barriers to the inclusion of African-Americans in American political, social, and economic life, Quayle admitted. But that decade had also witnessed the development of "a culture of poverty" distinctly different from previous eras, in which poverty was "a stage through which people pass[ed] on their way to joining the great middle class." This "culture of poverty" had resulted only partly from the Great Society's welfare programs, and more fundamentally from what Quayle called "changes in social mores" during the 1960s in which "it was fashionable to declare war against traditional values." "The inter-generational poverty that troubles us so much today," Quayle observed, "is predominantly a poverty of values."

But the vice president also, of course, called for reform. Quayle sketched out a political agenda, a vision of the American future put forward by the Republican administration he represented, including many of the party's long-standing urban initiatives. The Bush-Quayle program promoted home ownership, personal responsibility, urban enterprise zones, community-based policing, cuts in capital gains taxes, the encouragement of marriage, and the enforcement of child support payments. It was in this context that Quayle made his famous reference to the television character played by Candace Bergen:

> Bearing babies irresponsibly is simply wrong. Failing to support children one has fathered is wrong and we must be unequivocal about this. It doesn't help matters when primetime TV has Murphy Brown, a character who supposedly epitomizes today's intelligent, highly paid professional woman, mocking the importance of fathers by bearing a child alone and calling it just another lifestyle choice.

Perhaps most importantly, however, Quayle portrayed Murphy Brown's decision not merely as a wrongheaded personal one, but as a departure from previously dominant *religious* teachings. In closing, he turned directly from a critique of the present to a vision of the future that would reclaim something from the past:

> So, I think the time has come to renew our public commitment to our Judeo-Christian values in our churches and our synagogues, our civic organizations and our schools. We are, as our children recite each morning, one nation under God. That's a useful framework for acknowledging a duty and an authority higher than our own pleasures and personal ambition. If we lived more thoroughly by these values, we would live in a better society.

In true jeremiadic fashion, Quayle concluded his remarks with a call for renewal and an expression of hope in the promise of America: "Though our hearts have been pained by the events in Los Angeles, we should take this tragedy as an opportunity for self-examination and progress." As in the darkest days of King Philip's War and in the depths of the Civil War's carnage, so in San Francisco that day in May 1992: through the painful present loomed the promise of a brighter American future, if only the nation would return to its founding traditions and most basic values.

Much of the resulting dustup surrounding the vice president's remarks (at least, that part of it not devoted to ridiculing him for picking a fight with a fictional character) involved various and competing theories about the black underclass. But the critique that Quayle voiced that day—one that took issue with mainstream media for mocking "Judeo-Christian" values and undermining the traditional family; that criticized the moral, cultural, and spiritual consequences of 1960s counterculture and its Great Society programs; and that called for a recommitment to those traditional moral values as the key to the recovery of American greatness—was hardly new. Indeed, Quayle's own political career owed much to the political mobilization of the Christian Right that had gathered steam during the late 1970s, helped propel Ronald Reagan to the presidency, and would continue to buttress (primarily) Republican candidates into the twenty-first century. (Quayle was elected to the Senate on Reagan's coattails in 1980, defeating three-term incumbent Senator Birch Bayh and becoming the youngest person ever elected to the Senate.) From the beginning, the Christian Right had been driven by a powerful narrative of imperiled national promise, of a prodigal yet once chosen nation that had forsaken its moral and spiritual foundations in favor of secular humanism.

THE JEREMIAD FROM CIVIL WAR TO PROHIBITION

Of course, the American jeremiad did not simply vanish in the hundred-odd years that elapsed between Lincoln's Second Inaugural and Dan Quayle's castigation of Murphy Brown. In fact, a brief look at the period between the Civil War and World War II provides an intriguing perspective on the rise of the Christian Right. In the words of Gaines M. Foster, "A tradition of religion in politics based on faith in law to make right, or at the very least, to create a moral order capable of making people behave morally, has always existed alongside the dominant voluntary and revivalist traditions" in America. Just as clergy hammered home themes of chosenness and sinfulness throughout the Revolutionary, Founding, antebellum, and Civil War eras, these themes continued to animate public debate during the Gilded Age and into the early twentieth century. In fact, the success of a concerted political (and military) effort to purge the nation of the "national sin" of slavery may well have emboldened other Jeremiahs, later in the nineteenth century, to target other potential sources of American moral decline.[3] The targets of such campaigns were not new (we encountered most of them in previous chapters), and they represent some of the long-standing concerns that American Jeremiahs had been voicing since the early days of the American republic: intemperance, avarice, vice, greed, inappropriate sexual behavior, the lack of recognition of God in the nation's founding documents, and so on. New and troubling developments, such as Darwinism and concerns over the effects of the nation's rapid post–Civil War urbanization, put a particular late-nineteenth-century twist on these long-standing worries.

Concerns about the Constitution's omission of God (let alone His Son), as well as worries over the nation's changing demographic makeup in the wake of a major influx of immigrants from southeastern Europe, played a significant part in this post–Civil War activism. The National Association to Amend the Constitution was formed even before the war ended, and expressed a fear that unless the government took a clear stand endorsing Christianity, the moral decline that activists saw all around them would spiral out of control. But despite orchestrating an avalanche of petitions to Congress in 1868 and 1869, this movement repeatedly failed to gain congressional support. Renaming itself the National Reform Association in 1875 and taking on a broader agenda of moral and religious activism did not yield any greater success. Persistent campaigns for Sabbath closing laws also proved unsuccessful.[4]

More promising was the cause of temperance, which as we saw in chapter 3 also predated the Civil War. The National Temperance Society was formed in 1865, followed nine years later by the Women's Christian Temperance Union (WCTU), a group whose name denotes the close association between religion and moral reform during these years. The WCTU, especially, linked liquor and intemperance to a number of related social vices, including but not limited to those affecting women (abandonment, domestic abuse, etc.), while Billy Sunday tied the "unprecedented increase of crime" to the doctoring up of illegal liquor in his famous "Booze Sermon."[5] Along with the Anti-Saloon League, the WCTU agitated unsuccessfully for years. The coming of World War I changed the dynamics of this debate, however, and the Volstead Act (implementing Prohibition under the Eighteenth Amendment) went into effect in 1919. The political effort to enact Prohibition relied on both the particular dynamics surrounding American involvement in World War I (anti-German sentiment as well as fears about the corruption of American soldiers on military bases) and the concerted efforts of religious Americans over the course of many years.

Underlying all these issues lay such larger social transformations as urbanization, immigration, and the birth of a consumer society. In his 1885 best seller *Our Country*, Josiah Strong surveyed this landscape, noting with concern the increasing numbers of "Romanists" in the cities and the ongoing threat of Mormonism in the West. Strong linked these new Catholic immigrants with the nation's rapid urbanization, tied both developments to the moral decline he saw in the late nineteenth century, and worried about the future implications of such social trends. Billy Sunday's "muscular Christianity" appealed to many Americans' concerns that young boys were growing up soft and effete, the result of transformations in the economy away from hard physical labor to commercial pursuits. The early history of the YMCA movement reflects this fear of effeminacy among the nation's young men, and Clifford Putney has shown that

> as antebellum men increasingly chose business over leadership in the churches, church leadership fell into the hands of less "manly" men (mainly ministers) and women....Many nineteenth-century reformers, first in England, then in America, expressed faith in the power of strenuous activity to overcome the perceived moral defects of urbanization, cultural pluralism, and white-collar work.[6]

The influx of Catholic immigrants from southern Europe worried a broad spectrum of American Protestants, and showed just how powerful the combination of Anglo-Saxon racism and long-standing American anti-Catholicism could be when they joined forces.

Finally, the rising influence of Darwinism also played into concerns about American moral decline. William Jennings Bryan's closing argument at the Scopes trial—never delivered in court, but published soon after the trial—connected the spread of evolutionary ideas, and more specifically the adoption of evolution among the nation's educational elite, with an increase in unbelief among the young, and went on to make the further connection to moral decline in his own time:

> Evolutionists say that back in the twilight of life a beast, name and nature unknown, planted a murderous seed and that the impulse thus originated in that seed throbs forever in the blood of the brute's descendants, inspiring killings innumerable, for which murderers are not responsible because coerced by a fate fixed by the laws of heredity. It is an insult to reason and shocks the heart. That doctrine is as deadly as leprosy; it may aid a lawyer in a criminal case, but it would, if generally adopted, destroy all sense of responsibility and menace the morals of the world....If all the biologists of the world teach this doctrine—as Mr. Darrow says they do—then may heaven defend the youth of our land from their impious babblings.[7]

Bryan's account of the influence of Darwinian theory on the moral state of twentieth-century America contains clear echoes of the jeremiad form: lamenting a current crisis, identifying a historical point in time where the source of decline was introduced (and implicitly identifying a point before which moral health prevailed), and calling for reform and action—in this case, the conviction of Scopes.[8]

In the wake of these developments, many American fundamentalists withdrew from politics, alienated from mainstream American culture and politics. But they stayed busy, embarking on ambitious educational and communications programs of their own, creating Bible institutes, radio (and, later, television) ministries, evangelical and fundamentalist seminaries, and religious publishing ventures. Such undertakings went hand in hand with attempts to facilitate a national revival to address these perceived national crises, and the rise of Billy Graham provides just one example of American fundamentalism's enduring commitment to revivalism. Though disillusioned with the direction of American culture, fundamentalists continued to display a strong sense of patriotism toward the nation they still considered God's country, as Joel Carpenter has elaborated: "Haunted by the 'Christian America' of their memory and imagination, fundamentalists could not shake the proprietary responsibility they felt for their nation's character."[9]

OUT OF THE WILDERNESS: THE (RE)EMERGENCE OF THE CHRISTIAN RIGHT

The reemergence of conservative Protestants in American life was driven by a backlash against the social protests and counterculture of the 1960s and 1970s and Supreme Court decisions on school prayer and abortion, as well as an increasingly powerful federal government with an increasingly long reach into areas previously left to local institutions. Believers saw these developments as further proof of a deep-seated corruption in American culture. Given their reticence about engaging in politics, fundamentalist leaders framed their reentry into politics as a defensive one, a response to a hostile mainstream culture increasingly dominated by secularism and liberalism. Jerry Falwell put it this way:

> Things began to happen. The invasion of humanism into the public school system began to alarm us back in the sixties. Then the *Roe v. Wade* Supreme Court decision of 1973 and abortion on demand shook me

up. Then adding to that gradual regulation of various things it became very apparent the federal government was going in the wrong direction and if allowed would be harassing non-public schools, of which I have one of 16,000 right now. So step by step we became convinced we must get involved if we're going to continue what we're doing inside the church building.[10]

In the words of Carl Henry, "Conservatives were provoked into public involvement by federal intrusion into areas of moral and religious concern such as funding of abortions and prohibition of prayer in public schools." Entering politics during the 1980s, fundamentalists drew on the earlier, and politically quite different, movement for civil rights, in which the nation's churches played a significant role. James Findlay points out that the "tactics of the liberal churches were a double-edged sword, which could be used to advance conservative as well as liberal ends. It was not long before exactly that happened. Perhaps ironically, then, the political successes of the mainline churches in the 1960s served as a precondition for the emergence of Jerry Falwell, Pat Robertson, and the Moral Majority in the 1980s."[11]

Clergy played a key role in convincing skeptical evangelical and fundamentalist congregations that a reentry into politics need not come at the expense of their spiritual health. Jerry Falwell—described by one scholar as "a fundamentalist ventriloquizing evangelicalism"—devoted enormous energy to building bridges between the two communities, and to crafting a public language of American moral decline to which both groups could subscribe. Besides preaching sermons at countless conservative churches around the country, Falwell spearheaded the formation of the Moral Majority in 1979, building that organization into a formidable public voice in American politics. In 1980, disappointed with the presidency of Jimmy Carter (especially given the high hopes with which many had welcomed the evangelical Carter's election four years earlier), many Christian Right leaders supported Ronald Reagan, whose personal religiosity was far less orthodox (and whose personal life included a divorce) but who was skilled at evoking the imagery of American chosenness. Philip Jenkins locates a key difference between Reagan and Carter in their divergent understandings of the United States as a chosen nation. Carter emphasized the American loss of confidence in the wake of the 1960s and 1970s, sentiments expressed most vividly in his famed "malaise" speech. Reagan, on the other hand, "agreed that the United States had gone astray [yet] asserted that its worst sin was to weaken the godly nation in the face of its numerous external enemies, which threatened to bring down the shining city. This image of national chosenness was central to Reagan's vision, the foundation on which stood his entire political philosophy."[12] In Jenkins's telling, Americans vastly preferred Reagan's emphasis on chosenness over Carter's dour fixation on sinfulness.

It would be naïve to view the emergence of the Christian Right as a wholly spontaneous eruption of popular outrage at the counterculture or the Supreme Court's liberal direction. In fact, the interests of religious conservatives dovetailed with those of secular-minded ones, who shared the Christian Right's anticommunism and concern about the increasing reach of the federal government. Such secular conservatives supported these nascent Christian Right organizations and offered their expertise on topics like direct mail, fund-raising, organization, and operations.[13] Given the rhythms of American politics, a backlash against the 1960s was bound to happen at some point, providing a market for the cultural products the Christian Right was selling. Secular forces helped this process along.

Critics of the Christian Right have long noted its lack of concrete policy successes—the failure of Pat Robertson's 1988 campaign for the Republican presidential nomination, the continuing inability to achieve either the reversal of *Roe v. Wade* or a constitutional amendment banning abortion, the reelection of Bill Clinton—as evidence of the movement's failure to take hold in American politics. But such shortsighted dismissals radically underestimate the power of the fundamentalist-evangelical alliance, which thrived on opposition to the Clinton administration (and whom Clinton provided with more than enough ammunition to bolster claims about moral decline at the highest levels of government) and clearly reestablished itself during the presidency of George W. Bush. Ralph Reed made this argument in 1994, regarding critics who saw Falwell's closing of Moral Majority—it would be revived in 2004—as a sign of the movement's failure:

> What these critics did not realize was that even as they danced on the grave of the Moral Majority, a new pro-family movement was rising, phoenix-like, from its ashes....Falwell had accomplished his objective of reawakening the slumbering giant of the churchgoing vote. He had passed the torch to a new generation of leadership who launched new organizations and redirected the pro-family impulse in a more permanent, grassroots direction. These leaders tended to be young (under forty), enjoyed extensive Washington experience, boasted impressive academic or legal credentials, and were generally political professionals rather than pastors or preachers.[14]

It is difficult to argue with Reed's analysis. The Christian Coalition emerged from Robertson's failed campaign for the 1988 Republican presidential nomination, and drew on his extensive database of political supporters to provide the Coalition's foundation and to encourage state- and local-level activism throughout the 1990s.[15] But it is also undeniable that in recent years the Christian Right has been forced to deal with generational change. Falwell and D. James Kennedy (whose Coral Ridge Presbyterian Church sponsored the Center for Reclaiming America for Christ) passed away in 2007, and the senior statesmen of the Christian Right (Robertson, Charles Colson, James Dobson) increasingly share the limelight with a new generation of leadership, including David Barton's WallBuilders, which takes on the mantle of the biblical hero Nehemiah, and Tony Perkins's Family Research Council. This new generation of leaders has been energized by such emerging issues as gay marriage, stem-cell research, the Terry Schiavo case, assisted suicide, and the ongoing concerns about abortion, school prayer, school choice, and pornography. In addition to religious activists, a new generation of American officeholders sympathetic to Christian Right positions on social issues has contributed mightily to the ability of the Christian Right to keep its agenda at the forefront of American politics into the twenty-first century.

Both religious and political figures have shown a new interest in asserting evangelical interests in foreign policy, beyond the Christian Right's traditional anticommunism and support for Israel, and in recent years have raised concerns about sex trafficking and the worship rights of Christians around the world. Such developments show the increasing sophistication of the Christian Right as a movement and a powerful political player, and have resulted in occasional tensions with other segments of the American conservative community. And regardless of the political influence of self-identified Christian Right groups, it seems clear that the broader ideological affinities between religious and secular conservatives will serve the interests of the Christian Right in years to come. In the words of Ronald E. Hopson and Donald R. Smith, "The place of the Christian Right on the American scene is best measured by the extent to which their ideas and meanings are absorbed within the larger culture and begin to define the 'mainstream.'"[16]

Far from a brief flutter on the political scene, then, the contemporary Christian Right jeremiad has proven enormously effective in mobilizing traditionalist Americans concerned with the secularization of public life. The internal politics of the Republican Party have been transformed by this mobilization, and the presidency of George

W. Bush has made abundantly clear how powerful evangelical ideas and rhetoric remain at the highest levels of American government.

Given this contemporary resonance of the Christian Right and the ways in which it continues to engage (and polarize) the American electorate, it is incumbent to define clearly my use of the term. I use the term "Christian Right" to denote a political alliance of evangelical Protestants and politically like-minded Catholics who share their social, political, and moral concerns. The specific targets of this alliance include legalized abortion, the Equal Rights Amendment, the sexual revolution, the increasing acceptance of homosexuality in American culture, and the counterculture of the 1960s more generally. Of course, one cannot automatically assume that the leaders of a movement represent exactly the views of the rank and file. Christian Smith claims that the relative unanimity among fundamentalist leaders and their evangelical allies masks significant diversity among their followers, whose views more closely parallel those of the American public. At the same time, the continuing importance of evangelicals in American electoral politics provides evidence that, at the least, Christian Right leaders are skilled at highlighting issues of particular concern to traditionalists and mobilizing such voters accordingly. The strength of evangelicals as a voting bloc in recent years also suggests that, though surely not monolithic, a cluster of moral-cultural issues does lie at the heart of this group's political concerns.[17]

In other words, I am offering a *political*, and not a *theological*, understanding of the term "Christian Right," and thus shall not delve into the definitional difficulties inherent in distinguishing "evangelicals" from "Pentecostals" and "fundamentalists," for example—be they distinctions regarding millennialism, the end times, or biblical interpretation. In this sense, not every individual or group associated with what I call the "Christian Right" jeremiad will necessarily be evangelical or fundamentalist, although clearly the movement's driving ideological force and most significant funding come from conservative Protestants. Indeed, one of the more interesting developments in American Protestantism in recent years has been the growing alliance between evangelicals and Roman Catholics. The group Evangelicals and Catholics Together, for example, referred to their alliance as "theologically rooted" and not merely one of political expediency. "Our culture's sickness is far too deep for mere political remedies.... [The American culture war presents] a clash of worldviews that involves fundamental differences about truth and ultimate reality, the nature of God, the created order, the moral law, and the human condition.... [in which] these two communions stand shoulder to shoulder." The political and social concerns identified by the Christian Right have proven important to a broad political alliance including orthodox Jews, Muslims, and secular traditionalists of various sorts.[18]

THE INTERNAL NARRATIVE: THE CHRISTIAN RIGHT ON AMERICAN MORAL DECLINE

As we have seen time and again in the previous two chapters, the jeremiad is first and foremost an indictment of national sin, a story of a prodigal nation that has fallen away from its covenant. In the Christian Right narrative, American society is awash in sin and the fruits of sin: crime, divorce, illegitimacy, drug use, media violence, abortion, dishonesty, and sexual libertinism. Although the symptoms of decline are often framed in moral, political, or cultural terms, these critics present a distinctly *spiritual* diagnosis of the problem and its solution: American society has turned away from its fundamental religious values and is showing symptoms of spiritual illness. Ed Dobson provided an exhaustive list of the encroaching "forces of secularism" in American culture, including *Roe v Wade*, the removal of God from the nation's public schools, the breakdown of the traditional family, a pornography epidemic, the gay rights movement, the Equal Rights Amendment, and the growing federal involvement in church affairs. All of these developments, he argued, "generated a perception among fundamentalists that a new religion of secularism was evolving and that it threatened the extinction of the Judeo-Christian values."[19]

Nor were such concerns limited to evangelical activists: on the floor of the United States Senate, Robert Byrd (D-W.V.) observed symptoms of moral decline all around, paraphrasing Dickens by describing the United States as experiencing "the best of times materially...the worst of times spiritually." Despite the economic prosperity of the late 1990s, Byrd pointed to gratuitous public displays of sexuality and violence, the denigration of religion in the legal and public spheres, the crumbling of the American family, and rampant crime—in short, "a general decline in morals throughout the nation." The critique was also ecumenical: in a book produced by Evangelicals and Catholics Together, Richard John Neuhaus and Charles Colson advanced the view that debates over abortion, media, and the traditional family provide evidence of a profound cultural shift: "Our culture is drifting away from its Judeo-Christian foundations and adopting an entirely different set of presuppositions."[20] But what exactly were those foundations, and what were these new presuppositions?

The Nation's Sins: Sex, Secularism, Schools

In the eyes of the public spokespersons for the Christian Right during the late 1970s and early 1980s, perhaps the most significant change in American morality concerned understandings of human sexuality and appropriate sexual behavior. Concern about the loosening of traditional sexual moral standards following the upheavals of the 1960s and 1970s linked a series of hotly contested issues: abortion, homosexuality and the growing movement for gay and lesbian rights, the increasing acceptance of pre- and extramarital sexual activity, pornography, divorce, feminism, the Equal Rights Amendment, and traditional family structures and gender roles. George Weigel argued that the two central issues of the 1980s and 1990s were abortion and gay rights, both of which went to the heart of sexuality and its role in the nation's public life. A related concern about the prevalence of pornography—"a cancer that is changing the character of our republic"—also figured prominently in this critique. None of these campaigns were wholly new—as we have seen above, social movements in favor of morals legislation are as old as America itself—but the upheavals of the 1960s gave them a new urgency in the minds of religious conservatives.[21]

Most basically, critics decried a steady departure from traditional standards of sexual behavior, the foundation of which was a prohibition on sex outside of marriage. No one claimed that Americans had always lived up to the ideal, but there was a public stigma attached to the blatant flouting of standards of sexual behavior, and a legal environment that criminalized homosexual conduct, that buttressed traditionalist understandings of proper sexual behavior in years past.

The Christian Right jeremiad pointed to a number of specific threats to the traditional family: rising divorce rates, the overturning of traditional gender roles and the consequent assault on male headship within the family, and the growing acceptance of cohabitation by unmarried couples and/or children born to unmarried parents. "The philosophy today is trial and error; divorce is not so bad any more; broken homes are not so terrible any more," lamented Falwell. He linked sexual promiscuity, feminism, and the entry of women into the workforce alongside the acceptance of divorce and cohabitation as key factors undermining the traditional family. Such developments, he argued, were ominous, since "[t]he strength and stability of families determine the vitality and moral life of society." Carl Henry connected confusion in the home with a lack of moral consensus in America. And continuing trends in unmarried parenthood and cohabitation throughout the 1980s and 1990s contributed to a rising tide of what was traditionally called "illegitimacy."[22]

Into the 1990s and beyond, defense of the traditional family continued to play a central role in the Christian Right critique. Ralph Reed anchored the movement in more widely accepted political terms, advancing a "pro-family agenda" of smaller government, tax relief for families, and a balanced federal budget, all representing an effort to "restore the centrality of the two-parent, intact family as the foundation of our democratic society." William Bennett's *Index of Leading Cultural Indicators* traced with alarm the shifts away from traditional two-parent heterosexual norm.[23]

The increasingly organized movement for gay and lesbian rights— and its scattered legal and political successes—attracted attention as yet another way in which traditional sexual restraint was threatened. In his 1980 book *Listen, America!*, Jerry Falwell lamented that what was once widely understood as "the zenith of human indecency" had become an acceptable lifestyle. "We would not be having the present moral crisis regarding the homosexual movement if men and women accepted their proper roles as designed by God," Falwell continued, arguing that homosexuality "is a symptom of a sin-sick society." The growing movement for gay rights figured heavily in Falwell's explanation of why he formed the Moral Majority: "The entire homosexual movement is an indictment against America and is contributing to its ultimate downfall." The revived movement for gay rights and same-sex marriage in the 1990s and beyond—particularly the Supreme Court's ruling in *Lawrence v. Texas*, and the movement for same-sex marriage that it sparked—energized Christian Right activists in a number of statewide and national elections, and spawned a number of organizations dedicated to the preservation of marriage as a covenant between one man and one woman.[24]

Of all these sexuality-related issues, however, it is difficult to overstate the importance of legalized abortion in the Christian Right's narrative of American moral decline. Abortion is to the Christian Right narrative what slavery was to the abolitionist: the single, overriding national sin, beside which all others pale by comparison, that threatens to bring God's judgment on the nation. The Supreme Court's decision in *Roe v. Wade* (1973) was a wake-up call for conservative Christians of many stripes; "If we expect God to honor and bless our nation, we must take a stand against abortion," wrote Falwell in 1980, and he coauthored a book devoted entirely to explaining how abortion had led him to see the necessity for Christians to engage in political activism. Carl Henry linked *Roe v. Wade* to a host of sexuality-related issues: "Surely," he opined, it is "not America at her best when we chart the massacre of a million unborn children a year, the flight from the monogamous family, two and a half million persons trapped in illegal drugs and alcohol...the normalizing of deviant sexual behavior...the proliferation of AIDS..." For George Weigel, "the abortion issue has become *the* icon of the sexual revolution, and the sexual revolution has become *the* symbol of the liberal politics in which freedom means autonomy." Pat Robertson included *Roe v. Wade* among his twenty-three "Dates with Destiny" (under the general heading "Losing Our Way") as indicating "the loss of human rights for unborn children." Other prominent Christian Right figures—Edward Dobson, Ralph Reed, Richard John Neuhaus, James Dobson, and William Bennett—invoked abortion as a singularly important marker of the nation's rejection of traditional sexual morality and consequent moral decline.[25]

Although for much of the 1980s the Christian Right could boast little in the way of concrete progress on the abortion issue, the Hyde Amendment (which barred the use of Medicaid funds to provide abortions) and rhetorical support from President Ronald Reagan—who wrote an antiabortion pamphlet while in office—kept their position before the public eye. The election of a pro-choice administration in 1992, and again in 1996, represented both a setback and an opportunity to regroup for those who linked legalized abortion with a threat to the nation's spiritual health. In the mid-1990s, Evangelicals and Catholics Together attempted to unite theologically and ecclesiastically disparate (indeed, mutually suspicious) traditions in common cause against "an encroaching culture of death," the leading edge of which was represented by abortion.[26]

But if these sexuality-charged issues formed a central part of the Christian Right's narrative of American decline, they by no means exhausted it. A series of broader laments—driven by a concern about the marginalization of religion, and especially of traditionalist or "Judeo-Christian" religion, in American public life—animated support for voluntary school prayer, opposition to "activist" courts, and denunciations of the mainstream media for liberal or anti-Christian bias. And turning from concern about the internal health of the nation, the Christian Right jeremiad lamented the decreasing willingness of

American foreign policy makers to confront godless communism in the Americas and around the world.

The first two critiques—of school prayer and activist judges—formed two sides of the same coin. Christian Right leaders pointed to the state of American public education as symptomatic of a declining public morality, and laid responsibility for that decline at the feet of a Supreme Court that had removed prayer and Bible reading from the public schools in its 1963 *Schempp* decision. According to Jerry Falwell, "We have outlawed Bible reading and prayer. We have kicked God out the back door. The result of the exclusion of God from the public school scene is evident. There is a drug epidemic raging....moral permissiveness literally pervades the atmosphere of the public school." Falwell noted that, for many years, American public schools were the best in the world, incorporating Bible reading, singing, and prayer with an education in basic knowledge and skills. However, "our public schools no longer teach Christian ethics.... [T]he decay in our public school system suffered an enormous acceleration when prayer and Bible reading were taken out of the classroom by our United States Supreme Court." Richard John Neuhaus also noted the importance of the school prayer decisions in marking the nation's moral decline, arguing that the *Schempp* decision "set asunder what had been a unified tradition."[27]

In the twenty-first century, such a critique was heard from the highest levels of American government: Senator Byrd focused on the Supreme Court's decisions "since 1962" to disallow public school prayer as a fatal break with the traditions of the nation, while Zell Miller (D-Ga.) decried "the terribly wrong direction our modern judiciary has taken us in." Pat Robertson lamented that, since 1963, "despite 340 years of biblical education of our children, one atheist and a handful of judges stripped the Bible from all the schools of the nation. The moral education of our children was trampled underfoot by a tiny left-wing minority." While acknowledging that correlation does not indicate causation, Ralph Reed could not help noticing that the nation had seen a 560 percent rise in violent crime since 1960, along with overcrowded prisons that led a decreasing number of criminals to serve out their sentences; as well as declining SAT scores, a rise in divorce, and so on. Still, he noted, "there can also be no doubt that there is a correlation between a decline in the role of religion in our society and the rise of social pathologies of every kind."[28]

Removal of prayer and Bible reading from public schools represented just one example of a shift in the nation's broader culture, especially among elites in government, media, and the educational establishment. Evangelicals and Catholics Together contended that "[r]eligion, which was privileged and foundational in our legal order, has in recent years been penalized and made marginal." Religion's important role in American public life, Senator Byrd argued, has been rejected in recent years in favor of a "prejudice against the influence of religious commitment and moral values upon political issues." This Court fails to realize that "[e]very single value upon which this country was so painstakingly built—individual sacrifice for the greater good, fairness, charity, truthfulness, morality, personal responsibility, honesty—all of these are, at root, qualities derived from Judeo-Christian teachings," and as a result the Court is leading us "down the road to becoming a godless nation[.]" Hostility to religion in the schools did not come only from distant institutions like the U.S. Supreme Court, but often from local school administrators, who discriminated against students' legitimate expressions of religious belief and forbade any discussion of religion whatsoever. Even in the absence of overt hostility to religion, public schools often fostered an ignorance of the role of religion in the nation's history, thanks to textbooks that slighted America's religious heritage and its importance to national development.[29]

Implicit—at times explicit—in some of these critiques of the marginalization of religion is a critique of the increasing scope of the federal government's reach. Such centralization represents a threat to local vitality and sovereignty, a thriving free-market culture, and the ability of parents to make decisions regarding the environment in which their children would be raised. Robert Bork, whose controversial nomination to the Supreme Court gave his thoughts on such developments a wide hearing, noted how the courts' embrace of liberalism had weakened intermediate institutions like families and schools.[30]

The Christian Right critique of mainstream American media focused on its role in undermining traditional family values, its glorification of violence and sexual gratification, and its liberal political bias in the reporting of news. The first two elements of this critique gave rise to an increasingly vigorous critique of sexually explicit, violent, and/or countercultural lyrics in popular music, a movement that in the 1980s brought Christian Right thinkers together with other like-minded individuals and groups (including Tipper Gore, wife of then-Senator Al Gore [D-Tenn.]) around the issue of parental warning labels on popular music CDs. The infamous Super Bowl halftime show in January 2005 motivated Senator Zell Miller (D-Ga.) to berate his Senate colleagues for doing nothing to address "made-in-the-USA filth masquerading as entertainment." With regard to the press, Jerry Falwell lamented thirty years ago that "[t]he leadership of all three networks has fallen into evil hands," while Pat Robertson viewed the mainstream media as a sort of fifth column, "working at cross-purposes with the traditional goals and moral values of the American people." Not only are members of the press and Hollywood disproportionately liberal and secular in their personal lives, critics assert, but they have used their positions of public trust to push an antireligious, antitraditional crusade on the nation. The founding and increasing prominence of Robertson's own Christian Broadcasting Network, not to mention the more mainstream Fox News, represent self-conscious attempts to take some action against liberal media bias.[31]

Finally, the Christian Right identified several important international issues as containing a strong religious component. Most significant, perhaps, was the Cold War: American evangelicals and fundamentalists had long spoken out against "godless" communism, and against any American capitulation to the Soviet Union or China. The humiliation that the United States endured while dozens of its citizens were held hostage in Iran served to highlight how far the Chosen Nation had fallen by the late 1970s, and how betrayed it had been by inept leadership at a particularly dangerous time. The fear that President Carter was "soft on communism" and that Ronald Reagan promised a more aggressive military defense of Western (read: "Judeo-Christian") values played an important role in the Christian Right's mobilization behind the decidedly non-evangelical Reagan in 1980. As popular support for the nuclear freeze movement grew during the 1980s, Christian Right figures denounced such a move as threatening the liberties preserved by American institutions, and as dangerously naïve about human nature and international affairs.[32]

Tying together all of these concerns—"the collapse of ethical principles and habits, the loss of respect for authorities and institutions, the breakdown of the family, the decline of civility, the vulgarization of high culture, and the degradation of popular culture"—is a critique of a new, post-1960s ethic, variously labeled by critics as hedonism, selfish individualism, paganism, secularism, secular humanism, or moral relativism. Francis Schaeffer described this development as a conflict between Christianity and humanistic materialism, and others decried the increasing emphasis on individual fulfillment at the expense of transcendent moral law. "For some time," Pat Robertson observed, "a major shift has been taking place in our culture. Where we once worshipped and held in high esteem the God of the Bible and His laws, we now worship another god—that is, the individual."[33]

Such a rootless, relativistic individualism is hostile to the moral order that characterized American society in earlier times: it "frays the social fabric," and modern liberalism has "constantly moved away from...constraints on personal liberty imposed by religion, morality, law, family, and community." Furthermore, such individualism goes hand in hand with a materialistic worldview in which spiritual values are progressively eroded by an increased emphasis on economic success or material well-being. According to Jean Bethke Elshtain, "we are creatures who have forgotten what it means to be faithful to something other than ourselves." Bruce Frohnen laments that contemporary Americans "have come to reject their duty to God's will because they have come to identify the good, not with the holy, but with the pleasant." Attempts to ennoble such hollow individualism—like Alan Wolfe's valorization of "moral freedom"—only show how far we have fallen.[34]

The implications of this turn away from what Carl Henry calls "divine-command morality" are felt across the spectrum of issues outlined above. According to David Popenoe, "The cultures of most developing and developed societies today...are moving or have moved toward individualism," and thus "America's fundamental problem...is cultural disintegration, a weakening of the ties that bind." Behaviors long relegated to the fringes of American society—unbelief, homosexuality, skepticism of authority, extramarital sexual activity—have in recent years become normalized. Practices once engaged in, as quietly as possible, by just a countercultural few, were now common. Thus William Bennett took issue with widespread views that Bill Clinton's sexual misconduct was "merely" private behavior, arguing instead that "the widespread loss of outrage against this president's misconduct tells us something fundamentally important about our condition," which he likened to "moral and intellectual disarmament."[35]

Founders and the Decline from Founding Virtue

As we saw in chapters 2 and 3, American Jeremiahs do not merely critique the present; they look to the past. The Christian Right jeremiad offers two primary examples of the virtuous past, of a time of national spiritual health and well-being that provides a template for what a redeemed and reformed polity might look like: the founding era, and 1950s America. These two periods are intimately connected in the narrative; Christian Right Jeremiahs see the 1960s as the decade that severed America from its traditional Judeo-Christian foundations, and life just prior to the 1960s as the last generation really in touch with those foundations. The founding is important because it provides an example of a time in which liberty, religion, and authority coexisted in a proper balance; while post–World War II America offers an echo of this founding moment that is still a vivid memory for many Americans. (I discuss nostalgic and Golden Age politics more fully in chapter 7.)

Many Christian Right accounts trace the religious impulse in American history back to the origins of American colonial settlement. Falwell highlighted the Jamestown settlement, the Mayflower Compact, the early histories of New England and Pennsylvania, and the role of churches in colonial universities as especially significant roots of America's religious heritage. According to Senator Byrd, these early settlers imbibed the notion of an Elect Nation from their English Protestant background, and as a result "religious conviction permeated the bloodstream of American Constitutionalism and American statecraft as far back as 200 years prior to the writing of the Constitution." Byrd repeatedly invoked the specifically religious nature of the American experience: "[E]arly American documents reflect aspirations, which are, at their core, based on a belief in a Supreme Being and on the existence of a human soul."[36]

Both revolutionary action and the nation's foundational documents, according to Paul Johnson, illustrate "the centrality of the religious spirit in giving birth to America." Certainly not all figures in the movement would necessarily agree with Pat Robertson's description of the founders as "students of the Old and New Testaments and…deeply influenced by the life and teachings of Jesus" who "founded the nation on principles basic to our Judeo-Christian heritage." But all agree that the founders—Washington, Madison, Adams, and so many others, even the religiously heterodox Jefferson—represent moral exemplars who never shrank from the opportunity to link Judeo-Christian piety and American national identity. The American Revolution, as opposed to the French, was fired by and friendly toward Christianity, and religious and political notions of liberty informed and supported each other. The founders "were united by a common belief in the importance of religion as an aid and a friend to the Constitutional order [and] spoke with one voice about the importance of religion in civic life," wrote William Bennett. Regardless of their degree of personal belief, the founders understood the importance of a public faith that cemented citizenship, shared sacrifice, personal piety, and the common good. Terry Eastland argues that "[a]s a matter of historical fact, the Founding Fathers believed that the public interest was served by the promotion of religion."[37]

Although official disestablishment was the law of the land under the First Amendment, a general culture of (Protestant) religiosity, and a publicly influential role for churches and church leaders remained the backbone of the nation's public life well into the twentieth century. According to Bruce Frohnen, "For early Americans the link between justice and fear of God was clear," and the vision of the good life in early America, "deriv[ed] from the Bible, shows the roots of American liberty in a religious understanding of man and society that transcends even as it affects politics." The American democratic proposition, according to Neuhaus, "emerges from and is sustained by prior propositions about God and his ways in the world."[38]

In addition to the early history of American colonization and the founding period, the Christian Right narrative also highlights the period before the 1960s as a time of national virtue. Echoing Dan Quayle, Gertrude Himmelfarb argues that the 1960s represented "a genuine moral and cultural revolution," and despite advances also brought about "rapid acceleration of crime, out-of-wedlock births, and welfare dependency." According to Paul Hammond,

> It was the prevalent, established religion of the 1920–1960 period that was assaulted by the social revolution arising in the 1960s, and continuing today…[W]hat was being assaulted was the assumption that church involvement…was a good thing because it signified conventionality and fundamental attachment to core American values.

The link between the litany of sins, the sexual revolution of the 1960s and 1970s, and a pre-1960s America, is clearly made by Pat Robertson:

> There was a time not long ago that the Christian view of sexuality prevailed. Sure, there was kissing and petting between couples. Yes, young men were considered predators, but young men and women were taught that sexual intercourse was for marriage, and sex outside of marriage was a sin. I can remember clearly the college days after World War II.…Even the wildest fraternity crowd did not condone adultery.

Jerry Falwell linked drugs with socialism, hedonism, and welfarism; Ralph Reed placed the "drug culture" alongside the sexual revolution, Vietnam, Watergate, and the growth of the welfare state" as things that tore the cultural fabric of the United States late in the twentieth century.[39]

Such a close connection between piety and American public life has eroded in the wake of the 1960s: "Where once men believed they served God by caring for their families, neighbors, and communities, today we seek to fulfill ourselves by controlling our own lives." Alongside this rejection of religious commitments goes an increasing cynicism about America's role in world politics as well as an increasing questioning of the notion that religious issues have any legitimate place in public discourse. Neuhaus describes the rise of the "religious new right" as due in part to "an uneasiness...about the public loss of transcendence, about a perceived moral vacuum at the heart of our public life, about the absence of a sense of interest-surpassing content and consequence in the American enterprise.... [M]atters of history and cultural tradition are being drained from our public discourse." Christian Right Jeremiahs thus see the loss of an earlier context of self-restraint as a sort of engine of contemporary spiritual decline, closely bound up with the loss of public religiosity; the authors of the manifesto *Evangelicals and Catholics Together* claim that "we contend for the truth that politics, law, and culture must be secured by moral truth" and, in making such a contention, link themselves to "the Founders of the American experiment."[40]

Such changes in post-1960s American mores—religious, political, sexual, legal—represent the tip of a much broader iceberg of social transformation, founded on a departure from the intentions of the nation's founders on the subject of church and state. According to Ralph Reed, "The Founders never intended for the First Amendment to restrain government, in its legitimate role of fulfilling a secular purpose, from accommodating religious faith.... Sadly, American legal culture has shifted from neutrality to hostility towards religion, something the founders never intended." It is to rectify this situation—problematic for any nation, to be sure, but especially so given the religious character of so much of American history—that Senator Byrd calls for the reinstatement of voluntary school prayer as a way to combat the "drift towards materialism and radical secularism"[41] that the Court's decisions and the wider culture have fostered.

Such an account of decline from godly foundations certainly evokes those New England Jeremiahs who lamented *their* society's spiritual decline three centuries before Falwell's rise to fame. Says Falwell, "Wallowing in our materialism, self-centeredness, and pride, we decided that we really didn't need God after all. We began to tamper with his absolute standards, making them subject to our own opinions and decisions." In a passage penned during the Clinton years, Pat Robertson distilled this larger narrative of American decline into a remarkable indictment of the 1960s and its ongoing influence on American life:

> Until modern times, the foundations of law rested on the Judeo-Christian concept of right and wrong and the foundational concept of Original Sin....Modern, secular sociology, however, shuns such biblical teachings in favor of an evolutionary hypothesis based on the ideas of Darwin, Freud, Einstein, and others. This view, often called "secular humanism," takes the view that man has evolved from the slime and that with time and ever greater freedoms, mankind will ascend to the stars. These ideas, which are contrary to the Word of God, have led directly to the bitter conflict and social chaos of our day....
>
> The legacy of the 1960s is still with us today. The free-love, anti-war, psychedelic 1960s proclaimed not only the right of dissent but the right to protest against and defame the most sacred institutions of the nation....Free love, the rise of pagan cults, and the New Age movement have all thrived in this atmosphere of defiance. And what may prove to be the greatest holocaust in history—the abortion movement—is one of its most sinister expressions.[42]

Call for Renewal

The Christian Right jeremiad has always been closely aligned with a particular vision of the American future and a particular political agenda designed to advance that vision. The main features of that agenda follow rather directly from the traditionalist character of the narrative: outlawing abortion; banning gay marriage and, indeed, any notion of rights for homosexuals as homosexuals; returning voluntary prayer into the nation's public schools; public campaigns against pornography and violent or sexually explicit media; shrinking the size and scope of the federal government and its reach into private and religious sectors; a strong national defense; and school choice programs.

Since much of the Christian Right jeremiad focuses on human sexuality, its call to national repentance naturally highlights the importance of a restoration of traditional sexual mores. Jerry Falwell saw this clearly: "We have to teach [our boys and girls] how to date. We have to teach them to love one another rightly. We have to teach them how to marry and how to raise children again. The whole country has forgotten that..." Indeed, four of the five major national sins identified by

Falwell in 1979—abortion, homosexuality, pornography, humanism, the fractured family—involved sexual matters.[43]

Since the Christian Right jeremiad sees religious liberty as integral to the American experience—given its importance to the founders and its status as a bedrock American political value—and considering the ways in which the courts have restricted the exercise of certain types of public Christianity, reversing the legal transformations of the past thirty years is also high on its agenda. Since "the Court has enunciated a First Amendment jurisprudence that is increasingly hostile to the free exercise of religion, and that has in effect inverted the First Amendment's religion clause," regaining religious liberty for American Christians represents an urgent priority. One way to accomplish this is to appoint judges and Supreme Court justices who, in the words of Tony Perkins, chair of the Family Research Council, "will simply interpret the Constitution as it is written." Appellate as well as Supreme Court nomination battles have become increasingly protracted, with exhaustive vetting of candidates, increasingly rancorous confirmation hearings, and the use of filibusters to prevent votes on controversial candidates. Perkins's "Justice Sunday" event referred to this process as a "filibuster against people of faith."[44]

Yet the Court, such critics note, has not proven hostile to *all* expressions of religiosity. The Christian Right jeremiad notes the paradoxical fact that the removal of religion from public schools and institutions since 1962 has paralleled the *entrance* into American public life of a host of non-Western, meditative, therapeutic, or occult practices. This legacy of the 1960s—increasing penetration of the nation by "alien religious influences that the West once unhesitatingly called alien, such as witchcraft, cults, mosques, shrines, and temples"—frames the Christian Right's call for the reestablishment of religious liberty and Judeo-Christian values. Support for school choice programs and home schooling seeks further to enhance the ability of born-again and traditionalist Christians to live lives free from the legal and bureaucratic reach of the secular school system, as they did in times past, before the infiltration of American life by the federal government.[45]

Overall, then, the Christian Right jeremiad's vision for America evokes an earlier and simpler age, in which families and local communities were at greater liberty to express their religious faith in public without having to worry about complaints from religious minorities or the intervention of secularizing liberal judges or the Supreme Court. Ralph Reed's statement of this vision provides a glimpse of *both* historical ideals mentioned above, the founding/early national period and the pre-1960s view of America. If religious conservatives had their way, he assured his audience,

> America would look much as it did for most of the first two centuries of its existence, before the social dislocations caused by Vietnam, the sexual revolution, Watergate, and the explosion of the welfare state. Our nation would once again be ascendant, self-confident, proud, and morally strong. Government would be strong, the citizenry virtuous, and mediating institutions such as churches and voluntary organizations, would carry out many of the functions currently relegated to the bureaucracy.[46]

This America, suggests Reed, most closely approximates the one that the founders intended to bequeath to us. By electing sympathetic candidates, confirming judges who share this vision, and (re)inculcating these values in America's citizens, the Christian Right seeks to "take America back" from the forces of secular humanism.

EXTERNAL CONTEXT: AMERICA'S DIVINE MISSION

Of course, as we have seen in the previous chapters, narratives of decline are never the whole story when considering the American jeremiad. A sacred story always surrounds, enfolds, and gives meaning to the mundane tale of decline from virtuous foundings. In the Christian Right jeremiad, such a sacred story interprets the American experience as part of God's unfolding plan for human history. Vern McClellan gleaned religious significance from Christopher Columbus's journals, while Falwell noted that only twenty-five years separated Columbus's voyage to America from the beginning of the European Reformation: "It was as if God had preserved a great 'Island in the Sea' as a place of refuge for persecuted believers from continental Europe." From there, the narrative generally moves ahead to Jamestown, the Mayflower Compact, and especially John Winthrop's idea of the New England settlement as "a city on a hill." "This image of the City upon a Hill was in time to become secular," Paul Johnson admits. "But in its origins the idea was religious." Through the revolutionary experience—Robertson sees the colonists' victory as nothing short of miraculous—and into the early national period, God blessed the Americans in their bold experiment in self-government, since such an enterprise was undertaken in a covenantal relationship with God. Of course, as we saw in our consideration of the New England jeremiad, this sort of typological interpretation of Scripture could be a double-edged sword, and Falwell invokes a Deuteronomic understanding of history: "America must not forget where she came from. Let us not forget the warning God gave the Israelites, which is the same warning that applies to America today."[47]

If the founders were a uniquely religious set of men, then it stands to reason that their political achievements would provide evidence of God's blessing: "God promoted America to a greatness no other nation has ever enjoyed because her heritage is one of a republic governed by laws predicated on the Bible..." The United States' rise to global power and influence is generally presented as causally following from the religious foundations of American liberty. According to Falwell, "God has blessed this nation because in its early days she sought to honor God and the Bible, the inerrant Word of the living God....[The founders] developed a nation predicated on Holy Writ. The religious foundations of America find their roots in the Bible." The implication is clear: there is something unique and powerful, something out of the ordinary, about the American rise to power, a kind of theological "American exceptionalism" that interprets American history not only against the background of Western history, but as a key part of God's plan for human history. David Barton traces the Christian influences on America through the influence of John Locke on the founders. Nothing is accidental in such a providentialist worldview, and even the United States' defeat in Vietnam can be read as an expression of God's displeasure at the increasingly liberal and secular direction that the nation has taken since the 1960s.[48]

As we have seen time and time again, the jeremiad contains both lamentations of decline and invocations of national chosenness and promise, often tacking back and forth between the two depending upon political context. Indeed, George W. Bush gained the White House in 2000 by playing on a lament over the loss of honor and character at the nation's highest levels of government, and clearly shared many of the concerns about American moral decline that have appeared in this chapter, as well as a vocal evangelical religious commitment. In the wake of September 11, however, Bush sharply condemned Jerry Falwell's remarks attributing the attacks to American moral decline, and reaffirmed the fundamental notion of American chosenness repeatedly in his post–September 11 speeches. "The advance of human freedom...now depends on us....Freedom and fear...have always been at war, and we know that God is not neutral between them." America's "responsibility to history is already clear: to answer these attacks and rid the world of evil." In fact, the president linked the attacks directly to the nation's *virtue*, not its decline, and tied that goodness to virtuous ancestors: "In every generation, the world has produced enemies of human freedom. They have attacked America because we are freedom's home and defender, and the commitment of our fathers is now the calling of our time."[49]

I mentioned in the previous chapter that the appeal of "chosen nation" thinking seems almost irresistible, especially in times of war and conflict. Note how George W. Bush's Second Inaugural Address, clearly beckoning toward a post–September 11 world and delivered as American forces were deployed in Iraq, *declines* the mantle of chosen nation in one sentence, yet reclaims the idea of America as instrumental to the "visible direction" of history, "set by liberty and the Author of liberty."

> We go forward with complete confidence in the eventual triumph of freedom. Not because history runs on the wheels of inevitability; it is human choices that move events. Not because we consider ourselves a chosen nation; God moves and chooses as He wills. We have confidence because freedom is the permanent hope of mankind, the hunger in dark places, the longing of the soul. When our Founders declared a new order of the ages; when soldiers died in wave upon wave for a union based on liberty; when citizens marched in peaceful outrage under the banner "Freedom Now"—they were acting on an ancient hope that is meant to be fulfilled. History has an ebb and flow of justice, but history also has a visible direction, set by liberty and the Author of Liberty.[50]

INTO THE TWENTY-FIRST CENTURY:
9/11 AND AFTER

As we have seen, the nation's founders, and their colonial predecessors, serve an important role for the Christian Right jeremiad. Given what we have learned about the jeremiad in the previous chapters, this should not come as a surprise: the jeremiad has always held founding virtue up to present-day degeneracy. I suggested in the previous chapter, however, that for thinkers like Lincoln, Henry Ward Beecher, and Gilbert Haven, the founders were important less for their concrete achievements—they had allowed slavery to persist, for example, and left behind a political system that proved ripe for monopolization by a slave conspiracy—than for the sea change in political *ideas* that they introduced (in Lincoln's words, Jefferson's "abstract truth, applicable to all men and all times"[51]). For the Christian Right jeremiad, on the contrary, the concrete particularities of the nation's founding are paramount: the faith of the Founding Fathers, if not in evangelical Christianity, at least in a form of theism friendly to religion in the public realm; their vision for small federal government; their willingness to countenance local establishments of religion or at least to favor religious over nonreligious practices; as well as the more general claims about family structure, male headship, and so on.[52] Perhaps the most prominent element of the Christian Right critique of the "naked public square" is that the secularizing impulse behind such a view flies in the face of the practices of earlier generations of Americans.

It is no accident, therefore, that so many (though by no means all) Christian Right Jeremiahs also turn out to endorse a form of strict constructionist and/or original intent jurisprudence, in which the Constitution ought to be interpreted in ways that mirror what the founders could have intended from their vantage point in the late eighteenth century. These terms—originalism, original intent, strict constructionism—are of course highly charged politically, and not interchangeable, but refer to a general approach to constitutional interpretation (in the words of sympathetic politicians, that judges should simply "interpret the Constitution as written" and not impose their own values).[53] The reasoning for such claims is fairly straightforward: the nation's founders were religious, they viewed religion and morality as essential props to government in a free society, and, while championing the institutional separation of church and state, they had no objection to governmental legislation on moral matters, or to a close association between religious institutions and the government. Accordingly, therefore, the Christian Right political vision involves a return to the friendly, if institutionally separate, relationship between mainstream Christianity and the American government that obtained earlier in the nation's history. Not surprisingly, the notion of a "living constitution," in which basic constitutional values must be viewed as subject to renegotiation in response to changing mores, is anathema to originalists.[54]

The tendency to privilege original intent parallels the Christian Right's emphasis on timeless and unchanging truths, derived from the Bible, in that precise aspects of the past (family structure, gender roles, sexual codes) are taken as authoritative regardless of time or place. Vincent Crapanzano has argued that a certain literalist approach to authoritative texts predominates among both culturally conservative Christians and originalist judges in contemporary America. Crapanzano's particular articulation of this parallel fails to do justice to the nuances of each position, but the general thrust of his observations does demonstrate some significant cultural and methodological overlapping between the Christian Right political agenda and broader ways of thinking about religion, law, and American society.[55]

In his fine study of the Christian Coalition, Justin Watson sheds a great deal of light on the way in which the Christian Right jeremiad figures into the broader contours of American history and politics. Watson sees a twofold agenda at work in the Coalition's career. First, we find a defensive agenda, driven by a sense of threat: recall that Christian Right Jeremiahs often narrated their entry into American politics as motivated by the sense that a secularizing, liberalizing federal government was threatening traditionalist Americans' ability to structure their lives around the values they held most dear. In this vein, the Christian Right embraces a commitment to American values such as freedom of speech, religion, and assembly. In other words, in a pluralistic public sphere, there is no reason why traditionalist and/or religious Americans, like Americans of countless other groups, should be frustrated in their attempts to raise their children as they see fit and organize themselves to seek to reform society and politics. But there is another, "offensive," agenda, a restorationist one that seeks to restore traditional religious values and practices to the center of national life. Such an agenda can easily shade into a desire for "Christian America," especially to those concerned about civil liberties or the rights of religious minorities and who view Christian Right positions as hostile to the very pluralism on which Christian Right activism depends. Watson identifies this tension between two divergent impulses—between recognition and restoration—as lying at the heart of the Christian Coalition's uneven political career since the 1990s, and sees the management of these tensions as central to the future prospects of the Christian Right more generally.[56]

All jeremiads, as we have seen, exist in a larger social and political context. Politically speaking, the Christian Right jeremiad has always faced a formidable rival, namely the narrative of the 1960s as a hallmark in the history of American freedom, a staple of the American left. Certainly a decade that saw the passage of the Civil Rights Act, the Voting Rights Act, Medicaid, and the immigration legislation of 1965, to name only a few, will hold a powerful rhetorical appeal for many, and some scholars and activists have sought to valorize the expansion of rights to minorities and women during these years.[57] By contrast, the Christian Right jeremiad presents the 1960s as a fundamental break with a continuous American religio-political regime, and the source of a host of spiritual and social ills. Politically speaking, such an approach entails risk, and thus we find Christian Right Jeremiahs taking great pains to distance themselves from the segregationist elements of the very time period that they are valorizing, and to endorse rights for women and minorities that were not honored until the 1960s or after.[58] The history of the Christian Right as a social movement, even its most ardent supporters admit, has been characterized by a great deal of racial mistrust, and the fact that both African-Americans and evangelical Protestants share socially conservative views on sexuality-related issues has not been enough to allow the two groups to forge political alliances. Without such alliances, D. James Kennedy's oft-stated goal of "reclaiming America for Christ" will likely continue to elude the Christian Right.

PART II

THE JEREMIAD IN AMERICAN CULTURE

❊

FIVE

Competing Jeremiads

As we have seen, the story of American moral decline and divine punishment has served as a powerful tool for political mobilization throughout the nation's history, beginning with the migration to America itself and continuing down to the twenty-first century. All jeremiads represent efforts at persuasion, in which speakers attempt to fire the imaginations of their listeners and call them to action by using skillfully crafted political narratives. Those listeners, in turn, enter the political arena, enacting their own stories of American chosenness, sinfulness, and redemption, playing their part in the attempt to bring a prodigal nation home again.

And yet, when we look more closely at the many American jeremiads canvassed in Part I, we begin to see an important distinction between two ways of presenting its basic elements (lament over the present, evocation of the past, call for renewal). Rooted in different ways of understanding the American past, these two types of jeremiads in turn offer sharply contrasting visions for the American future. *Traditionalist* jeremiads understand the past's value to lie in its concrete social practices, institutions, and traditions, and lament the community's falling away from those practices. Their political agenda, accordingly, involves recapturing key elements of social reality as, in their understanding, it once existed. *Progressive* jeremiads, while similarly lamenting present conditions, look to the past not for concrete practices to emulate, but for fundamental principles lying at the heart of American nationhood. The realization of those principles, according to the progressive jeremiad, has been repeatedly thwarted, and thus its expansive vision for the American future involves ever more fully realizing such ideals, in new and different circumstances.

THE PAST AS MODEL: THE TRADITIONALIST JEREMIAD AND THE ROOTS OF AMERICAN IDENTITY

At the heart of the traditionalist jeremiad's lament over present conditions lies an *empirical* contrast between "the way things are now" and "the way things used to be." The jeremiads of second-generation New England clergy like Increase Mather, Samuel Danforth, and William Stoughton presented New England history as one of declension, a falling off from the founding generation's piety. Danforth asked his audience to "call to remembrance the former days and consider whether it was not then better with us, than it is now." New England jeremiads contrasted the godly behavior of the colonies' founders with the lackluster commitment exhibited by the children of those founders, condemning emergent alternative religious movements (especially Baptists and Quakers), commercial growth, nascent social mobility, and "worldliness." Recall David Minter's observation that "Puritans found themselves in a situation defined by the curious intermingling of three elements: the crumbling of their design, the waning of their piety, and the waxing of their prosperity." New England Jeremiahs often suspected that the first two of these phenomena were caused, or at least aided and abetted, in some way by the third. Likewise, departures from traditional standards of sexual behavior played a key role in the Christian Right's anti-1960s jeremiad. In addition to the nation's growing tolerance of homosexuality, Christian Right leaders pointed to other sexuality- and family-related issues—abortion, rising divorce rates, the emergence of new and nontraditional gender roles, feminism, and the growing acceptance of cohabitation by unmarried couples and of children born to unmarried parents—as evidence of an increasing turn away from past behavioral standards anchored in Judeo-Christian piety.[1]

By highlighting the present generation's departure from the practices of their forebears, the traditionalist jeremiad makes a powerful claim that the value of the American past lies, in some key way, in *what people did in the past*. The fact that the American founders had tolerated slavery, for example—even to the point of forbidding Congress from prohibiting the importation of slaves until 1808, and ensuring the return of fugitive slaves—was a powerful weapon in the arsenal of proslavery rhetoric during the years leading up to the Civil War. Jeremiads produced by slavery's defenders thus viewed the rise of the Republican Party (and abolitionism more generally) as apostasy from the example of the founders, a decline in the willingness of nineteenth-century Americans to abide by the clear standards laid down by the nation's founders. Thus we encounter the complex, and only partially successful, attempts by Lincoln and other Republicans to claim *both* fidelity to the founders *and* opposition to the spread of slavery, by arguing that the founders had *intended* slavery to die a gradual death and a new social reality without slavery to take its place.

The Christian Right's traditionalist jeremiad emphasizes the religious motivations behind American colonization, the religious backdrop of the Revolution and early national period, and the relatively uncontroversial nature of public Christian practice during much of the nation's history. Whether it be prayer in public schools, traditional sexual mores, or the display of religious symbols on public property, the 1960s are significant, since they represent the point at which widespread Protestant consensus (or at least hegemony) on a number of issues broke down and the nation turned away from its traditional valuation of Christian piety in its public institutions.[2] During those years—and in the years since—both student protesters and Supreme Court justices showed a dangerous willingness to tamper with ways of relating church and state that had been in place for nearly 200 years. Judge Roy Moore, the former Chief Justice of the Supreme Court of Alabama who gained notoriety in 2003 for his refusal to remove a large monument to the Ten Commandments from his courtroom, noted that "Since the 1960s, federal courts have consistently removed all acknowledgments of God from the public sector, whether denominated as prayer, Bible reading, displays, mottos, or historical references.... Even references to God in our national laws are disparaged and tolerated as 'ceremonial deisms.'"[3]

Given this emphasis on the concrete particulars of previous times, the traditionalist jeremiad offers a vision for the future in which the past serves as model and a limiting condition, a sort of empirical checklist to guide a political agenda for the future. New England Jeremiahs repeatedly implored civil magistrates—whom they viewed as "nursing fathers" to the churches—to emulate the behavior of godly founders by upholding, with coercive measures if necessary, both religious orthodoxy and godly comportment in the civil sphere, forbidding displays of ostentatious luxury, for example, and long hair on men.

More recently, the Christian Right has offered a broadly similar picture of the nation's past as the key to the nation's future. In Jerry Falwell's words, "This is a Christian nation," by which he means—as we saw in the previous chapter—both that the founders themselves were men of Christian faith, and that Christianity has been intertwined with American public life since the nation's earliest days.[4] But given the kinds of political, religious, and cultural diversity that characterize American society in the twenty-first century, to proclaim the relevance of the past for the present and future is to emphasize *constraint* and limitation. Since the Christian Right constructs an American past dominated by a Protestant consensus, its jeremiad views the growth of new religious movements and Eastern religions since the 1960s not as the flowering of religious liberty, a basic American ideal firmly ensconced in the First Amendment, but rather as the loss of Protestant dominance. Similarly with the rise of gay rights: the Christian Right jeremiad sees not the next phase of the ongoing American civil rights movement but an assault on the traditional hegemony of heterosexual monogamy.[5]

Finally, traditionalist jeremiads display a distinct hostility to the pluralistic religious landscape of twenty-first-century America, a hostility intimately connected with their view of, and reasons for valuing, the past. On the one hand, a successful jeremiad represents a democratic moment, in which individuals (e.g., fundamentalists, abolitionists) enter the political system to act upon their deep concern for the health of their community. When American fundamentalists shook off fifty years of political disengagement and reentered the political fray, they brought with them a series of concerns and demanded that politicians take notice. In one way, of course, the Christian Right represented a reaction against the perceived excesses of the 1960s, but it was also a genuine populist movement that spoke out, in the name of traditionalist moral and religious values, against a political system that seemed deaf to its concerns. Indeed, the name "Moral Majority" was carefully chosen to suggest the movement's size and power. And yet although movements like the Christian Right narrate their entry into politics largely in "defensive" terms, their constructive vision is equally important to their activism. At the heart of the Christian Right jeremiad, as Justin Watson has articulated, lies a deep unease with pluralism and diversity as it has come to exist in the twenty-first century.[6]

This contemporary unease with pluralism is not new to the traditionalist jeremiad. Baptists, Methodists, and Anglicans only emerged as full members of the New England polity as the influence of Congregationalism over New England public life gradually waned. And the inability of Confederate leaders to envision a future without slavery played a crucial role in the eventual defeat they suffered at the hands of the Union armies. Proposals to free and arm the slaves, voiced with increasing boldness as military fortunes dimmed, were opposed by the Confederate government and slaveholders alike as "social and cultural suicide for the white South."[7] Their rejection showed the power of a constraining understanding of Southern identity that privileged the racial hierarchies of the South over competing values like political and economic independence.

Although I have emphasized the Christian Right jeremiad as an exemplary contemporary example of the traditionalist jeremiad, American liberals are equally prone to this sort of attachment to particularities of the past. Since the 1990s, for example, a revived American communitarian movement, which draws adherents from across the political spectrum, has lamented the decay of traditional forms of community involvement and civic engagement. Many works of communitarian and civic republican social criticism—most notably, in recent years, work by Robert Bellah, Amitai Etzioni, and Robert Putnam—have lamented the increasing individualism of American society and sought to revive, in practical ways, the spirit of community and social connection.[8]

But these accounts fail to entertain the possibility that we haven't so much lost something as developed something new. The constraining nature of such jeremiads is especially clear in Putnam's *Bowling Alone*, which draws its rhetorical power from the drastic membership declines in the dominant forms of postwar civic engagement—most particularly, the local chapter of national-level organizations like the Elks, Moose, Kiwanis, and Jaycees. But looking only at such concrete forms can easily blind us to the reality of *new forms* of engagement that emerged with new technologies, and to the differing modes of engagement among a younger generation more comfortable with the Internet and text-messaging.[9] As such, Putnam's account remains imprisoned by his exclusive focus on social interaction as it existed in the 1950s and 1960s. *Bowling Alone* was able to make such a pointed contrast between present and past levels of civic involvement only by refusing other modes of engagement—book groups, self-help programs, national-level environmental groups, forms of social engagement fostered by the Internet—the status of "social capital."

THE PAST AS PROMISE: PROGRESSIVE JEREMIADS
AND THE POWER OF FOUNDING PRINCIPLES

Like its traditionalist counterpart, the progressive jeremiad begins with a lament over present conditions and looks to the past for solutions. Its lament, however, is not over the way that society has departed from the actual practices of a previous era, and it spends little time arguing about "the way things used to be." Rather, the progressive jeremiad looks to the American past, most particularly to the founding period, as the source of emancipatory ideals and fundamental principles. Despite their power, the progressive jeremiad laments, such principles have been co-opted and frustrated by the apathy or, worse yet, the active collusion of elites eager to maintain their own positions of power. Consider two nineteenth-century practitioners of the progressive jeremiad. For both Abraham Lincoln and Frederick Douglass, the crisis of their time was clear: slavery, and a host of social and political disputes that involved slavery in one way or another. Although Douglass had agitated for the abolition of slavery since the beginning of his public career and Lincoln only arrived at such a position after several years of civil war, both saw slavery as implicated in the growing disunity, rancor, and sectional divisiveness of the 1840s and 1850s, and eventually the armed conflict of the 1860s.

The language of decline from past virtue, so prominent in the traditionalist jeremiad, is less pronounced in its progressive counterpart, and more often appears as a lament over the steady retreat from founding promise. During the 1850s, for example, important public figures like Gilbert Haven and Henry Ward Beecher condemned the rise of a "slave power" that had, in their view, gained control of the federal government and hijacked the radical potential of the American founding. For observers like Thomas Wentworth Higginson, only such a dark explanation could account for the continuing inability of American principles of liberty to prevail.[10] The Supreme Court's decision in *Dred Scott*—which sought to take slavery off the national political agenda entirely, by ruling that Congress had no power to interfere with slavery in federal territories—added credibility to claims about the slave power. Whether or not the slave power actually existed on the scale asserted by abolitionists and Northern sympathizers, its importance to progressive jeremiads is clear. In this narrative, the slave power represented a conspiratorial attempt to ensure an ever-greater distance between American founding promise and contemporary American practices.

The past serves as crucial a role for the progressive jeremiad as it does for the traditionalist jeremiad. When Lincoln and Douglass looked for a solution to the nation's difficulties, they looked to the past, and evoked the spirit of the nation's founders, not for their concrete practices—the failure to do away with slavery represented a grave, though perhaps politically necessary, founding error—but due to the radical *promise* of the founding, the birthright that the nation's founding documents had promised to all Americans. Douglass located the moral significance of the American founding in its radical *principles*, and not the mundane (slaveholding) *realities* of its time. Recall that in his famous speech of July 4, 1852, Douglass told his audience that "[t]he principles contained in [the Declaration of Independence] are saving principles. Stand by those principles, be true to them on all occasions, in all places, against all foes, and at whatever cost." In the midst of war, he exuberantly (if a bit hyperbolically) celebrated the "principles in the Declaration of Independence which would release every slave in the world and prepare the earth for a millennium of righteousness and peace."[11]

Lincoln, too, valorized the nation's founders, although like Douglass he made no claims that they had fully realized their own highest ideals. In his debates with Stephen Douglas, Lincoln described his own position as putting slavery "where Washington, and Jefferson, and Madison placed it...in the course of ultimate extinction."[12] When Lincoln did praise the founders (usually Jefferson) in more particular ways, it was always as propounders of an ideal, articulators of principles of liberty and equality. Jefferson, he claimed, was the man "who, in the concrete pressure of a struggle for national independence by a single people, had the coolness, forecast, and capacity to introduce into a merely revolutionary document, an abstract truth, applicable to all men and all times."[13] The jeremiads offered by Lincoln and Douglass emphasized the past not as a model for the future, not as a limiting set of empirical conditions to be replicated as closely as possible in perpetuity, but as a *promise* or birthright.

And, finally, like its traditionalist counterpart, the progressive jeremiad calls the nation to reform and political action, to realize founding principles ever more fully and completely. As Lincoln would finally, and reluctantly at first, come to see the matter after years of war, fidelity to the founders' ultimate concerns—those founders who had placed slavery "in the course of ultimate extinction" but left it intact in their own day—would require nineteenth-century Americans to strike the death knell of slavery.[14]

The notion of birthright provides a unique perspective on some of the progressive jeremiad's basic premises. Sheldon Wolin has observed how birthrights involve both historical inheritance and the necessity of growth and development to meet new challenges. His comments are directly pertinent to the ways in which progressive jeremiads seek to breathe new life into foundational ideals:

> A birthright is defined by the historical moments when collective identity is collectively established or reconstituted....Birthrights are transmitted, and because of their meaning will have to be reconsidered amid different circumstances. We inherit from our fathers, but we are not our fathers....We cannot, for example, experience the past directly. We can, however, share in the symbols that embody the experience of the past. This calls for a citizen who can become an interpreting being, one who can interpret the present experience of the collectivity, reconnect it to past symbols, and carry it forward.[15]

The "interpreting citizen" does not merely seek to re-create past ways of doing things, but to live in a new and radically different social context in which the ideas of liberty and equality, to name just two, might take quite different forms than those envisioned by the American founders, and yet remain legitimate expressions of those ideals.

Lincoln and Douglass called Americans to action, not in pursuit of a set of specific social structures or institutions that had existed in the past, nor to re-create an American Golden Age of harmony and unity, but rather to reclaim a birthright inherent in their founding documents. Each viewed his task, although structured and bounded by the examples of the founders, as essentially about moving founding ideals forward and building a new American future. For Lincoln and Douglass, the nation's promise lay in its ability to grow out of its earlier shortcomings; although it is not a jeremiad proper, Lincoln's call for a "new birth of freedom" on the Gettysburg battlefield suggests just this sort of evolving understanding of American fundamentals. And if the nation refused to evolve in the direction of freedom, Douglass reminded his listeners that "prouder and stronger governments than this have been shattered by the bolts of a just God."

The progressive jeremiad is not limited to these two nineteenth-century thinkers. Consider, for example, Franklin Roosevelt's articulation of an "Economic Bill of Rights" in his 1944 State of the Union Address. As he looked forward to the eventual end of the second world war, Roosevelt laid out the premises of his story of American nationhood— "This Republic had its beginning, and grew to its present strength, under the protection of certain inalienable political rights"—and went on to note that "[a]s our nation has grown in size and stature...as our industrial economy expanded...these political rights proved inadequate to assure us equality in the pursuit of happiness." He continued by linking his vision for the future with the language of the Declaration of Independence and the Constitution:

> We have come to a clear realization of the fact that true individual freedom cannot exist without economic security and independence....In our day these economic truths have become accepted as self-evident. We have accepted, so to speak, a second Bill of Rights under which a new basis of security and prosperity can be established for all—regardless of station, race, or creed.

A renewed campaign for "true individual freedom," then, the continuing struggle to achieve the ideals of 1776, will involve a commitment to economic opportunity and a political campaign against those economic royalists who have always sought to deny the radical implications of the Declaration's promise. Such themes had long occupied Roosevelt's rhetoric and joined political concerns with economic ones in a ringing endorsement of foundational American principles in a time of great crisis. In his State of the Union Address, Roosevelt beckoned to themes laid out as early as his 1936 nomination acceptance speech:

> Political tyranny was wiped out at Philadelphia on July 4, 1776....Since that struggle, however, man's inventive genius released new forces in our land which reordered the lives of our people...The age of machinery, of railroads; of steam and electricity; the telegraph and the radio; mass production, mass distribution...combined to bring forward a new civilization and with it a new problem for those who sought to remain free. For out of this modern civilization economic royalists carved new dynasties....Today we stand committed to the proposition that freedom is no half-and-half affair. If the average citizen is guaranteed equal opportunity in the polling place, he must have equal opportunity in the market place...[16]

Consider, too, Martin Luther King's celebrated 1963 "I Have a Dream" speech, which justifiably casts a long shadow over any study of American political rhetoric. King knew that it was no coincidence that his own great speech was delivered at the monument dedicated to Lincoln, that "great American, in whose symbolic shadow we stand today." King told the story of America as based most fundamentally on a founding promise, a birthright of sorts: the "check" written to all Americans by the nation's founders, "a promissory note to which every American was to fall heir." By pointing out the nation's default, that this check had been returned unpaid, King identified the crisis of his own day and tied it to an American promise. King reached deep into the American tradition and into the American past—as he put it, his dream was "deeply rooted in the American dream"—not to recapture a set of past practices, but to reclaim a promise, to make good on a debt, to fulfill the radical potential of those founding principles. Like Lincoln, King embraced an expansive understanding of the symbolic, and not merely the literal, meaning of the Declaration and Constitution: the promissory note "was a promise that all men—yes, black men as well as white men—would be guaranteed the unalienable rights of life, liberty, and the pursuit of happiness, a check that declared that all men were created equal." This promise was the American birthright.

One final distinction to note here between the progressive and the traditionalist jeremiads relates to issues of democratic pluralism and diversity. The victory of Lincoln's tentative jeremiad in the Second Inaugural, or Douglass's Fourth of July speech, and the gradual struggle toward the American future envisioned by figures like Gilbert Haven and Henry Ward Beecher, spelled the doom of the entire way of life that undergirded the antebellum South, while opening up an American future without slavery. (That it did so in the interests of a more capacious understanding of constitutional principles was a fact no doubt lost on those whose positions of power were eliminated in the process.) Such an opening, had it been implemented fully, would have been nothing short of transformative, as a previously excluded—indeed, brutally enslaved—group was slowly, but steadily, incorporated into the political life of the nation. As David A. J. Richards has observed, "The mission of the Reconstruction Amendments was and should have been the inclusion, on terms of equal rights, of black Americans in the American political community now understood to be a moral community of free and equal citizens..."[17] The progressive jeremiad—in distinct contrast to the traditionalist's constraining emphasis on "what people actually did" in the past, or at the nation's founding—presents a vision of democracy equally rooted in the American past, but rooted in an inclusive understanding of American ideals.

THE JEREMIAD AS AN AMERICAN NARRATIVE:
THE POWER OF POLITICAL STORIES

One can describe these jeremiads in any number of ways—tools for political mobilization, rhetorical justifications for policy agendas, power grabs by charismatic demagogues—but underlying all these possibilities (and many others not listed here), jeremiads are *stories* about how and why the American past has led to the American present. They present characters who propel a plot forward; through such plots, and such characters, they advance a moral tale.[18] As a story, the jeremiad contains both great hope and deep sorrow, hope at the nation's promise or previous achievements, and sorrow at its current moral or spiritual state. As I have stressed, both the hope and the sorrow are integral to the jeremiad's power, as they are to the prophetic tradition on which American Jeremiahs model themselves.

From John Winthrop to Jerry Falwell, the jeremiad represents one of the most enduring and deeply rooted "sacred stories" in the American repertoire. Understanding such stories is key to understanding the ways in which any community creates its self-image, and the United States is no exception. Stephen Crites has explored the importance of "sacred stories" to the formation of communal identities, and David Gutterman has shown how a variety of Christian thinkers—Billy Sunday, Martin Luther King, Jr., and, more recently, Promise Keepers and Call to Renewal—have brought the Exodus narrative into twentieth-century American politics, using the powerful imagery of God as deliverer and Israel as the chosen people to widely divergent political ends.[19] More generally, the rise of "narrative theology"—most widely associated with the work of Stanley Hauerwas—has emphasized the fact that "every social ethic involves a narrative."[20]

These insights bear on political communities as well as religious ones. Hauerwas refers to the power of narrative to "form a people" in ways they understand as consistent with their narrative's fundamental values. New England Jeremiahs evoked "God's New Israel" as a way of grounding collective identity both in the biblical story of a blessed but often-sinning people and in the first-generation heroes who risked everything to build a godly community in the American wilderness. In the years prior to the Civil War, both Northerners and Southerners used their image of each other to define themselves and their opponents, and to describe the crisis growing all around them: the Southern image of greedy, atheistic Yankee capitalists competed with the Northern view of indolent, dissolute slave-owners who preyed on slave women and separated families in pursuit of the highest bidder. Most recently, the Christian Right narrative of post-1960s decline in traditional values brought on by a secularizing ideology (abetted by liberal elites) represents both a statement of political identity and an appeal to members and potential members to join the cause and write the next chapter in the American story, to "take America back for Christ." In this respect, all jeremiads subdivide their respective communities into those deemed faithful to the founders' examples and those apostates who have squandered national promise. In doing so, they tell us far more about the *present* situation in which their rhetoric is produced, deployed, and consumed than about the *past* that they supposedly describe and evoke.[21]

And yet, the selectivity of narrative is integral to its ability to persuade and to impart the meanings a narrator wants to impart. After all, narratives are not merely sets of statistics or logical deductions, nor year-by-year chronicles of events, but moralized tales about how and why the past has led to the present. Narrators simply *must* ignore or hide elements of that social reality that do not comport with their plots if they expect those plots to be persuasive: "Narrative succeeds to the extent that it hides the discontinuities, ellipses, and contradictory experiences that would undermine the intended meaning of its story. Whatever its purpose, it cannot avoid a covert exercise of power: it inevitably sanctions some voices while silencing others."[22]

Narratives are effective to the degree that they present unified and coherent plots. Anyone dealing with political narratives would do well to remember the words of literary scholar Wesley Kort: "When most effective, plot draws little attention to itself; it seems unforced by tone, unplotted, natural." Of course, narrators are not generally eager to highlight their own role in the making of their story; the narrative form tends to masquerade as nothing more than a straightforward empirical account, a key element of what Henry Tudor identifies as "political myth." Robert Putnam, for example, disavowed his status as narrator, and creator, of his account in *Bowling Alone*: "One way to avoid nostalgia is to count things." But this notion that plots must seem natural should move us beyond the simple realization that narrators construct their stories and into a more subtle set of questions about how they fashion their stories to maximize the likelihood of acceptance by their target audience, how they seek to harness the power of narrative toward specific political ends, and so on.[23]

Let's return to Putnam's celebrated account of the decline of American community in the second half of the twentieth century.

Putnam valorized the "long civic generation"—the generation that fought World War II and that underwrote the expansion of social capital in the postwar years (peaking around 1960)—and tracked the effect of the generational change from this civically involved generation to their significantly less involved children and grandchildren. The results, plotted in a number of striking—if creatively presented—graphs, provoked a national orgy of self-reproach and a search for ways to reconnect as a nation. But if Putnam's single chapter called "The Dark Side of Social Capital" had played a more important role in the narrative, one would see a variety of unpleasant aspects of the early 1960s that he valorizes: its intensely racial nature, its restriction of women's social roles, and so on. But highlighting such unpleasant aspects of social capital in American history would defeat the entire purpose of Putnam's narrative.

This power of narrative is partly a power of particularly effective *narrators* (Mather, Lincoln, Douglass, King, Falwell) and partly inherent in the narrative form itself. This is perhaps most true in the case of New England elites, who controlled the press in their colonies and who sought to harness the jeremiad to promote godly conduct and obedience to authority. New England election sermons were not intended as dispassionate summaries of all that had transpired in the colony. Only the relevant data made it into the story, and that data was presented in ways consistent with the larger story of decline. Frederick Douglass understood as clearly as anyone the power of defining what the Civil War had been all about, and he lamented the nation's willingness, as the nineteenth century proceeded, to portray the war as an equally heroic effort on all sides or to downplay the issues of race and citizenship at stake. Douglass knew that competing interpretations of the war threatened the progress that blacks had made and represented a bid for power by a white elite uninterested in protecting Southern blacks' civil rights.[24] (The election of 1876 would prove him right.) And Dan Quayle's speech to the Commonwealth Club did not attempt to chronicle *all* the effects of the 1960s, but rather to highlight those that led to a culture of poverty and that were directly relevant both to his audience and his purpose for speaking to them that day. All of these narratives serve political mobilization by offering interpretations of contemporary events that place such events into a meaningful relationship with the past and with a yet-to-be-realized future, appealing to like-minded Americans to join in a crusade to recapture those lost virtues.[25]

Somewhere in the distinction between these two ways of valorizing the past—between the past as model and the past as promise—lies the difference between two quite different ways of envisioning the American future. These two categories, traditionalist and progressive, are meant as heuristic aids in the analysis of political phenomena, not rigid boxes within which one should seek to file particular social movements, narratives, or narrators. As we shall see in the next chapter, traditionalist and progressive jeremiads map, at least very loosely, onto the "orthodox" and "progressive" orientations identified by James Davison Hunter in his seminal account of the culture wars in American politics.[26] And I have suggested at several points that disputes between constitutional interpretations favoring "original intent" and those more inclined toward a "living constitution" epitomize some of the same dynamics and ideological conflicts that I have traced in the traditionalist and progressive jeremiads. But *both* types of jeremiad are deeply American, drawing on notions of American identity, the American past, and imagery of the Chosen Nation as crucial to understanding the United States' singular importance in world history.

In addition, although I intend the distinctions laid out in this chapter to be part of an analytic toolkit that can help us make sense of these complex cultural, political, and literary formations, any *particular* jeremiad (and certainly any particular political movement) will likely include elements of each approach. Consider, for example, an exchange that took place during the 2008 Republican Party presidential primary campaign. In a New Hampshire debate, former Arkansas governor Mike Huckabee offered the following reflection on the Declaration of Independence and the enduring significance of its "basic principles" in the American tradition, distinguishing those principles from specific policies that may change from year to year.

> I think the simple answer for me is all the way back to the document that gave us birth. And it goes like this. That we hold these truths to be self-evident. That we are endowed by our creator, with certain inalienable rights, these being life, liberty and the pursuit of happiness. That we are created equal.... That was a radical idea when those 56 signers put their name on that document, knowing the experiment of the government didn't work they would die for it.
>
> Those are principles. The things that you live for or die for. The sense that all of us have an essence of equality. And the primary purpose of a government is to recognize those rights did not come from a government. They came from God. They're to be protected, and then defined as the right to a life, the right to liberty, our freedom. To

live our lives how we want to live them without government telling us how to do it. And ultimately, not to be happy, but to have the pursuit of happiness....

Our policies often reflect what's going on at the time....I'm not saying we change our positions, but we change the policies in terms of the priority, but those principles don't change. The principles are still to make sure that we recognize the equality of each other and that we recognize where those rights come from and what those rights are.

Of course there are any number of ways to approach Huckabee's comments here, ranging from the cynical (he is being duplicitous, consciously using progressive rhetoric to promote a traditionalist agenda) to the more nuanced (his remarks show the Declaration's enduring appeal across a wide range of perspectives in American politics). The categories of traditionalist and progressive are meant to help us sort through the long history of Americans' struggle with these questions, but we should not expect the jeremiad as it appears in real political life to always display this sort of analytic precision. Huckabee's own political vision, to be sure, hewed closely to that of the Christian Right, and he endorsed all the major issue positions favored by its traditionalist jeremiad. This distinction between principles and policies, however, just might open up a space for progressives to engage the Christian Right jeremiad around a series of related queries, and to seek ways in which their own commitments and those of traditionalists overlap. How do these broad American principles—life, liberty, the pursuit of happiness—relate to particular policy agendas like health care or foreign policy? How might we bring new and different groups of Americans into a vibrant dialogue about both the principles and the policies as we move into an uncertain American future? As a war president, Abraham Lincoln referred to "the struggles our people are making for the preservation of their precious birthright of civil and religious liberty."[27] What might an American birthright look like in the twenty-first century? In seeking to realize it, which aspects of our past should we build upon, and which are best left behind?

Finally, my goal in distinguishing between the traditionalist and the progressive jeremiad has not been to leave the impression that there is a "true" narrative waiting to be discovered, a story that is more "authentic" to the evidence of American history than that of its opponents. As we shall see in the next chapter, when we take up questions of historical memory and narrative, *both* types of jeremiads construct an American past compatible with their political outlooks, the unity of their narrative's plot, and the contours of their vision of the American future. Both employ the narrative elements of character, setting, and plot to draw a moral lesson that advances a political agenda. In a sense, we can never get beyond narrative, and *all* stories of the American past are moralized tales seeking to advance political agendas in the present. Decisions about the adequacy of various jeremiads as historical accounts ultimately reflect *political* as much as *empirical* judgments.

SIX

Constructing a Usable Past

Men always praise (but not always reasonably) the ancient times and find fault with the present; and they are such partisans of things past, that they celebrate not only that age which has been recalled to their memory by known writers, but those also (being now old) which they remember having seen in their youth....

The jeremiads offered purification not history. Still, it might have been better for them—and for us—if they had abandoned Jeremiah now and then to take their texts from Ecclesiastes: "Say not thou, 'What is the cause that the former days were better than these?' For thou dost not inquire wisely concerning this (7:10)."[1]

O N JUNE 17, 1963, one year after it had ruled unconstitutional the practice of opening public school days with recitations of the Lord's Prayer, the United States Supreme Court issued its decision in *Abington v. Schempp*, striking down (by 8–1 vote) the practice of beginning each public school day with Bible readings or a short prayer. Edward and Sidney Schempp, Unitarians whose children attended school in Abington, Pennsylvania, brought the suit, accusing the state of attempting to establish religion through these practices, in direct violation of the First Amendment. (A similar suit contesting Bible reading in the Baltimore public schools, brought by atheist Madalyn Murray, was decided in *Schempp* alongside the Pennsylvania case.) Although student participation was not mandatory, and the specific verses were selected by students or teachers and not school administrators, the Court found that the practices, and the laws enacting them, "require religious exercises and such exercises are being conducted in direct violation of the rights of the appellees and petitioners."[2]

Writing for the majority, Justice Tom Clark acknowledged that religious belief and practice loomed large in American history, from the first colonizing enterprises to the opening of the Court's own sessions, which invoked the name of God. "It can be truly said, therefore, that today, as in the beginning, our national life reflects a religious people who, in the words of Madison," Clark observed, "are 'earnestly praying, as...in duty bound, that the Supreme Lawgiver of the Universe...guide them into every measure which may be worthy of his [blessing...].'" After acknowledging the traditional importance of religion—implicitly, of Christian religion—Clark reflected on the fundamental principles on which the American constitutional system had been based. Though religion may have been embedded in American history, so was a commitment to religious liberty. Such a commitment, as Clark understood it, required that the state maintain a "wholesome 'neutrality'" regarding religion. The Court rejected the claim that the religious exercises required by the Pennsylvania school district reflected the free exercise rights of the majority in the areas represented by the school districts, and that removing such exercises effectively established a "religion of secularism."[3]

But an even more intriguing set of observations—and ones more relevant to our purposes—are found in the concurring opinion of Justice William Brennan. Brennan looked to the history of the First Amendment's drafting and the views of the founders on religion, but realized that "an awareness of history and an appreciation of the aims of the Founding Fathers do not always resolve concrete problems....A too literal quest for the advice of the Founding Fathers upon the issues of these cases seems to me futile and misdirected." The social world of the Founders was simply too different in too many key ways for us to look to their example as a concrete model for our own.

> [O]ur religious composition makes us a vastly more diverse people than were our forefathers. They knew differences chiefly among Protestant sects. Today, the Nation is far more heterogeneous religiously, including as it does substantial minorities not only of Catholics and Jews but as well of those who worship according to no version of the Bible and those who worship no God at all. In the face of such profound changes, practices which may have been objectionable to no one in the time of

Jefferson and Madison may today be highly offensive to many persons, the deeply devout and the nonbelievers alike.

Ultimately, Brennan argued, the Court must decide such cases according to its best understanding of the broad principles underlying the American constitutional system, not the specific religious views of the nation's eighteenth-century founders. "Whatever Jefferson or Madison would have thought of Bible reading or the recital of the Lord's Prayer in what few public schools existed in their day," Brennan wrote, "our use of the history of their time must limit itself to broad purposes, not specific practices."[4]

The Court's lone dissenter, Justice Potter Stewart, took issue with the very notion of the "separation of church and state" as a metaphor: "[A]s a matter of history and as a matter of the imperatives of our free society," Stewart observed, "religion and government must necessarily interact in countless ways." Taking issue with the doctrine of "incorporation" advanced in the Court's *Cantwell v. Connecticut* (1940) decision—which held that the Bill of Rights' guarantees applied to the states as well as the federal government—Stewart appealed to the historical specifics of the First Amendment's drafting and adoption. "As a matter of history, the First Amendment was adopted solely as a limitation upon the newly created National Government," he wrote. In the school prayer cases Stewart saw "a substantial free exercise claim on the part of those who affirmatively desire to have their children's school day open with the reading of passages from the Bible," and suggested that majorities ought to be free to implement such practices so long as no coercive state powers were brought to bear on dissenters.[5]

The *Schempp* case sparked nationwide controversy among religious bodies, media, and in the halls of Congress, where members introduced numerous resolutions aiming to overturn the decision. Billy Graham denounced the decision, as did many evangelical leaders; mainline Protestant and Jewish leaders tended to be more sympathetic to it. In many places (not unlike the aftermath of *Brown v. Board of Education* a decade earlier), school districts attempted to evade or simply ignore the ruling. Late in the 1960s, the *New York Times* reported on teacher-led Bible readings in public schools in Pennsylvania and across the nation, spurred in part by widespread revulsion at the social upheavals of the 1960s and ongoing opposition to *Schempp*.[6] And as we saw in chapter 4, the *Schempp* decision continues to serve as a rallying cry for leaders of the Christian Right lamenting the nation's spiritual decline. On the same television program on which Jerry Falwell made his controversial remarks about September 11, his host Pat Robertson tied the attacks even more particularly to the *Schempp* decision. "[A]t the highest level of our government, we've stuck our finger in your eye," said Robertson. "The Supreme Court has insulted you over and over again, Lord. They've taken your Bible away from the schools. They've forbidden little children to pray. They've taken the knowledge of God as best they can, and organizations have come into court to take the knowledge of God out of the public square of America."[7]

This chapter explores the competing uses to which each jeremiad puts the American past, and the ways that such uses signal some of the larger differences between traditionalist and progressive jeremiads. If the past is the model for the future, for example—as we saw in the case of the traditionalist jeremiad—then we would expect traditionalist Jeremiahs to attend carefully to the details of that model, and to lay out specific aspects of the past to follow. If, on the other hand, the past is promise and birthright, as it is for progressive Jeremiahs, historical details are less important than the ability to lay out, in a compelling narrative, the power of that promise and the link between national promise and the contemporary political crisis.

THE SEARCH FOR USABLE PASTS: FACTS, PLOTS, NARRATIVES

Each type of jeremiad engages in the search for and construction of what Van Wyck Brooks, in *America's Coming of Age*, called a "usable past." In Brooks's understanding, the past is "an inexhaustible storehouse of apt attitudes and adaptable ideals."[8] In constructing these usable pasts, each jeremiad seeks to promote its own diagnosis of present ills as well as its vision of the nation's future prospects. And in so doing, each jeremiad prompts its critics to construct "competing pasts," counternarratives consonant with their vision of the nation's fundamental crisis.

Such constructed pasts, in order to be usable, need to be created; they do not just present themselves. Thus Jeremiahs must be skillful narrators and weave the facts of the American past into compelling stories. For example, no one would dispute the *fact* of the *Schempp* decision, its central holdings, its concurring and dissenting opinions, and the like. But claims about the *meaning* and *importance* of *Schempp*— what makes it "usable" and not simply "past"—require the construction of a larger plot to provide context and explain its significance.

Both the traditionalist and the progressive jeremiad present coherent plots, ones that have appealed to millions of Americans over the years. Each is an attempt to persuade an audience (or potential audience) of the superiority of its interpretation of American history over those of its competitors. In a democratic society, furthermore, such persuasive attempts take the form of social movements and electoral campaigns—the stuff of politics—and thus these narratives serve the purposes of community and subcommunity mobilization.

Different jeremiads interpret *Schempp* in quite different ways, and those interpretations show in the way that the story of the decision is told. The Christian Right jeremiad views *Schempp* as, in Richard John Neuhaus's words, having "set asunder what had been a unified tradition." Many traditionalist Americans view *Schempp* as deeply offensive to the sentiments of people of faith and contrary to the fundamental American value of religious liberty.[9] In other words, it is not just wrong on populist grounds (as contrary to the beliefs of a majority of the American people) or on constitutional ones (as Justice Stewart opined), but it is false to American history, which has always been characterized by a Judeo-Christian consensus and an accommodating relationship between church and state. Critics of the Christian Right, of course, point out the ways in which pre-1960s America tolerated a host of infringements on the religious rights of minorities, and offer an interpretation of American history that justifies *Schempp*'s removal of religion from the public schools in the name of steadily expanding religious liberty. Such a narrative views the rise of the Christian Right itself, during the 1970s and 1980s, as a threat to the liberties that *Schempp* sought to guarantee.[10] Yet these competing narratives are not easily resolved, and are likely unresolvable, since assessing narratives is not an entirely empirical undertaking. The question "What counts as a relevant or persuasive fact?" is itself a political question.

To complicate these questions even further, the Schempp decision resides, chronologically and narratively, within a larger construct called "the 1960s," which itself plays a crucial role as a turning point in the Christian Right jeremiad, the time in which so many Christian Right thinkers believe that the nation began its spiritual decline. Of course, a different jeremiad—say, the one offered by Martin Luther King in 1963—would likely see the 1960s as the time when the nation's citizens and leaders finally (albeit reluctantly and belatedly) began to wake up and claim the full potential of their founding ideals. How does one define the 1960s? Is it Martin Luther King at the Lincoln Memorial, and well-dressed black men carrying signs that read "I am a man"? Or is it Woodstock, LSD, and the nation's cities burning in the decade's later years? Is one or the other of these definitions more "true" than the others? Or—as seems more likely—is any such definition likely to be partial in important ways, and to depend on one's cultural, religious, and political preconceptions and commitments? In other words, the way that American Jeremiahs present the 1960s depends on what they see as the salient components of "the 1960s." which will in turn influence the story they tell about *Schempp*. And so on.[11]

The same questions could apply to other events that are important to the jeremiads considered in part I of this book. In chapter 2 I briefly considered the Halfway Covenant, which granted partial church membership to the children and grandchildren of members who lacked the experience of personal conversion but who nonetheless lived upstanding lives. Was the Halfway Covenant, as Increase Mather thought (at least initially), further evidence of the decline of piety in that once godly community? Or was it rather (as Solomon Stoddard maintained) a creative and faithful way of adapting the fundamentals of New England life to a dynamic and evolving social reality? Either of these positions could be defended, and in fact Mather himself reversed his earlier opposition and came to endorse the Halfway Covenant later in his life.[12] We could do the same for the Civil War—crucible of American liberty and nationality, or Northern capitalist aggression? Or Prohibition—democratic expression of American evangelical fervor or narrow-minded moralistic imposition? Or *Roe v. Wade*—key step in the march toward gender equality, or mass murder of the unborn? The "plain facts of American history" often turn out, upon closer examination, to be deeply contested.

NOSTALGIA AND THE GOLDEN AGE

Much of the jeremiad's rhetorical power has always resided in the historical nature of its critique, its dramatic contrast between a virtuous past and a degenerate present. By valorizing the 1950s, the Christian Right not only looked to a time of national virtue prior to the upheavals of the 1960s; it also evoked the childhoods of its target audience.

The term "nostalgia" emerged out of early modern European medicine, and referred to extreme forms of homesickness observed among seventeenth-century army recruits (even to the point of wasting away to death). By the twentieth century, however, "nostalgia" had come to describe not a medical condition but an affective state character-ized by positive, yet bittersweet, associations with some aspect of the "personally experienced past," a past that is favorably contrasted with the degenerate present. But nostalgia doesn't only affect malcontents and Luddites, or the disaffected elderly yearning for the world of their youth. Scholars of both individual psychology and social history view nostalgia as "a universal experience, present and prevalent across the lifespan" that "now attracts or afflicts most levels of society." It is at once both deeply personal—recalling to mind the world of child-hood—and political, capable of serving as a rallying cry, especially to individuals of the same generation or backgrounds.[13]

Nostalgia serves important psychological functions, including building a sense of personal identity, defending against existential crises that arise in times of rapid social change, and bolstering social bonds among groups and generations. At the same time, as a func-tion of human memory, nostalgia is susceptible to all sorts of distor-tions and biases. Nostalgic accounts of the "way things used to be" do *not* give us a privileged vision of how things actually were, but, in the words of Arthur Dudden, represent "a preference for things as they once were, or, more importantly, *a preference for things as they are believed to have been.*"[14]

Why is nostalgia so psychologically powerful and politically effec-tive? We should never underestimate the power of the particular com-bination of regret and longing that nostalgia offers, especially as this psychological effect is not randomly associated with the historical past, but returns individuals to times and places of real significance in their lives. "Nostalgic narratives…typically feature the self as central character, and revolve around interactions with important others…or momentous events." Indeed, Jason Leboe and Tamara Ansons argue that "the most potent nostalgic experiences occur in response to recol-lections that possess a vivid, story-like quality," where the act of remem-bering transports people to some prior circumstance and gives them the *subjective* impression that they are reliving the past.[15] Jerry Falwell, for example, recalled his days at Mountain View Elementary School, which included weekly chapel, Bible reading, singing, and prayer. But this was before the Supreme Court got involved. "[O]ur public schools no longer teach Christian ethics.…the decay in our public school sys-tem suffered an enormous acceleration when prayer and Bible reading were taken out of the classroom by our United States Supreme Court," he wrote. When fighting to retain his judicial office before the Alabama Court of the Judiciary, Judge Roy Moore justified his refusal to remove a statue of the Ten Commandments from his courtroom by drawing on his childhood, in which such symbols were prominent in public life.[16]

Nostalgia is a powerful coping mechanism, helping to maintain identity during times of social upheaval. And this coping mechanism seems to operate on a collective level as well, as nostalgia serves to strengthen bonds within subcommunities who perceive themselves as under threat. Here we see most clearly the *political* aspect of nostalgia. Defenders of traditional values, certainly, find an idealization of the past enormously appealing *politically* at a time when they perceive long-accepted standards of personal and public behavior to be under assault. Writing in the immediate wake of the 1960s, Fred Davis argued that "[t]he nostalgia wave of the 1970s is intimately related…to the massive identity dislocations of the 1960s."[17] By fashioning a narrative of imperiled national promise, Christian Right leaders brought a powerful (previously latent) political force into existence, one that highlighted the traditionally friendly relationship between American government and Christian piety, providing potent political arguments for such issues as public school prayer, tuition tax credits, traditional family structures, and the display of religious symbols on public property.

Scholars dealing with nostalgia often note its double distortions: an overly positive view of the reconstructed past on the one hand, and an overstatement of negative aspects of the present on the other. Certainly one can make such an argument about the anti-1960s jeremiad. For example, the 1960s saw the culmination of an American mass movement to undo a system of legalized apartheid that had been in place for nearly 100 years, as well as movements for women's equality and the beginnings of modern environmentalism. Attending too extensively to *these* elements of the American story, however, would weaken the very coherence and power of the narrative's plot, complicating the sense of inexorable downward movement so crucial to mobilizing a political movement for reform. Traditionalist Jeremiahs do generally acknowledge such progress, but quickly set it aside.[18] It is no accident, for example, that the much-heralded efforts by the Christian Right to expand its alliances with African-Americans have come largely to naught. African-Americans may hold conservative views on gay marriage, for example, but they have little nostalgia for a pre–civil rights era America. The same might be said for Christian Right outreach to nonwhite Christian immigrants who, despite sympathies with culturally conservative policies, seem unlikely to fall into alliance with a movement widely perceived as unconcerned with the discrimination faced by members of minority cultures.[19]

So in one way, the Christian Right's emphasis on the 1960s as a fundamental rupture in American history is an attempt to construct an ideal past and connect it with the experience of its audience's members. But it's not just the 1950s on which they look back longingly. They believe the 1960s destroyed traditions that had existed, virtually unchanged, since the founding. Ralph Reed describes his "religious conservative vision for America" in these terms, in a quotation I introduced in chapter 4 but which is worth revisiting in this context:

> America would look much as it did for most of the first two centuries of its existence, before the social dislocation caused by Vietnam, the sexual revolution, Watergate, and the explosion of the welfare state. Our nation would once again be ascendant, self-confident, proud, and morally strong. Government would be strong, the citizenry virtuous, and mediating institutions such as churches and voluntary organizations would carry out many of the functions currently relegated to the bureaucracy.[20]

Reed's vision, while deeply traditionalist in its view of the past and its hope for the future, runs together two very distinct ideals. The specific reference to "Vietnam, the sexual revolution, Watergate, and the explosion of the welfare state" suggests a nostalgic pre-1960s ideal worthwhile in its own right, while his invocation of "America...look[ing] much as it did for most of the first two centuries of its existence" suggests that the mid-twentieth-century ideal serves as a bridge to the nation's founding period, far beyond the personal experience of anyone in the audience. This distinction—between a yearning for the world of childhood and the praise of a distant founding period—is the difference between a rhetoric of nostalgia and a rhetoric of the golden age.

Talk of a "golden age," of course, has a long pedigree in the history of social and political thought, both Western and non-Western. The Greek poet Hesiod—who, if he did not coin the phrase, certainly is responsible for the widespread association of gold with an idealized past[21]—had the good sense (or perhaps the strategic foresight) to place his own version of the golden age *outside* human history, safe from the prying eyes of skeptical historians. Roman poets such as Juvenal generally located their golden ages in the realm of myth. But the traditionalist American jeremiad has always been bolder: not content to look *outside* history for an ideal toward which to strive, Jeremiahs have offered the nation's founding and early national period as a golden age worthy of emulation. Like nostalgic accounts, golden age narratives yearn for qualities thought to have been lost in the transition from past to present. By presenting an idealized portrait of a community's founding, golden age critics simultaneously make claims about the community's essential qualities and illuminate political fault lines in the present. Thus, like nostalgic narratives, the golden age is a story used by some members of a community against others, and serves as the basis for political movements dedicated to recapturing lost virtues.

In narrating such foundational moments in the life of a community, theorists of the golden age evoke concrete qualities of a bygone age—faith, political courage, selflessness, community spirit—as a distinct antidote to the many failings of the present. The qualities purported to have been present in the golden age vary from theorist to theorist, of course, yet they are always precisely those that the critic laments as having vanished in the present. David Lowenthal calls the golden age "an imagined landscape invested with all [critics] find missing in the modern world."[22] Unlike nostalgia, however, the landscape to which the narrator appeals is not personal or generational, but an even purer and in part mythic past.

Once again, the Christian Right jeremiad is instructive. Such accounts see the founding period as a national golden age, where individuals subordinated their particular interests to the common good, a Judeo-Christian consensus structured public life, and men of great character embarked upon the American experiment in self-government without attempting to separate religion from politics. The golden age, on this traditionalist telling, possesses precisely the qualities that contemporary society lacks: sexual restraint, public religiosity, a commitment to the common good, and deference to traditional sources of authority.[23] In fact, for the Christian Right—not coincidentally—religion and its public role play a central part in what makes the golden age golden. Although the new nation disestablished churches as a matter of national policy under the First Amendment, a general culture of Protestant religiosity, and a publicly influential role for churches and church leaders, characterized the nation's public life during these years.[24]

Nostalgia and the golden age offer two important and different ways of valorizing the past. And yet, although they usually do so, nostalgic and golden age politics need not represent radically separate time periods. Early New England is an interesting example. Looking back to the piety and godliness of the founding generation—which was, after all, their parents' generation—second-generation New England Jeremiahs saw a communal golden age and longed for a reinvigoration of that spirit. In New England, the founders themselves were often the objects of nostalgic reverence, and as a second-generation phenomenon, the New England jeremiad did not need to manufacture its golden age out of whole cloth or to evoke mythic figures from the mists of time, but could point to actual historical figures known, at least indirectly, to most members of their audience. By invoking first-generation colonists and their leaders as heroic figures, New England Jeremiahs linked their audiences to the founding itself, a historical ideal that in turn evoked their parents and the world of their childhood. Indeed, many of their sermons concluded with appeals to the "ancient members" of the community, who were not so ancient. They were, in fact, often still alive.

But regardless of whether the historical ideal is said to have existed at the nation's birth or just several decades ago, traditionalist American Jeremiahs always present such ideals as possessing a few key qualities—unity, community, self-sacrifice, commitment to the common good, religious faith, deference to traditional authority—in sharp contrast to current society, with its division, fragmentation, individualism, and unbelief.

A Competing Political Past: Challenging the Traditionalist Jeremiad

Insofar as traditionalist jeremiads make historical claims—it was like this in the past, it ought to be like this in the future—they lay themselves open to objections from historically minded skeptics. Indeed, recent scholarship in American religious and cultural history—much of it, to be sure, spurred by political objections to the Christian Right's view of a lost Judeo-Christian consensus—has complicated the rather homogenous view of the American past advanced by traditionalists. But the more important lesson here is that *each* type of jeremiad shapes a past conducive to its own diagnosis of what is wrong in the present and to its vision of the American future, thus leaving itself open to critics only too eager to present competing counternarratives. We have a name for this process of sifting, assessing, and passing judgment on these narratives and counternarratives; we call it politics.

We have seen that, to be effective, narratives require compelling characters and coherent plots. First-generation New England could only be made into a land of pristine piety, in which godly magistrates administered a harmonious community, through an act of rhetorical construction by narrators with a particular ideological aim in mind: to present this idealized portrait to a younger generation that seemed increasingly uninterested in (if not hostile to) the biblical aims of those founders. In other words, from the universe of potential characters and plots that clergy might choose, the jeremiad required narrators to minimize instances of dissent and discord in the colony's early years. The ejection of Roger Williams and the banishment of Anne Hutchinson; the deep divisions between Thomas Shepard, John Cotton, and John Wilson during the 1630s; the controversial tenure of Governor Henry Vane in 1636; tension within the ruling elite between, for example, Winthrop and Thomas Dudley; economic acquisitiveness among the first generation; the surprisingly large numbers of prosecutions for sodomy, bestiality, and other sexual transgressions; the inroads of Quakers and Baptists during the second and third decades—few, if any, of these episodes found any place in the jeremiads of second-generation New England.[25]

The aforementioned events are not merely discrete pieces of counterevidence to claims of primitive unity. They are, more powerfully, elements of potential *counternarratives* of early New England history. The most obvious examples here are the expulsions of Williams and Hutchinson from Massachusetts Bay—Williams, for his vocal dissent from religious and political orthodoxy; Hutchinson, for her role in divisive religious conflicts that convulsed the churches—between 1636 and 1638. Hutchinson's expulsion, for example, might be seen as the triumph of orthodoxy over dissent, but it might also represent "the opening salvo in a series of debates concerning communal definition, theological boundaries, and socioeconomic goals that remained hotly contested down to the end of the century and beyond." Disputes over not only theology but also the division of land, interactions with the natives, and a variety of other contentious issues dropped out of the New England past as presented by the second-generation jeremiad, as clergy like Increase Mather "refashion[ed] the early years of the colony's settlement... erasing the doubt, confusion, and greed that Winthrop recorded, and sketching in their place a picture of the founders as men driven by a humble and holy urge to worship God in the way they thought best."[26]

By minimizing dissent and disharmony in the first generation, New England Jeremiahs also magnified the discord and disunity of the present. The frequent use of terms like "worldliness" and "luxury" shows how the economic dimension of New England life drew the ire of second-generation Jeremiahs. (A society as diligent about its worldly duties as New England was bound to become prosperous, almost in spite of itself.) And given their providential understanding of God as the ultimate cause behind all things, Puritan elites, in the words of Perry Miller, "could not regard the deleterious consequence of opulence merely as an effect of a environment upon an organism, but were compelled to see it rather as a symptom of innate depravity."[27] As Miller put it elsewhere, "France and Spain are unlucky, or they miscalculate, or smallpox ravages them, and that is that. But a nation in covenant is systematically punished, the degree of affliction being exquisitely proportioned to the amount of depravity."[28]

Counternarratives appear in contemporary contexts as well. The Christian Right jeremiad has long called attention to the importance of the "traditional family" or "family values." The traditional family serves as a point of departure for a host of other gender- and sexuality-related issues—the entry of women into the workforce (reentry, since many were forced *out* of the workforce after World War II); the rise of feminism and the movement to pass an Equal Rights Amendment; the growing movement for gay and lesbian rights—all of which are traced to the 1960s or the 1970s.[29] Yet Stephanie Coontz has argued that the traditional family turns out, on closer examination, to be "an ahistorical amalgam of structures, values, and behaviors that never coexisted in the same time and place." Coontz offers a history of the American family in which the traditional family of the 1950s was *itself* a novel phenomenon, arising in the immediate postwar years and dependent on economic prosperity and an ethic of domestic consumption, as well as the willingness of (or successful cultural pressure on) women to return to the home from their positions in the workforce during the 1940s. Not only was the ideal far more scarce than the public pronouncements of Christian Right leaders would lead us to believe, but those families that did approximate the ideal depended on the labor of women, and often children, of lower socioeconomic status. Coontz does not simply present data to refute the Christian Right's valorization of the traditional family, but proposes a counternarrative, arguing that in certain key ways today's families are in fact *more* connected than those that existed in days gone by.[30]

PROGRESSIVE JEREMIADS: CONSTRUCTING AN AMERICAN PAST FULL OF PROMISE

The progressive jeremiad looks to the past as well, but it looks in a quite different way, seeking to restate founding principles in language appropriate to changing times. Thus the progressive jeremiad is not concerned so much with making claims about the way "things really were" in the past, and even less in casting the future into that mold.

But the progressive jeremiad's past, containing such a powerful founding promise, is equally constructed, and equally mythic. In its telling, liberty and equality become the birthright of every American, despite the limitations of previous ages in the realization of those ideals. And birthrights require narratives, since they forge connections and obligations between generations.[31] We considered Franklin Roosevelt's "Economic Bill of Rights" in chapter 5, and Martin Luther King's dream at several points in this book. Each of these American Jeremiahs saw the solution to the crisis of his own time as the creative reappropriation of founding principles, envisioning an American future both deeply faithful to the nation's founding spirit and flexible enough to adapt to new challenges for new times.

In fact, for the progressive jeremiad, the new nation *must* look different from the old if it is to be faithful to the principles that underlie American democracy. As we saw in chapter 5, Lincoln certainly knew that the nation over which he was presiding, and the nation that he foresaw emerging after the Civil War, would *have to* look radically different from the one that the founders "brought forth" four score and seven years ago if it were to redeem the birthright of liberty that he read as applying to all Americans. And yet it must also be deeply faithful to the basic ideals that those founders held dear.

Like its traditionalist counterpart, the progressive jeremiad constructs a national past, and is itself a selective and partial narrative, depending for its political success on a set of claims about the potential of fundamental American ideas to continually expand and incorporate new groups. Martin Luther King refused to believe that the bank of American justice was empty, but others have not been so charitable. Intentionally or not, the progressive jeremiad avoids some of these thorny empirical questions that we saw in the previous section by leaning on imagery of national promise and birthright, claims that are less easily refuted because they are not, ultimately, empirical questions at all. But the progressive jeremiad has a historical element as well, and that historical account, not surprisingly, has attracted its own critics.

A Competing Political Past: Challenging the Progressive Jeremiad

The claim that the meaning of the American founding, for example, is not exhausted by the concrete conditions of 1776—as we saw in Lincoln's objections to Stephen Douglas, in Franklin Roosevelt's invocation of economic rights, and in King's confidence in bringing the "check" back to Washington—represents an extraordinary confidence in the emancipatory potential of American ideals, and requires tremendous optimism about the willingness of Americans to support the expansion of such concepts as liberty and equality. Certainly there have been many in American history who did not share this understanding of American ideals. William Lloyd Garrison, Stephen Douglas, the leaders of the Black Power movement who denounced King, and other American skeptics were not somehow less "American" than King, or Frederick Douglass, or Lincoln. They denied the progressive jeremiad's hopeful narrative of American founding promise, either by denying that there *was* any promise beyond what they could see around them or by asking why, if these concepts had such radical potential, it had not been realized sooner.

The examples of King and Lincoln, in fact, suggest that such promise may not really be "in" those founding ideals at all, that at the same time one is telling the American story, one is simultaneously involved in creating national meaning. And for political success to be a realistic possibility, one needs more than simply a compelling narrative or faith in American founding promise. For such a view to get a widespread hearing, one also needs a powerful political interest to align with a particular expansionist reading of the American founding.[32] We might go even further and note that what one really needs is an army. Lincoln's vision for a transformed Union would have been stillborn without Grant's Virginia campaigns of 1864 and 1865 and Sherman's March to the Sea to back it up. Franklin Roosevelt pointedly linked the successful prosecution of the war to his promotion of the Economic Bill of Rights.

Of course, Martin Luther King's place in the American pantheon is due in large part to his heading of a mass movement that eschewed violence. Yet in the "I Have a Dream" speech King skillfully invoked the threat of social unrest—

> This is no time to engage in the luxury of cooling off or to take the tranquilizing drug of gradualism....It would be fatal for the nation to overlook the urgency of the moment. This sweltering summer of the Negro's legitimate discontent will not pass until there is an invigorating autumn of freedom and equality....Those who hope that the Negro needed to blow off steam and will now be content will have a rude awakening if the nation returns to business as usual. There will be neither rest nor tranquility in America until the Negro is granted his citizenship rights. The whirlwinds of revolt will continue to shake the foundations of our nation until the bright day of justice emerges.

—only to quickly disavow it:

> Let us not seek to satisfy our thirst for freedom by drinking from the
> cup of bitterness and hatred. We must forever conduct our struggle
> on the high plane of dignity and discipline. We must not allow our
> creative protest to degenerate into physical violence. Again and again
> we must rise to the majestic heights of meeting physical force with soul
> force.

So to realize the promise of the American past as the progressive
jeremiad sees it depends on a rare confluence of circumstances, including a sympathetic populace (or at least one willing to be awakened to
sympathy), a political and legal environment amenable to the expansion of rights (coerced, if necessary), and a compelling narrative (and
narrator) who can articulate the connection between the controversial
proposed *extension* of American ideals and the relatively uncontroversial
text of the Declaration or Constitution. Might there be some inherent
limits to the project of imagining ever more "perfect" incarnations of
the American union? Twenty years ago, Roderick Nash made an argument for animal rights as the latest frontier in the ongoing march of
liberty and dignity that began in July 1776.[33] Is the species jump that
Nash is calling on Americans to make different in kind, or merely in
degree, from the leaps of sympathy that were required to end slavery in
the 1860s, or legalized segregation in the 1960s? Or will Americans be
looking back 100 years from now, wondering how anyone could have
failed to see that the Declaration of Independence required Americans
to press beyond species borders and extend rights to animals? And if
the latter is the case, will it be due to something inherent in the ideals
themselves, or to a fortuitous confluence of political circumstances?

We might also ask just how capacious the progressive jeremiad can
be, just how expansive its birthright, so long as it remains wedded to
an image of the United States as God's chosen nation, or to some form
of American exceptionalism that relegates other nations to a secondary or inferior status. This is a very important question, and at the
same time a very difficult one to answer. For one example of how such
"pressing of the outer bounds" might look, we might consider Martin
Luther King Jr.'s late speech "Beyond Vietnam," a blistering critique
in which he admits that "[t]he world now demands a maturity from
America that we may not be able to achieve."[34] King here calls his
nation to move beyond such metaphors as "Chosen Nation" and "last,
best hope of Earth" and into a more subtle relationship with the rest
of the world. His later career provides an intriguing example of the

convergence between the political rights championed by Douglass and Lincoln, and Roosevelt's notion of economic rights mentioned above (especially in his final efforts, such as the Poor People's Campaign). It is no accident that as King's disenchantment with America's role in the world increased—from the soaring rhetoric of "I Have a Dream" to the profound disillusionment of "Beyond Vietnam"—he became an increasingly unpopular, controversial, and polarizing figure.

CONSTRUCTING A USABLE PAST

While both traditionalist and progressive jeremiads construct a past in order to inspire their contemporaries, the contest between these two ways of understanding the American past is not a historical one, but a *political* one.

It seems unrealistic—and probably not desirable—to expect to purge political thinking of such a universal aspect of human experience as nostalgia. Nor would anyone, I suspect, anticipate a diminution in Americans' reverence for their founders or founding principles. And if the reinvigoration of the study of narrative across the humanities has taught us anything, it is that the need to make coherent sense of our lives, both individually and collectively, is a deeply rooted one. As democratic citizens, though, we can and should approach each type of jeremiad with a clear understanding of the partiality of narrative and an acknowledgment that any "American past" is a construction, a partial set of insights created in the service of *someone's* political agenda.

As we have seen in this chapter, constructing a usable past can be a contentious undertaking. Seeing the jeremiad as a political narrative leads to a deeper appreciation of the ways in which, to quote political theorist Joshua Dienstag, "the project of political theory is often not so much to reform our morals as it is to reform our memories."[35] The politics of memory and the politics of history are each deeply important to the politics of the jeremiad. In the next chapter, we will examine a particular contest in which traditionalist jeremiads do battle against progressive jeremiads: the American "culture wars."

SEVEN

The Jeremiad and the
Culture Wars

My friends, this election is about much more than who gets what. It is about who we are. It is about what we believe. It is about what we stand for as Americans. There is a religious war going on in our country for the soul of America. It is a cultural war, as critical to the kind of nation we will one day be as was the Cold War itself…

For a variety of reasons…I have chosen to jump into the fray and become a warrior in the vicious culture war that is currently under way in the United States of America. And war is exactly the right term. On one side of the battlefield are the armies of the traditionalists like me, people who believe the United States was well founded and has done enormous good for the world. On the other side are the committed forces of the secular-progressive movement that want to change America dramatically: mold it in the image of Western Europe.

In one way or another, this is the oldest story in America: the struggle to determine whether "we, the people" is a spiritual idea embedded in a political reality—one nation, indivisible—or merely a charade masquerading as piety and manipulated by the powerful and privileged to sustain their own way of life at the expense of others. The failure of Democratic politicians and public thinkers to respond to popular discontents…allowed a resurgent conservatism to convert public concern and hostility into a crusade to resurrect social Darwinism as a moral philosophy, multinational corporations as a governing class, and the theology of markets as a transcendental belief system.…Their stated and open aim is to change how America is governed—to strip from government all its functions except those that reward their rich and privileged benefactors. They are quite candid about it, even acknowledging their mean spirit in accomplishing it.…It is the most radical assault on the notion of one nation, indivisible, that has occurred in our lifetime.[1]

TWO CULTURE WARRIORS

Pat Buchanan, Culture Warrior

On August 17, 1992, Pat Buchanan rose to deliver the opening night address to the Republican National Convention in Houston, Texas. Buchanan had run a surprisingly strong second to President George H. W. Bush in the New Hampshire primary earlier that year, garnering 40 percent of the vote there and more than 3 million Republican primary votes across the country. Throughout the spring of that year, Buchanan had persisted in his campaign to return the Republican Party to its conservative roots. In a sense, Buchanan's speech represented the swan song of this failed presidential candidacy, one final chance to rally his troops (the "Buchanan Brigades," he called them) before falling into line and supporting the incumbent.

And fall in line he did, with perhaps a bit more relish than Republican Party officials might have wished. In his speech to the convention, Buchanan drew a stark contrast between a mainstream, traditional, religious America, represented by George Bush, Buchanan himself, and the Republican Party, and a relativist, secular, unbelieving minority that had insinuated itself at the highest levels of American society, which he tied to Bill and Hillary Clinton and the Democratic Party. Buchanan insisted that the cultural war was at root "a religious war...as critical to the kind of nation we will one day be as was the Cold War itself."[2]

Buchanan linked the Clinton agenda to the 1960s, the decade where it all went wrong: "The American people are not going to buy back into the failed liberalism of the 1960s and '70s, no matter how slick the package in 1992." Buchanan proceeded to roll out a host of other issues of concern to the Christian Right—anticommunism, abortion, gay rights, feminism, threats to Judeo-Christian values, strict constructionist jurisprudence, law and order—each time linking the traditionalist position with the Republican Party and George H. W. Bush. At the end of this list of virtues, Buchanan offered his famous assessment of the contemporary American scene, the one for which his speech would be remembered, referring to a "religious war" for the soul of the country in which "Clinton and Clinton are on the other side, and George Bush is on our side." Buchanan distinguished Bush's Republican conservatism from "[t]he agenda Clinton and Clinton would impose on America—abortion on demand, a litmus test for the Supreme Court, homosexual rights, discrimination against religious schools, women in combat—that's change, all right," he continued. "But...it is not the kind of change we can tolerate in a nation that we still call God's country."

Buchanan's convention speech was denounced by many—and cheered by many others—for its plainspoken and pugnacious proclamation of a "cultural war" in the United States, and his stinging personal attacks on Bill and Hillary Clinton as exemplars of all that was wrong with America. Many analysts saw Buchanan's prime-time address, with its strident moralism and thinly veiled race-baiting, as contributing to Bush's later loss to Clinton in the general election. (The morning after his speech, moderate Republicans were tripping over themselves, and each other, in an effort to distance themselves from Buchanan.) At the same time, it was far from a swan song. Buchanan's speech was actually the opening salvo of what would become a decadelong struggle against everything that Bill Clinton (and his wife) represented: politically, culturally, and socially, not to mention economically.

The 1990s would witness a resurgent conservatism in American culture, even while Bill Clinton presided over the executive branch for eight years. It was the decade of conservative talk radio, epitomized by the enormous popularity of Rush Limbaugh; the decade of the "Republican Revolution," which returned the House of Representatives to Republican control for the first time in four decades and sent a political neophyte named George W. Bush to the Texas governor's mansion; and the decade of the Kenneth Starr inquiry and the impeachment of Bill Clinton, driven by moralized outrage over a president's infidelity, salacious behavior in the Oval Office, and perjury. Buchanan himself was sidelined, but never silenced: he would run for president two more times, including a run in the general election as Reform Party candidate in 2000. The winner of that election, George W. Bush, repudiated Buchanan's culture war rhetoric (and the larger system of thought of which it formed a part, often called "paleoconservatism") with his claim to "compassionate conservatism," while at the same time endorsing a Republican platform crafted by a committee heavily influenced by Christian Right activists.

But the culture war language would prove durable into the twenty-first century, and a decade after Buchanan delivered his speech Fox News commentator Bill O'Reilly would publish his own book, *Culture Warrior*, with its contrast between "armies of traditionalists like me" and "committed forces of the secular-progressive movement."[3]

Bill Moyers, Culture Warrior

On June 4, 2003, public broadcaster—and Lyndon Johnson's former press secretary—Bill Moyers addressed the Take Back America Conference, sponsored by the Campaign for America's Future, a left-leaning political organization. Media accounts claimed that Moyers's speech, in accepting the Campaign's Lifetime Leadership Award, fired up the conference delegates far more than those of the Democratic presidential hopefuls at the same meeting. Moyers decried "the most radical assault on the notion of one nation, indivisible, that has occurred in our lifetime" in the politics and policies of the George W. Bush administration, and rooted his criticisms in the ideals of the American founding. "Look at our history," Moyers urged his audience. "For the Great Seal of the United States the new Congress went all the way back to the Roman poet Virgil: 'Novus Ordo Seclorum'—'a new age now begins.'...Through compromise and conciliation the draftsmen achieved a Constitution of checks and balances that is now the oldest in the world."[4]

But even the greatest of ideals can be hijacked. Despite such promising beginnings, Moyers went on, "hardly a century had passed since 1776 before the still-young revolution was being strangled in the hard grip of a merciless ruling class....Conservatives—or better, pro-corporate apologists—hijacked the vocabulary of Jeffersonian liberalism and turned words like 'progress,' 'opportunity,' and 'individualism' into tools for making the plunder of America sound like divine right." Moyers admitted no illusions about earlier times: "For all the rhetoric about 'life, liberty, and the pursuit of happiness,' it took a civil war to free the slaves and another hundred years to invest their freedom with meaning. Women only gained the right to vote in my mother's time." But the *ideals* of the founding, in Moyers's telling of the national story, were instrumental to the American struggle for liberty.

For a historical example of a successful movement to realize American ideals, Moyers looked to the Populist and Progressive movements, heirs to American revolutionary ideals, and assured the audience that "[w]hile the social dislocations and meanness that galvanized progressives in the nineteenth century are resurgent so is the vision of justice, fairness, and equality." Although the Campaign for America's Future was primarily concerned with issues of economic fairness, Moyers made abundantly clear that economic issues were *moral* issues, grounded in the most fundamental questions about human personhood and the meaning of American citizenship:

[A] Social Security card is not a private portfolio statement but a membership ticket in a society where we all contribute to a common treasury so that none need face the indignities of poverty in old age without that help.... [T]ax evasion is not a form of conserving investment capital but a brazen abandonment of responsibility to the country.... [I]ncome inequality is not a sign of freedom-of-opportunity at work, because if it persists and grows, then unless you believe that some people are naturally born to ride and some to wear saddles, it's a sign that opportunity is less than equal.... [S]elf-interest is a great motivator for production and progress, but is amoral unless contained within the framework of community...

But to fully appreciate Moyers's role in the culture wars, and his use of the jeremiad, we must read this speech alongside a keynote address he delivered just about a year later to Jim Wallis's Call to Renewal, a progressive Christian social justice coalition.[5] Although the themes of his earlier speech remained consistent—corporate greed, economic inequality, the need for a new egalitarianism—Moyers made the moral and religious basis of his political vision more explicit to the religious audience. "We are heading into a new religious landscape," he observed, one that would require religious sensitivity and an embrace of the fundamental premise of American religious politics articulated by the founders: the separation of church and state. Moyers both affirmed the essential rightness of the cause and admitted that obstacles often stood in the way of its fulfillment:

It was a noble sentiment often breached in practice. The red man who lived here first had more than his pockets picked; the Africans brought here forcibly against their will had more than their bones broken. Even when most Americans claimed a Protestant heritage and practically everyone looked alike we often failed the tolerance test; Catholics, Jews, and Mormons had to struggle to resist being absorbed without distinction into the giant mix-master of American assimilation.

Noting that religion could foster both healing and violence, Moyers contrasted "the soul of democracy" (which, he assumed, he and his audience represented) with "a triumphalist theology in the service of an imperial state" (represented by the George W. Bush administration). This was no minor disagreement: "At stake is America's role in the world. At stake is the very character of the American experience—whether 'We, the people' is the political incarnation of a spiritual truth—one nation, indivisible—or a stupendous fraud."

These two options—political incarnation of spiritual truth, or stupendous fraud—framed Moyers's vision of the polarizing dichotomy that we saw in Buchanan's speech. He identified "two Americas today," and offered a narrative that showed how the nation's founding ideals had been hijacked. The passage is worth quoting at length:

> What has been happening to the middle and working classes is not the result of Adam Smith's invisible hand but the direct consequence of corporate activism, intellectual collusion, the rise of a religious orthodoxy that has made an idol of wealth and power, and a host of political decisions favoring the powerful monied interests who were determined to get back the privileges they had lost with the Depression and the New Deal. They set out to trash the social contract; to cut workforces and their wages; to scour the globe in search of cheap labor; and to shred the social safety net that was supposed to protect people from hardships beyond their control. *Business Week* put it bluntly: "Some people will obviously have to do with less....It will be a bitter pill for many Americans to swallow the idea of doing with less so that big business can have more." To create the intellectual framework for this revolution in public policy, they funded conservative think tanks—the Heritage Foundation, the Hoover Institution, and the American Enterprise Institute—that churned out study after study advocating their agenda. To put political muscle behind these ideas, they created a formidable political machine....Big business political action committees flooded the political arena with a deluge of dollars. And they built alliances with the religious right—Jerry Falwell's Moral Majority and Pat Robertson's Christian Coalition—who happily contrived a cultural war as a smokescreen to hide the economic plunder of the very people who were enlisted as foot soldiers in the war. And they won.

This "stupendous fraud" was not simply the result of mistakes or erroneous judgments, in Moyers's telling, but of a conscious effort at deception. These fraud peddlers, Moyers told his audience, don't really believe their culture wars rhetoric, which is in fact just "a smokescreen" for economic interests, the fruit of intellectual collusion. Moyers concluded his speech with a rousing call to political action, exhorting his audience to "get Jesus back" in the service of progressive ideals.

"CULTURE WARS" IN AMERICAN POLITICS: THE JEREMIAD DURING THE CLINTON YEARS

Both Buchanan and Moyers—in their remarks and in their public careers more generally—drew on the language of the American jeremiad that we have seen laid out in the pages of this book. In each case, the ills of the present were contrasted with a virtuous past, which was closely tied to a vision of the future and a political agenda to achieve that future. Buchanan spoke of a "cultural war," while Moyers referred to a "radical assault" on the idea of the American nation. Each of them spoke against the backdrop of the politics of the Clinton years (and, in Moyers's case, the contested election of George W. Bush in 2000), in which talk of "culture wars" filled the airwaves.

James Davison Hunter's influential 1991 book *Culture Wars: The Struggle to Define America* first laid out the general terms and parameters of the concept; Hunter used the term to refer to a series of linked disputes in American society, disputes that involve government but are at their root about fundamentally conflicting moral worldviews. Cultural conflict—"political and social hostility rooted in different systems of moral understanding"—was of course not new in the United States: what *was* different in the waning years of the twentieth century, according to Hunter, was the way in which such conflict had exploded *within* the dominant "biblical culture" and across previous lines of conflict. Hunter sketched out an American cultural-political landscape populated by two "competing moral visions." On the one hand, Americans holding "orthodox" views tend to see truth and morality in *fixed* terms, and occupy tightly bounded communities that locate the sources of moral authority in an unchanging transhistorical or transcendent essence. Such a position views moral obligations as fairly concrete, personalized, and inflexible, unaffected by the passage of time or by scientific or technological progress. On the other side of the cultural battleground Hunter located "progressives," who understand moral obligation and commitment as requiring a sensitivity to historical or situational contexts, and who view ethical obligations as unfolding and evolutionary in nature. In Hunter's words, the impulse toward orthodoxy involves a "commitment...to an external, definable, and transcendent authority," while the progressive point of view represents a "tendency to resymbolize historic faiths according to the prevailing assumptions of contemporary life."[6]

What does such a theory about morality have to do with politics? Each side of the culture wars seeks to tie its own moral vision to the fundamentals of American national identity, and to enlist the government to take its own side in political disputes that raise cultural and moral issues. The orthodox camp's insistence on the fixed nature of moral truth is apparent in such issue positions as opposition to abortion and same-sex marriage and support for public school prayer and traditional gender roles, as well as newer issues (ones that have become prominent since the publication of *Culture Wars*) like opposition to stem-cell research and physician-assisted suicide.

These two moral worldviews involve fundamental issues of personal and political identity in the present, to be sure, but they also bear on the kinds of questions about national meaning and purpose that Americans have always asked themselves, and that have fired the language of the jeremiad since the nation's earliest days. The cultural struggle between these two sides is "a struggle over national identity—over the meaning of America, who we have been in the past, who we are now, and perhaps most importantly, who we, as a nation, will aspire to become," Hunter wrote. Since the earliest years of the republic, various groups had viewed each other with suspicion and outright hatred due to competing notions of moral truth or religious practice. Cultural conflict, in his interpretation, is far more deeply rooted than political conflict, though in certain situations one can lead to the other. As Hunter put it in a 2006 forum sponsored by the Pew Foundation, "the Civil War, when it finally broke out, was preceded by thirty years of a culture war on precisely the issue that the real war was fought over. And the Civil War wouldn't have happened had it not been for the kinds of polarizations that had happened culturally, symbolically, thirty years prior."[7] For decades, North and South held vastly different self-perceptions and, consequently, vastly different understandings of each other. Though few would claim—and Hunter did not—that these cultural divisions *caused* the Civil War they certainly contributed to the misunderstandings and conflicts that led to it.

Hunter was not the first to point out these cultural, political, and religious dynamics. He acknowledged that his thesis represented a validation and extension of Robert Wuthnow's earlier findings in *The Restructuring of American Religion*. Wuthnow's book chronicled the declining importance of denominationalism in the United States, and an increasing cultural cleavage between religious conservatives and liberals *within* the same denominations. In other words, traditionalist Protestants, Catholics, and orthodox Jews increasingly felt that they had more in common with each other than with liberal or progressive members of their own religious communities, and political alliances between culturally conservative Roman Catholics and evangelical Protestants (two groups with a history of distrust, to say the least) illustrate the weakening of denominational loyalties and the increasing importance of extra-church organizations and agendas. (The example of Evangelicals and Catholics Together, which we encountered in chapter 4, is a case in point.) The same can be said for coalitions of religious progressives, although, lacking the bitterness of alienation from the mainstream and the righteous anger of the Christian Right, such alliances attracted fewer headlines. (Their relative lack of success may also explain their relative lack of publicity.) Nor are the culture wars the exclusive property of American Christians: such dynamics are beginning to appear among American Muslims as well.[8]

Although it made sense of the polarized political culture of the 1990s, the culture wars thesis was controversial from the start. A number of critics pointed out that survey data simply do not show a yawning cultural gap within the American electorate and that therefore, if such a culture war exists at all, it must reflect merely elite opinion. Alan Wolfe argued that the American people were largely moderate in their social and political views, and that they accepted neither the orthodox nor the progressive position in toto. With the important exception of homosexuality, Wolfe argued, Americans are basically "one nation, after all," and he took issue with the metaphor of war as a description of what was happening in American politics. Although Hunter did admit, at several points in the book, that "culture wars" rhetoric was often spurred on by elites seeking to mobilize Americans for their particular causes, and that these elites were more polarized than the American public at large, his propensity to use the language of war and combat often left the impression that such cultural polarization afflicted the nation as a whole.[9]

Despite the shortcomings of culture war analysis as an explanation for the entirety of political disputation in late twentieth-century America, cultural politics *do* appear central to the ability of Republican candidates to win the White House repeatedly over the past four decades, despite the party's national minority status, and to a number of other political developments in late twentieth-century America. Kenneth Wald and David Leege describe post–New Deal America as "the epitome of cultural politics," echoing the view that cultural appeals explain a great deal of post–World War II American political life. In an extensive analysis of cultural rhetoric over the course of the past sixty years, Leege and Wald argue that such appeals have spurred defections from the Democratic Party and fostered Republican identity among Southern whites. They point to the Reagan administration's use of "religious traditionalism" to appeal to culturally conservative Democratic Catholics while simultaneously solidifying the allegiance of evangelical Protestants. Of course *both* parties use cultural appeals and cultural politics, but Leege and Wald argue that such efforts are especially important to the minority party, who must not only assemble coalitions and mobilize their supporters but also look for ways to *discourage* members of the majority party from turning out to vote. Geoffrey Layman has also examined the empirical data on cultural politics, and argues that America's political parties "are fully engaged in a new form of religious and cultural political conflict." Cultural issues clearly continue to influence American politics, and a number of empirical analyses of American politics have shown that the cultural dimensions highlighted by Hunter and Wuthnow remain relevant to political analysis, especially as regards the political allegiance of white evangelicals.[10]

I mentioned at the end of chapter 5 that the traditionalist and progressive versions of the American jeremiad map, in at least general ways, onto the orthodox and progressive impulses in the American culture wars, respectively. The connection between the jeremiad and the culture wars, then, is a specific example of the larger connection between narratives and politics. The Republican Party's national success in post–World War II American party politics has been due in large part to the ability of its evangelical, traditionalist, and culturally conservative wing to employ the language of cultural conflict more skillfully than its opponents (either within the party or among Democrats), crafting a narrative that resonated with Americans' cultural uncertainties. Hunter's war analogies may be overheated, but they certainly seem in keeping with the participants' views on the matter, if Buchanan and Moyers are any indication. And it does seem clear that a number of important institutions in American society (religious bodies, political parties) face increasing cultural conflict between those who view issues of moral truth as firm and unchanging and those more willing to countenance adjusting long-established practices in the service of what "the times" require. Each side in these cultural conflicts constructs a narrative of the American experience in service of their views. Let's consider two of these in a bit more detail.

NARRATIVES AND POLITICS: THE JEREMIAD AND THE CULTURE WARS

Competing moral principles and visions do not insert themselves into political life; they are drawn upon, articulated, and narrated by political elites. In American political discourse, Hunter's "impulse toward orthodoxy," for example, rarely appears as a set of abstract principles, but rather comes packaged in a narrative about how these principles have contributed to the American past, how they figure into the nation's present, and why they are important for the future. With some variations (on isolationism and immigration, where Buchanan's rhetoric became increasingly shrill and led to his virtual repudiation of, and by, the Republican Party), Buchanan's cultural conservatism provides a concrete manifestation of the orthodox side of Hunter's culture wars analysis. Buchanan was particularly emphatic that American greatness had always been a reflection of its dominant *culture*, which he identified as white, Anglo-Saxon, and Judeo-Christian.[11] Buchanan's convention speech contrasted Clinton's hedonistic relativism with the religious and moral consensus of pre-1960s America—before the sexual revolution, the counterculture, and antiwar demonstrations undermined many Americans' respect for traditional sources of authority. Buchanan called the faithful to political arms in a religious and cultural war "as critical to the kind of nation we will one day be as was the Cold War itself."

Conversely, the progressive jeremiad stresses the ongoing and always difficult search for the realization of American ideals of liberty and equality, and views the entry of racial, religious, and sexual minorities into full citizenship as fully in line with the vision of American life articulated by the nation's founders, even if it far outstrips anything those founders could have imagined. Moyers's narrative of national promise constantly threatened by entrenched interests evoked the earlier examples of Martin Luther King and those antebellum Americans who decried the rise of the slave power. Moyers too called his audience to action to rescue the American birthright of liberty and equality from those who would hijack it for their own political purposes (in his case, from the grasp of corporate and antidemocratic interests).

Thus each side in the culture wars presents a jeremiad in support of its worldview and account of American history, a narrative of present decay, the solution to which is a recapturing of some lost quality: Judeo-Christian values and traditions on the one hand, founding promise on the other. These jeremiads serve to bind members of each camp both "horizontally" and "vertically," forming and maintaining the bonds of each community (often by demonizing the other camp), and linking those groups up with a transcendent cause. As *political* narratives, jeremiads serve the cause of collective solidarity, and do for groups what personal narratives do for individuals: they anchor the group in historical time, giving a larger meaning and context to that history by connecting the moral truths that lie at the core of its vision of the good life to a concrete American story.

Furthermore, as narratives, both the orthodox and the progressive jeremiad offer *plots* that solidify the identities of those who affirm them, and that appeal to wavering Americans to see events through the lens they offer. As David Carr has argued, "There is no doubt that much of the communal rhetoric which addresses a group as *we* is putative or persuasive rather than expressive of a genuine unity and an already accepted sense of communal activity. In some cases such story-telling attempts to create a community where none existed before." In other words, American Jeremiahs do not simply *describe* existing divisions in American society, they provide compelling narratives that attempt to *shape* the way that Americans understand the issues of their times. Yet another way of saying this is that each side of the culture wars, each of these two competing jeremiads, seeks to reduce the political choices facing its audience into two competing, and polarized, options. (Thus Alan Wolfe may be right that the metaphor of "culture wars" overstated the degree to which the American people were polarized on various issues during the late twentieth century, but at the same time "culture wars" may accurately describe the way that partisan politics operated during those years.) Layman's work on the increasing cultural polarization of party activists suggests that something like this sort of polarization has been happening in American politics in recent years.[12]

Both Moyers and Buchanan provide glimpses of these processes at work, of the jeremiad aiming to cement the allegiance of those already on board and convince the wary. Buchanan began his address by speaking to the "Buchanan brigades"—"We took the long way home," he told them, "but we finally got here"—and then broadened his remarks to speak on behalf of Republicans as a group. In narrating his *own* reconciliation with Bush, Buchanan appealed to his supporters to see that Bill Clinton represented an even *greater* threat to American culture than an insufficiently conservative George H. W. Bush. For Moyers, sketching out the "collusion" that unifies the cultural, economic, and political aspects of the conservative takeover of American politics aims to convince his audience that seemingly disparate belief systems are in fact linked by a larger, and more nefarious, conspiracy, making the enlistment in a progressive cause all the most important.

But jeremiads do not only serve to bond speakers to listeners, and listeners to each other; they create a connection between the community and something more transcendent. Defending the political, social, sexual, or economic principles that obtained during the nation's early history, when religious orthodoxy sat rather comfortably atop the national culture, grounds orthodox identity not just in a series of principles but in a transcendent story of national purpose and power. When a member of the Christian Right takes action to defend traditional understandings of marriage, for example, the claim that heterosexual marriage has deep roots in the Judeo-Christian tradition and has served as the foundation of civilized society since the dawn of time is never likely to be far away. Identifying with the religious basis of the nation's founding, and presenting the American founders as men of faith and deep piety, links the orthodox jeremiad not only to the foundations of its own country but also to ultimate truth. Furthermore, it grounds individuals in a community of like-minded fellow believers, and links that contemporary community with a concrete historical entity.

The progressive jeremiad also links its adherents up to transcendent truths, rooted deeply in the American ideals of life, liberty, and the pursuit of happiness, and is committed to realizing those values in circumstances and forms that might differ substantially from those in which they were originally articulated. For example, in supporting antidiscrimination statutes regarding gays and lesbians, abortion rights, or environmental protection, progressive Jeremiahs do not evoke the unity of a bygone time period. Rather, they seek to link like-minded, or potentially sympathetic, Americans to a particular understanding of the *spirit*, if not the letter, of the nation's founding ideals, and provide a story about the gradual expansion of founding promise from its cramped beginnings to the present day.[13]

As we have seen, narrators are able to put forward an effective plot only if they populate it with compelling *characters*, and both sides in the culture wars do so. Of course, the orthodox position draws heavily on powerful imagery of godly founders. But even more central to this narrative are the faithful orthodox, who are called to withstand the onslaught of such corrupting movements as radical feminism, secularism, liberalism, and relativistic hedonism. These corrupting influences are not merely abstract presences in the orthodox narrative, but are themselves manifested in a *different* set of characters: intellectuals, liberal media elites, and meddlesome social workers who harass hardworking, God-fearing Americans. In his convention speech, Buchanan lauded a cast of ordinary Americans: New Hampshire mill workers; a legal secretary; the brave people of Koreatown, Los Angeles, who "took the worst of the Los Angeles riots, but still live the family values we treasure, and who still believe deeply in the American dream." The progressive jeremiad presents its own cast of characters as well: founders articulating noble principles; oligarchs and greedy elites seeking to insulate themselves from popular movements and hijack founding promises; progressive Americans who fight in every generation to advance those ideals and free the slaves, gain women the vote, and so on. And—in both cases—perhaps most importantly, the audience itself, the newest generation of Americans whom Moyers, Buchanan, and all their fellow Jeremiahs call to action in support of their most fundamental principles against all their foes.

Plots and characters intersect to give us narratives, and narratives pivot on *turning points*. The orthodox narrative, with its traditionalist jeremiad, identifies a set of godly founders who presided over a society in which individualism was tempered by obligations of religion, family, and community. As time went by, such influences as modern science, Darwinism, and growing individualism began to threaten this religious and moral consensus. The turning point, for the orthodox narrative, comes in the 1960s, with its sexual revolution, growing disrespect for authority of many sorts, and widespread hedonism.[14] The 1960s play an important role in Moyers's jeremiad as well. Although the Progressive movement peaked in the early 1900s, its egalitarian ideals would continue to shape much of the twentieth century. "The progressive impulse," he said, "had its final fling in the landslide of 1964 when LBJ...won the public endorsement for what he meant to be the capstone in the arch of the New Deal." That election, though, which must have appeared so overwhelming at the time, was actually to be a turning point, as "a resurgent conservatism [converted] public concern and hostility into a crusade to resurrect social Darwinism as a moral philosophy, multinational corporations as a governing class, and the theology of markets as a transcendental belief system."

The jeremiads that we encounter in the American culture wars are *political* narratives, not only because they offer interpretations of American history and culture, but in the circumstances of their delivery as well. Both Buchanan and Moyers delivered their stem-winders in the service of political mobilization. Context is key. In each case, the narrative remains unfinished, the future steps in the plot are not predetermined, since in a democratic society the prospect of returning to virtuous foundations is always just an election away, if only the critic can wake up his or her fellow Americans to seize the opportunity and elect the right candidates. Thus Pat Robertson ended his 1986 book *America's Dates with Destiny* with Election Day 1988, and called Americans to take up their responsibilities as active citizens and elect politicians who would reverse the country's moral decline. Nearly twenty years later, from the opposite side of the political spectrum, Moyers exhorted his own audience: "Democracy doesn't work without citizen activism and participation....So go for it."

EIGHT

The Past, Present and Future
of the American Jeremiad

The recognition of the broken covenant does not mean to me the rejection of the American past. We are not innocent, we are not the saviors of mankind, and it is well for us to grow up enough to know that. But there have been Americans at every point in our history who have tried to pick up the pieces, tried to start again, tried once more to build an ethical society in light of a transcendent ethical vision. That too is part of our tradition, and if we can find no sustenance there, our prospect is even darker than it now seems....

As a first step, I would argue, we must reaffirm the outward or external covenant and that includes the civil religion in its most classical form. The Declaration of Independence, the Bill of Rights, and the Fourteenth Amendment to the Constitution have never been fully implemented. Certainly the words "with liberty and justice for all" in the Pledge of Allegiance are not factually descriptive. But while I can understand the feeling of a Garrison that such hypocritically employed documents should be rejected, I would follow the course of a Weld and insist that they be fulfilled. If they have never been completely implemented, neither have they been entirely without effect.[1]

THE JEREMIAD AND AMERICAN NATIONAL IDENTITY

What are we ultimately to make of all these stories of national chosenness and sinfulness, of fallenness and repentance, of decline and renewal? I have argued that the American jeremiad, in both its traditionalist and progressive variants, has long offered a comprehensive and coherent account of the American experience—its original promise, its successes and failures, and its future prospects—and that American Jeremiahs have used the image of a prodigal nation to rally supporters to their social, political, and religious visions. At its heart, though, *every* American jeremiad—from Increase Mather's *Day of Trouble* to Bill Moyers's speech to Call to Renewal—is a salvo in the continuing battle over the nation's identity. What does it mean to be an American? Or, in the words Samuel Huntington chose for the title of his provocative book on American national identity: "Who are we?"

Anthony D. Smith, who has written about nationalism and national identity more than any other recent scholar, defines national identity as "the maintenance and continual reinterpretation of the pattern of values, symbols, memories, myths, and traditions that form the distinctive heritage of the nation, and the identity of individuals with that heritage and its pattern." A number of powerful symbols and myths have presented themselves over the course of this book: city on a hill, Chosen Nation, godly founders, prodigal nation, and so on. The "maintenance and continual reinterpretation" of such symbols often take place in highly visible acts of patriotism. We have seen jeremiads delivered in the midst of war, in public speeches on July 4 or other national occasions, in houses of worship, and at political rallies. More frequently, perhaps, one suspects that national identity is forged, and continually reforged, in countless, virtually unnoticed everyday interactions. Such processes are spurred along by political myths, "[tales] concerned with past events, giving them a special meaning and significance for the present and thereby reinforcing the authority of those who are wielding power in a particular community."[2] National identity is formed out of the confluence of myths and origin stories that each generation inherits from those who have come before, refashions into something bearing its own imprint, and passes on to subsequent generations. *Both* the traditionalist and the progressive jeremiad are deeply involved in this process, with one locating national identity in the demographic, ethnic, and religious characteristics of past generations of Americans and the other emphasizing founding principles as a kind of national birthright always in need of reinterpretation in radically different circumstances.

But before going any further, a word about the "American" in this term "American identity." Aspects of American national identity *predate* the political entity known as the United States. As George McKenna puts it, the Puritans "managed to envisage an America long before there was a United States of America." Put another way, in the words of Liah Greenfeld, "*National* identity in America...preceded the formation not only of the specific American identity (the American sense of uniqueness), but of the institutional framework of the American nation, and even of the national territory..." Yet another way of putting this point is to emphasize that the United States has not one but *several* sets of founders. Focusing on the colonizing endeavor and cultural preeminence of New England yields a set of Calvinist Puritan founders—John Winthrop, John Cotton, the Mathers, Thomas Dudley—who sought to erect a godly commonwealth in this new world. Of course there were other groups of American founders as well: the Catholic families involved in the Chesapeake; the Anglicans in Virginia; the Quakers and Dutch in the middle Atlantic territories. These colonial founders, labeled "Planting Fathers" in Frank Lambert's recent account of American religious liberty, provide one trajectory for understanding the complicated mix of religion and politics in the early history of the nation.[3]

This diverse assortment of founders laid the rhetorical foundations and set the larger context for the *nation's* founders, and those most responsible for eighteenth-century revolutionary rhetoric and action: Jefferson, Washington, Adams, Franklin, Madison, Hamilton, and so on. By any description, the cultural milieu, the political theory, and the communal vision of these national founders differed radically from those of their predecessors 100 years, or more, earlier. Yet the Puritan inheritance did not disappear. It would continue to shape American society and politics for years to come, as so many authors in recent years—George McKenna, Matthew Holland, and Robert Jewett, to name just three—have so powerfully articulated.[4]

The American jeremiad, then, is a river that draws from a number of different tributaries. Chief among these have been the early New England rhetoric of a chosen but sinful people seeking a godly commonwealth in the American wilderness; the meditations on national purpose that emerged just prior to, and during, the Civil War; and the ongoing ramifications of the reentry of American fundamentalists and their allies into the political sphere during the 1980s. As McKenna has observed, "The one constant running through all forms of this [Puritan-derived] Protestantism is the belief that Americans are a people set apart, a people with a providential mission."[5]

THE CHOSEN NATION: AMERICAN MYTH, AMERICAN IDENTITY

The American jeremiad goes hand in hand with the myth of the United States as a chosen, yet imperiled, nation. Claims of national chosenness are certainly not unique to the United States; many nations have considered themselves "chosen" for a special historical and religious destiny. One study identified no fewer than nine such nations, while

Anthony Smith has devoted an entire book to the notion of "chosen peoples," in which his analysis ranged from medieval Armenians to nineteenth-century Afrikaners.[6] But no nation, it seems safe to say, has so successfully combined a myth of chosenness with the sort of militarized global supremacy (and destructive potential) of the United States in the twenty-first century. It's a dangerous mix, especially when influenced by a powerful jeremiad in which military weakness in the face of communism (or, more recently, Islamic militancy) has been interpreted as a sign of American decline.

The most ambitious narratives of American national chosenness—Cotton Mather's *Magnalia,* or later versions of Manifest Destiny and westward expansionist triumphalism—are certainly no longer in fashion among historians. They appear on the fringes of mainstream political debate, if at all. Nonetheless, the idea of the United States as a nation uniquely destined to play a world-historical role does not need religious orthodoxy to underwrite it; it can function as a secular narrative as well (though a messianic secular narrative with religious overtones, to be sure). From the Puritans to Ronald Reagan, this idea has motivated Americans of many political stripes to take action in support of national ideals.[7]

In their account of the "Captain America" complex, Robert Jewett and John Shelton Lawrence lay out two ways in which American civil religion has shaped American nationalism. On the one hand, we see throughout American history countless examples of "zealous nationalism," in which the nation seeks to *impose* its missionary task on other countries—in their words, "to redeem the world by destroying enemies." On the other, we find a far different tradition, a "prophetic realism" that seeks to work for justice alongside other nations with tact and sensitivity, cognizant of the immense responsibility that comes with such power. In keeping with the jeremiad's roots in the prophetic tradition, Jewett and Lawrence trace these two options back to the Hebrew Scriptures, from the imagery of Israel as a rod of iron or as a light to the nations. It is a short step—rhetorically, at least—as readers of this book will know by now, from those ancient Israelites to our own early New Englanders.[8]

How have the American jeremiads we have encountered contributed to this notion of national chosenness? The New England jeremiad, as we have seen, understood the American experience as part of God's plan for human history. This encompassed the conversion of the Indians, combating Catholic influence in the "New World," and the search for a refuge from God's coming wrath at England. Most generally, New England was integral to the westward movement of the Christian Gospel.[9] Out of such concerns, and out of the bloody war that divided the country midway through the nineteenth century, grew an American civil religion and, later, a missionary impulse that would thrust the United States into a leading global role for much of the twentieth century, inaugurated by World War I and the grander dreams of Wilsonian internationalism. Emerging out of the history of fundamentalist anticommunism, the Christian Right jeremiad always viewed the American nation as a godly force in a dangerous world, and viewed military strength as the surest way to combat the rise of an atheistic system with global designs. But the danger was not only from communists or, later, "Islamofascists," but was from *within* as well, from Americans unwilling to comport themselves as befits members of a chosen nation. Thus the constant need of a prodigal America for its Jeremiahs: to defend us from those most dangerous enemies of all, those in our midst.[10]

Perhaps, one might think, we should simply jettison this problematic notion of chosenness. An "unchosen" United States might appear attractive, especially if one focuses on the unsavory and exclusionary potential of such language, or its especially violent and exclusionary episodes. William Pfaff has recently articulated such a critique in the wake of the American invasion of Iraq:

> It is something like a national heresy to suggest that the United States does not have a unique moral status and role to play in the history of nations, and therefore in the affairs of the contemporary world. In fact it does not. This is a national conceit that is the comprehensible result of the religious beliefs of the early New England colonists…which convinced them that their austere settlements in the wilderness represented a new start in humanity's story…A claim to preeminent political virtue is a claim to power, a demand that other countries yield to what Washington asserts as universal interests.[11]

And lest we consider Pfaff's critique as post hoc sour grapes, consider words penned more than forty years ago, *before* Vietnam, by Reinhold Niebuhr, hardly someone given to reveries about past virtue:

> A sense of mission may be a source of confusion when it tempts nations with a messianic consciousness to hide the inevitable vital impulses of collective existence, chiefly the will to power, under the veil of its ideal purposes. Such nations are inclined to pretend that they have triumphed over the baser impulses and to be wholly devoted to ideal ends. In the

American case the temptation is compounded by the obvious success of a nation which has grown so rapidly in strength by grace of various geographic, economic, and historical factors.... Our history in the nineteenth century, when we were engaged in occupying our portion of the continent from ocean to ocean... naturally revealed few pointers toward our future destiny as a world power... It did reveal some very telling manifestations of the temptation to screen the political lust and ambitions of a healthy young nation behind the ideal purposes with which our sense of mission had endowed us.[12]

Pfaff's critique makes a valuable point about American chosenness producing a militarized, unstable international political system and leading to all sorts of disastrous American interventions around the world. And Niebuhr highlights the moral blind spots that such national self-images can enable. Perhaps they are right. There certainly are times and presidents for whom American chosenness leads to reckless military adventures (the reader in 2008 need not look far). At the same time, American chosenness has also contributed to a sense of national responsibility to alleviate suffering at home and abroad. If a sense of American mission underwrote President William McKinley's pledge to "Christianize" the Philippines at the turn of the twentieth century, it also played an important role in the enormous relief effort assembled for victims of the Indian Ocean tsunami in 2005. Many Americans have used the biblical injunction from Luke's gospel—"from those to whom much has been given, much will be expected"—to justify higher levels of American foreign aid for the impoverished global South. In Robert Bellah's words, chosenness "accounts for much of the best in America as well as the worst."[13] The progressive jeremiad need not jettison the notion of national mission or founding promise, as we have seen in the case of King, who despite his disillusion retained a deep faith in American founding values. After all, as he put it, his dream, which was deeply rooted in the American dream, allowed him to hew a stone of hope out of a mountain of despair.

If this sense of American chosenness has been fostered by the continuing cultural significance of the Puritan inheritance, however, one might ask how robust such an inheritance will remain in an American society that looks less European, even less Christian (and certainly less white) than ever before. The explosion of religious diversity—not to mention diversity in general—since the immigration reforms of the mid-1960s relates directly to the two types of jeremiad explored in the preceding chapters.

THE TRADITIONALIST JEREMIAD AND AMERICAN NATIONAL IDENTITY

With the revival of immigration (legal and illegal) as an explosive political issue in 2007, a raft of jeremiads—by such prominent public figures as Pat Buchanan, Samuel Huntington, and Lou Dobbs—have been appearing in print recently.[14] But perhaps the most striking was not a book or newspaper column about immigration, but a letter written by a United States representative. On December 7, 2006, Rep. Virgil Goode (R-Va.) responded to a constituent who had contacted him expressing concern about the plans of newly elected African-American Muslim representative Keith Ellison (D-Mich.) to place his hand on the Koran during his private swearing-in ceremony. Goode's letter occasioned much controversy. He wrote:

> When I raise my hand to take the oath on Swearing In Day, I will have the Bible in my other hand. I do not subscribe to using the Koran in any way. The Muslim Representative from Minnesota was elected by the voters of that district and if American citizens don't wake up and adopt the Virgil Goode position on immigration there will likely be many more Muslims elected to office and demanding the use of the Koran...I fear that in the next century we will have many more Muslims in the United States if we do not adopt the strict immigration policies that I believe are necessary to preserve the values and beliefs traditional to the United States of America and to prevent our resources from being swamped.
>
> The Ten Commandments and "In God We Trust" are on the wall in my office. A Muslim student came by the office and asked why I did not have anything on my wall about the Koran. My response was clear, "As long as I have the honor of representing the citizens of the 5th District of Virginia in the United States House of Representatives, The Koran is not going to be on the wall of my office."[15]

Now clearly, not all traditionalist jeremiads display this sort of overt hostility to the varieties of American diversity. But Goode's letter is worth lingering over for a moment, because it crystallizes some of the elements of the politics of constraint that we find in the traditionalist jeremiad at this point in American history. Goode clearly identifies with the Christian Right's agenda: at the time of this incident he was a member of the Republican Study Committee, a group of roughly 100 House conservatives that opposed same-sex marriage, abortion, and embryonic stem-cell research and sought to reclaim a Christian presence in the public square.[16]

What, specifically, did Goode find objectionable about Ellison's plan to swear on a Koran? At first glance, it appears that Goode objected to "more Muslims elected to office." But since the Constitution forbids religious tests for officeholding, Goode could hardly be calling for members of a specific religion to be excluded from consideration for service in Congress, or denied seats once elected. Indeed, in an opinion piece for *USA Today*, Goode explicitly denied advocating a religious test for officeholding.[17] When Goode linked election of Muslims with their desire to swear on a Koran instead of a Bible, he seemed to be objecting not simply to their election but to their manner of behavior once elected: not just the election of Muslims, but Muslims "demanding the use of the Koran." But the swearing-in of Congressional representatives on the House floor does not involve *any* holy books: members raise their right hand, but do not put their left hand on anything. Ellison planned to swear on the Koran only in a private ceremony for friends, supporters, and family members.

What, then, might lie at the heart of Goode's concern? "I fear," he wrote, "that in the next century we will have many more Muslims in the United States if we do not adopt the strict immigration policies that I believe are necessary to preserve the values and beliefs traditional to the United States of America and to prevent our resources from being swamped." Goode's comments about Islam in America linked the rise of Islam in America with immigration, ignoring important domestic factors in the growth of American Islam. As Ellison pointed out to the news media, he was not an immigrant: he could trace his American ancestors back to the eighteenth century.[18] In fact, Goode was able to make the connection between Islam, a religious category, and immigration because he clearly viewed Islam as something fundamentally alien to the "values and beliefs traditional to the United States of America."

In this dispute, Goode hits all the notes of the traditionalist jeremiad. First, the identification of crisis, the increasing threat of non-Christian immigrants who claim the right to bring their religion into the American public square, and indeed the halls of government. Second, the contrast with a virtuous past: contemporary immigrants, in Goode's narration of the story, stand in sharp contrast to a past founded on "values and beliefs traditional to the United States of America." Thus the proliferation of Muslims in America represents a kind of invasion—a matter for immigration policy—and the lack of attention to this invasion is largely responsible for the nation having fallen away from its traditional roots in Judeo-Christian piety. Finally, we find the call to political action: "adopt the Virgil Goode position on immigration." For Goode, immigration—and especially immigration from Middle Eastern countries—was primarily responsible for the September 11 attacks. As Goode put it in an op-ed piece in *USA Today:*

> [W]e were not attacked by a nation on 9/11; we were attacked by extremists who acted in the name of the Islamic religion. I believe that if we do not stop illegal immigration totally, reduce legal immigration and end diversity visas, we are leaving ourselves vulnerable to infiltration by those who want to mold the United States into the image of their religion, rather than working within the Judeo-Christian principles that have made us a beacon for freedom-loving persons around the world.[19]

Notice, however, how such a view remains imprisoned within a worldview that equates what is most fundamentally or traditionally American with concrete demographic facts about the past: the predominance of Christianity in public life and the tiny fraction of Muslims in the American population. On this traditionalist understanding of what made the nation great, and the ways in which that greatness can be imperiled, the presence of "many more Muslims in the United States" represents a direct threat to the "preserv[ation of] the values and beliefs traditional to the United States of America." The past is a model for the present.

This way of thinking goes to the heart of debates over national identity and cultural diversity. What is American nationhood essentially about? Is there a "core" and, if so, what is it? Prominent thinkers such as Samuel Huntington and Arthur Schlesinger Jr.—not to mention politicians from both parties—have voiced deep concern about the future of American culture, due either to uncontrolled immigration or to the reluctance of such immigrants to adopt the traditional trappings of American culture. Alarm at the rise of multiculturalism in American higher education, history writing, and culture more generally led Schlesinger to lament "the decomposition of America."[20]

Religion is never far from these debates, and most critics voicing these concerns link their worries with the declining Protestant character of recent American immigration. As Huntington puts it,

[Revitalizing America's] core culture....would mean a recommitment to America as a deeply religious and primarily Christian country, encompassing several religious minorities, adhering to Anglo-Protestant values, speaking English, maintaining its European cultural heritage, and committed to the principles of the Creed. Religion has been and still is a central, perhaps the central, element of American identity.[21]

Huntington makes clear that he is referring to Anglo-Protestant *culture*, and not making an argument about racial supremacy. But the highly charged rhetoric around immigration politics has led others to eschew such careful distinctions. By 2006, for example, Pat Buchanan had left the Republican Party whose convention he had so forcefully addressed in 1992. In his book *State of Emergency*, Buchanan ties American cultural decadence to the disappearance of a white majority. Even more provocatively, Buchanan tied the 2007 shootings at Virginia Tech University to an overly permissive immigration policy, in an especially revealing column that illustrated his view of the racial and ethnic bases of American nationhood.

What happened in Blacksburg cannot be divorced from what's been happening to America since the immigration act brought tens of millions of strangers to these shores, even as the old bonds of national community began to disintegrate and dissolve in the social revolutions of the 1960s. To intellectuals, what makes America a nation is ideas—ideas in the Declaration of Independence, Bill of Rights, Gettysburg Address and Dr. King's "I Have a Dream" speech. But documents no matter how eloquent and words no matter how lovely do not a nation make. Before 1970, we were a people, a community, a country. Students would have said aloud of Cho: "Who is this guy? What's the matter with him?" Teachers would have taken action to get him help—or get him out. Since the 1960s, we have become alienated from one another even as millions of strangers arrive every year. And as Americans no longer share the old ties of history, heritage, faith, language, tradition, culture, music, myth or morality, how can immigrants share those ties?[22]

Perhaps no single statement so neatly encapsulates the distinction between traditionalist and progressive ways of understanding American national identity than Buchanan's claim that "documents no matter how eloquent and words no matter how lovely do not a nation make," along with his downplaying of ideas and principles in favor of history, heritage, faith, language, tradition, and culture. Although many traditionalist Jeremiahs would shy away from Buchanan's abrasive style and his blunt statements in the wake of tragic violence, his general point is far more widely shared. Here, in the arena of national identity, we see again the traditionalist jeremiad's attachment to concrete social conditions: American national identity is an ethnic (European) and religious (Protestant) identity. Ergo, things not European or Anglo-Protestant must prove themselves worthy of inclusion.[23]

THE JEREMIAD IN AMERICA: BERCOVITCH'S LONG SHADOW

It has now been thirty years since Sacvan Bercovitch's *The American Jeremiad* shed much-needed light on this most important genre of American political rhetoric. Since the book's publication, numerous studies have appeared looking at various aspects of the jeremiad: some reinforcing Bercovitch's general conclusions, others taking issue with them, and still others seeking to extend his insights into new territory. This book's identification of two types of jeremiad, the traditionalist and the progressive, aims to add nuance to Bercovitch's pathbreaking analysis.

"The ritual of the jeremiad bespeaks an ideological consensus—in moral, religious, economic, social, and intellectual matters—unmatched in any other modern culture," Bercovitch argued. In his view, the jeremiad's critique is immediately co-opted into a national consensus around middle-class values. "[T]he jeremiad not only allowed for but actually elicited social criticism," Bercovitch wrote, "but it did so by and large to enlist the criticism in the cause of continuing revolution" and a continued commitment to middle-class American values. Despite the jeremiad's surface anxiety, he argued, we should not mistake its lament over present circumstances with any real crisis of confidence on the part of America's Jeremiahs. After all, "their punishments confirmed their promise," and despite the rhetoric of disaster and decline, "restoration is already a foregone conclusion in God's mind."[24] As Bercovitch put it, "the jeremiads attest to an unswerving faith in the errand," and *presume* that the called-for reform will eventually take place, given America's central role as a "chosen nation" in God's plan for the world:

> Jeremiah...both laments apostasy and heralds a restoration....The chosen people had sinned and continued in sin, had been punished with exile and were being threatened with more severe punishments unless they reformed; but they remained chosen nonetheless, still the keepers of the ancient promise to Abraham.[25]

Bercovitch's powerful analysis of the jeremiad's influential role in American history focused largely on colonial New England, the founding, and the early national period. Taking the story down through the Civil War years and into the twentieth century has allowed us to see further complexities inherent in the jeremiad, including the distinctions articulated in chapter 5 between its traditionalist and progressive strands. I have suggested, at several points throughout this book, that Bercovitch's interpretation understates the sense of deep existential despair that American Jeremiahs have often experienced. It is not so clear-cut, to many of the Jeremiahs considered in this book, that America "remained chosen nonetheless," nor that "restoration...is already a foregone conclusion in God's mind and will."[26] In fact, the sacred backdrop can make American decline appear *worse* than that of other societies, and the consequences of continued disobedience all the more frightening. I quoted Perry Miller in chapter 2, but his words are worth repeating as this book concludes:

> France and Spain are unlucky, or they miscalculate, or smallpox ravages them, and that is that. But a nation in covenant is systematically punished, the degree of affliction being exquisitely proportioned to the amount of depravity. While thus being chastised it is still in covenant— or, at least, as long as it has not committed the unpardonable sin which conclusively severs the covenant. Until that moment, no matter how bleak the prospect, there is always hope: if it reforms, it will recover the blessing. But where is that point of no return?[27]

The idea that there might be a "point of no return" was quite real— and, not surprisingly, quite unnerving—to many American Jeremiahs over the years. New England Jeremiahs, as we saw in chapter 2, often considered it a distinct possibility that God would, in fact, forsake their land once and for all, and they said so regularly.

In his work on African-American notions of chosenness, Eddie Glaude has taken issue with Bercovitch's strong claims about the consensual nature of the American jeremiad. The material presented in part I of this book supports Glaude's argument that the jeremiad has been deeply divisive as often as it has served to reinforce an ideological consensus. Certainly the jeremiad *is* a reformist impulse, and not one that calls for transformations of the deep structures of American life. Such movements as Prohibition, abolition, civil rights, and the Christian Right all hold on to the notion of national promise, in spite of their critique of American practice. But we should not understate the radical challenge that such reformers can pose and have posed to

American society, nor the significance of the transformations that they have helped to bring about by holding up to Americans both their noble aspirations *and* the damage done by their continued inability to live up to those aspirations.[28] Martin Luther King may have become a secular saint of the American civil religion—especially given his early and untimely death—but by the end of his life he was deeply critical of fundamental American beliefs in exceptionalism and the way they seemed inseparable from military adventurism and consumerism.

TRADITION AND PROGRESS: TOWARD A MORE EXPANSIVE JEREMIAD

I argued above, with regard to Rep. Goode and the politics of national identity, that the traditionalist jeremiad, while as deeply rooted in the American tradition as its progressive counterpart, is unable to do justice to the full citizenship of the broad and diverse American populace of the twenty-first century. Its use of the past is too limiting, its view of the present too despairing, its vision for the future too divisive. The traditionalist jeremiad remains imprisoned in an exclusionary "Judeo-Christian" paradigm—more specifically, in a white European Judeo-Christian paradigm, one that ignores the ever-increasing diversity *within* American Christianity itself, not to mention American society at large—that makes it difficult to see how non-Christian religions can be both radically unique and wholly American.[29] With their attachment to concrete particularities of the American past, traditionalist jeremiads tend to miss, downplay, or denigrate such developments as civil rights, the explosion of new religious movements, the women's movement, the expansion of the franchise, and the emergence of a variety of nontraditional spiritual activities in late-twentieth- and early twenty-first-century America.

Furthermore, many of these new social and political developments were themselves spurred on by progressive Jeremiahs. The progressive jeremiad has possessed enormous appeal in times of great upheaval and has, over the years, sketched out a vision of an America bound together by principles of liberty and equality, principles open to critique and reformulation in new circumstances. It is a narrative that can boast a number of impressive achievements: in the twentieth century alone, as we saw in chapter 5, the progressive jeremiad has underwritten Roosevelt's New Deal and King's vision for civil rights. Thus it has shown itself to be a practical and politically effective way of telling the American story, with impressive policy successes as evidence of its power to shape American politics. Following traditionalist calls for reform that evoke a simpler, earlier time of virtue, on the other hand, threatens to undo many of the important twentieth-century advances made by women and racial, ethnic, and religious minorities.

By decoupling a vision for the American future from concrete particularities of the past, progressive jeremiads have urged the nation on to new understandings of the bonds (and the responsibilities) of American citizenship. Indeed, one of the most important arguments for rejuvenating the progressive jeremiad lies in its ability to comprehend, and to value as deeply American, the sorts of diversity that characterize the nation at the dawn of the twenty-first century. By highlighting the fact that, to take a recent example, religious diversity has *always* been part and parcel of the American experience, progressive jeremiads provide a more expansive understanding of our past as well as a more capacious understanding of our future. A heightened appreciation of American religious diversity does not always yield a peaceful social space, but it does promise a more constructive acknowledgment of the important role that *all* religious groups have to play in the American future.[30] Similar arguments might be advanced with regard to post-1965 immigration policy: the progressive jeremiad's ability to speak a language of national purpose while simultaneously expanding the parameters of what counts as authentically American bodes well for an increasingly pluralistic, twenty-first-century United States.

Both jeremiads, I have shown, build their visions of the future on understandings of the past. The traditionalist jeremiad has long functioned to give voice to popular skepticism of elites, to remind its audience of the importance of preserving the community's cultural and religious heritage, and to insist that the values present in the wider culture be reflected in the policy and politics of the nation at any given point in time.[31] The progressive jeremiad looks to the past as well, of course, but in a less linear and empirical way, and in a way less captive to the particularities of bygone eras. The language of the progressive jeremiad has appeared in times of crisis—antislavery, civil rights—as public figures have sought to call Americans to new understandings of their most basic commitments, and to new understandings of the relationship between their past, present, and future. Both of these visions of America—and, more importantly, the productive political struggles *between* the two—have brought Americans into the twenty-first century, a nation radically transformed from its earlier self yet shaped in fundamental ways by the legacy of evangelical Protestantism, its

Puritan past, and its sense of national mission. Incorporating new groups and perspectives into this national culture is a process that is always ongoing, never easy, and continually contested.[32]

And yet in an American society that grows more ethnically and religiously diverse with each passing year, the progressive jeremiad has the capacity to bring the ever-increasing pluralism of Americans to the fore, and to give voice to the experience of often-marginalized communities in ways that seem increasingly challenging for the traditionalist jeremiad. After all, although the United States has always been referred to in ways that highlight its ethnic and cultural diversity— "nation of immigrants," "melting pot," "salad bowl"—never have these labels been more appropriate than today. The U.S. Census Bureau estimates that 90 percent of the nation's population growth in the next half century will occur in racial and ethnic "minority" groups—groups that will represent a full 40 percent of the American population by 2040 and whose cultural, political, religious, and social influence will only continue to increase. Such developments carry important ramifications for the way in which political debate is carried on in the United States, for the relationship between the state and the myriad religious groups represented by these fast-growing segments of the American population, and for the possibility of religious talk as a venue for inclusion and recognition rather than exclusion and divisiveness. So long as what is essentially American is defined by a Christian consensus (or, put slightly differently, a "Judeo-Christian" consensus), the shifting of the American religious and political landscape can only appear as a falling off from those standards of purity, and never as a new and vibrant cultural development in its own right.

The progressive jeremiad, then, possesses both practical and conceptual advantages over its traditionalist rivals. In proposing a rejuvenation of the progressive jeremiad, I am suggesting that we move beyond nostalgic laments over declining bowling leagues or a naked public square and employ the jeremiad in ways that speak to a religiously and politically vibrant American future from deep within the American tradition. We must resist the urge to allow American nationhood to be defined by the demographic, cultural, or religious profile of a previous time: there is simply no going back to America as it once was, and traditionalist Jeremiahs preach to an ever-shrinking choir. A rejuvenation of the progressive jeremiad will involve both a capacious understanding of American identity and skillfully crafted narratives: John Higham and David Hollinger have called for new narratives that do not surrender the idea of a larger American identity to the divisions of class, gender, and race or make discredited appeals to the kinds of universals that underwrote assimilation and homogenization in years past.[33]

Nor are these sorts of expansive understandings of American identity only the product of a post-1960s multiculturalism. In the concluding paragraphs of his *Democratic Vistas*, Walt Whitman offered the following meditation on the American future, one directly related to the tension between the traditionalist and the progressive jeremiads:

> We see that the real interest of this people of ours in the theology, history, poetry, politics, and personal models of the past, (the British islands, for instance, and indeed all the past,) is not necessarily to mould ourselves or our literature upon them, but to attain fuller, more definite comparisons, warnings, and the insight to ourselves, our own present, and our own far grander, different, future history, religion, social customs, &c. We see that almost everything that has been written, sung, or stated, of old, with reference to humanity under the feudal and oriental institutes, religions, and for other lands, needs to be re-written, re-sung, re-stated, in terms consistent with the institution of these States, and to come in range and obedient uniformity with them.[34]

The progressive jeremiad offers a national narrative deeply grounded in the American past yet open to a dynamic and changing American future. It appeals, as Lincoln said in his First Inaugural, to the "better angels of our nature," and to King's acknowledgment that "we cannot walk alone." Only a capacious understanding of the American past can explain Frederick Douglass's remarkable admission in 1852 that, despite the severe oppression being visited on his people, "I do not despair of this country." Twenty-first-century Americans could do far worse than to follow these exemplars into an uncertain and evolving future.

Notes

Chapter 1

1. Jeremiah 3:19–22, 5:24–29; New Revised Standard Version.

2. A partial transcript of Falwell's original remarks can be found online at http://www.beliefnet.com/story/87/story_8770_1.html (accessed 25 May 2007); his partial retraction and clarification of the remarks, at http://www.beliefnet.com/story/87/story_8781_1.html (accessed 25 May 2007).

3. Transcript of Nagin's remarks in *The Times-Picayune* (New Orleans), Tuesday, January 17, 2006; online at http://www.foxnews.com/story/0,2933,181851,00.html (accessed 25 May 2007).

4. *Oxford English Dictionary*, "Jeremiad"; the reference is to Roberts, *Memoirs*, I: 186.

5. Bruegemann, *Old Testament Theology*, 51, 67, 79; also 115ff. For Bruegemann, the book of Jeremiah is "completely geared toward the crisis of 587 BCE and the demise of Jerusalem" (5), an attempt to "make *theological sense* out of a *geopolitical crisis*" (7, emphasis in original). Or, as he puts it elsewhere in the book, "[T]he army belongs to Nebuchadnezzar, but the intent belongs to YHWH" (103). See also van Seters, "Historiography in Ancient Israel."

6. See Burke, "Tradition and Experience," 137–52; Spengler, *Decline of the West*; and, rather more partisan, Herman, *Idea of Decline*. See also my "Augustine and the Rhetoric of Roman Decline" and "Environmentalism and the Recurrent Rhetoric of Decline."

7. In addition to the talk programs and media commentary associated with Limbaugh and O'Reilly, see Buchanan, *Death of the West*; O'Reilly, *Culture Warrior*.

8. On the left, see Ritzer, *McDonaldization*; Rifkin, *End of Work*.

9. Putnam, *Bowling Alone*; Bellah et al., *Habits of the Heart*.

10. Alito endorsement taken from the Focus on the Family Web site (family.org). The endorsement was posted during Alito's confirmation hearings, and is apparently no longer available on the group's Web site.

11. See especially the Epilogue to Morone, *Hellfire Nation*.

12. Bellah, *Broken Covenant*; see also Hughes, *Myths*; and Hatch, *Sacred Cause*.

13. Aamodt, *Righteous Armies*, 10; 3.

14. Guyatt, *Providence*, 8. One of these strands of providentialism is directly connected with the sort of apocalyptic rhetoric that we saw above; others spoke to the more general idea that God works through nations to accomplish divine purposes. Still others interpreted a community's successes and failures as evidence of God's pleasure or displeasure, respectively. Guyatt's work draws on earlier studies—Winship, *Seers of God,* and Walsham, *Providence*—but takes these works' insights into explicitly political directions.

15. Moorhead, *American Apocalypse*, 11. Contrast the complex admixture of lamentation and hope found in the American jeremiad with the sorts of narratives canvassed in Oliver Bennett's *Cultural Pessimism.* Such cultural pessimism, Bennett argues, "arises with the conviction that the culture of a nation, a civilization, or of humanity itself is in an irreversible process of decline" (1).

16. Murphy, "'A Time of Shame,'" 401–14; on the migration of Puritan ideas, see McKenna, *Puritan Origins.*

17. A less overtly theological, but no less grandiose, view of the significance of the United States in world history understands the American experience as charged with spreading democracy and freedom around the globe.

18. Howard-Pitney, *African American Jeremiad,* 13; see also King, *Where Do We Go,* 44.

19. "Fourth of July," 121, 122; "Appalling Developments," 134. Despite this deep cynicism about the American experience, however, Garrison did at times (when it worked to his advantage politically) point out the potentially radical nature of American founding principles to his contemporaries. "Was John Brown justified in his attempt? Yes, if Washington was in his; if Warren and Hancock were in theirs...Was John Brown justified in interfering in behalf of the slave population of Virginia?...Yes, if Lafayette was justified in interfering to help our revolutionary fathers" (Garrison, from *The Liberator,* December 16, 1859; in Nelson, *Documents of Upheaval,* 265). Garrison's newspaper, *The Liberator,* reported H. C. Wright's claim that "[t]he slaves of George Washington had as good a right to cut their master's throat as he had to throw his cannon balls and bombshells from Dorchester Heights upon the British in Boston Harbor," cleverly reminding his readers both that the founders were slaveholders and that their principles supported his political agenda ("Annual Meeting of the Massachusetts Anti-Slavery Society," 230). Garrison famously burned a copy of the Constitution, referring to it as "an agreement with hell" (*The Liberator,* July 7, 1854).

Chapter 2

1. John Higginson, "Epistle Dedicatory," in Noyes, *New-England's Duty.*

2. Mather's sermon was delivered on the occasion of a day of humiliation, 12 mo 11 1673 (that is, February 11, 1674, under the Julian calendar used throughout colonial America before 1751). In the following section, I explain the social context of such days of humiliation and fasting. The quotations regarding Mather are from Hall, *Last American Puritan,* 96, 99. On the war as "the great crisis" of early New-England history, see Slotkin and Folsom, *So Dreadfull a Judgment,* 3. The figure on Indian casualties is taken from Axtell, *Natives and Newcomers,* 293. Axtell bases this figure on Cook's "Interracial Warfare"; on King Philip's War, see esp. pp. 11–21.

3. Mather, *Day of Trouble,* 22. "Churches have not so performed covenant-duties towards their children, as should have been, and especially, the rising generation have many of them broken the covenant themselves, in that they do not endeavour to come up to that which their solemn vow in baptism doth engage them to before the Lord" (24).

4. *Day of Trouble*, 26; 17. This imagery evokes God as a "refiner's fire" who purges impurities; see Malachi 3:2–3, also Isaiah 1:25.

5. *Day of Trouble*, 23; 27.

6. Mather, *Brief History*, 27. Mather's dates are often unreliable, but on this occasion he seems accurate (Lepore, *Name of War*, 97–98).

7. The contested nature of the conflict's very name—the Indians' leader was a sachem, not a King; his name was Metacom, not Philip; and whether the word "war" accurately describes what happened was, and remains, debatable—is explored in Lepore, *Name of War*, xiv–xvii.

8. Lepore examines the variety of *types* of accounts, and the details of their publication information (*Name of War*, chap. 3). Scholars have noted, of course, the scarcity of accounts sympathetic to the Indians, not to mention the complete absence of any written *by* Indians: see Lepore, "Dead Men Tell No Tales," and Ronda and Ronda, "Death of John Sassamon."

9. Mather, *Earnest Exhortation*, "To the Reader"; also 6–11, 18–19. The *Earnest Exhortation* might represent the 1676 election sermon that Mather *would have* delivered in Boston, had he been invited to preach it. That honor went to his rival William Hubbard, perhaps indicating Mather's controversial status with the colony's civil leaders. See Nelsen, "King Philip's War," 616, and Hall, *Last American Puritan*, 113–26.

10. *Earnest Exhortation*, 7, 17.

11. *Earnest Exhortation*, 5, 12, 22, 25; see also Hall, *Last American Puritan*, 147–54. The synod's report was published as *The Necessity of Reformation*. Meanwhile, 700 miles away, Governor William Berkeley of Virginia knew full well why King Philip's War had afflicted New-England: English Puritans had put King Charles I to death in 1649, and their American brethren had raised no protest. Besides that, he argued, New-Englanders were greedy for Indian land, and used dishonest means to get it. See Washburn, "Governor Berkeley and King Philip's War."

12. Hudson, "Fast Days and Civil Religion," 7.

13. The quotation from Hooker is taken from *Thomas Hooker: Writings*, 244, 246, 250. For more on these issues, see my *Conscience and Community*, chap. 2. On England as chosen nation, see Foxe, *Actes and Monuments*; Smith, *Chosen Peoples*, 116–22; and Hudson, "Fast Days and Civil Religion," 14–16.

Defining a term like "Puritan" continues to provide fodder for scholarly disputes, and the details of such debates are not directly germane to this book. Furthermore, "Puritan" and "Anglican" did not denote hard and fast categories in sixteenth- or seventeenth-century England, nor were they mutually exclusive ones. Most basically, Puritans were English Protestants dissatisfied with the extent of reform in the English church; they sought fuller reformation and the purging of "Romish" or "popish" residues that remained in the Church of England (heavy-handed bishops, for example, or ornate church buildings and liturgies). That said, a range of theological, social, and political positions can be found within the ranks of Puritans (the name itself was a term of abuse, never sought by any self-respecting "Puritan"), and many views held by "Puritans" were not fundamentally different from those held by their Anglican contemporaries.

The classic works on such definitional questions remain those of Patrick Collinson, especially *The Elizabethan Puritan Movement* and *The Religion of Protestants*, as well as Bozeman, *To Live Ancient Lives*. The most recent and provocative salvo in these definitional debates—which proclaims that "Orthodox New-England was a Reformed Christian success story, on the whole, but puritan it was not"—is Winship, "Were There Any Puritans in New-England?".

14. Hooke, *New-Englands Teares*, 7–8, 21; Miller, *Errand into the Wilderness*, chap. 1. The quotation from Winthrop is taken from his "Model of Christian Charity" (1630), *Winthrop Papers*, vol. II: 282.

15. Stout, *New-England Soul*, 53; Delbanco, "Looking Homeward, Going Home." On Nathaniel and Samuel Mather, see Hall, *Last American Puritan*, 41–43. The divergent social and political development of Puritanism in England and America has led to a rich literature not entirely germane to the issues under consideration here. See Foster, *Long Argument*.

16. Bozeman argues that first-generation New-England Puritans emphasized the salvation of the soul, while the second generation articulated deep concerns about the world around them (Bozeman, *To Live Ancient Lives*, 308–10). On the second-generation nature of the jeremiad, see Elliot, *Power and the Pulpit*, 6–8; Arch, *Authorizing the Past*, 90–91; and Miller, *Errand into the Wilderness*, 9–11.

17. *New-England Soul*, 85. Elliot makes a similar point about the 1680s: see Elliot, "New-England Puritan Literature," 261–62. On the Glorious Revolution, see Lovejoy, *Glorious Revolution*; on the Halfway Covenant, see Pope, *Halfway Covenant*, and Hall, *Last American Puritan*, 55–60.

18. Gildrie, "The Ceremonial Puritan," 4; Stout, *New-England Soul*, chap. 4. Of course no society is free from internal divisions, and the selection of clergy to deliver election sermons in early Massachusetts Bay often reflected tensions between the magistrates and the Deputies. On the power of the press in early New-England see Hall, *Last American Puritan*, 131–40.

19. Stout, *New-England Soul*, 29; Foster, *Long Argument*, 216–17; Breen, *Character of a Good Ruler*, 97. See also Egan, "'This is a Lamentation,'" 402.

20. Elliot, *Power and the Pulpit*, 88, also 99–105; see also Miller, "Declension in a Bible Commonwealth," 23.

21. In writing about eighteenth-century clergy, James West Davidson could also be describing most of the seventeenth-century critics covered in these pages:

> God was responsible for all events in the world, whether directly or through mediate causes....For eighteenth-century New-Englanders, the natural and moral spheres were so well contempered with each other that it was not at all inappropriate to have a judgment accompanied by human instrumentalities accompanied by another one levied through natural means...

See Davidson, *Logic of Millennial Thought*, 100–01, 103; as well as Winthrop Hudson's explication of the "Deuteronomic" understanding of history, in "Fast Days and Civil Religion."

22. Whiting, "To the Christian Reader"; Hubbard, *Happiness of a People*, i, 49–50; Stout, *New-England Soul*, 78.

23. Cotton Mather, *Things*, 9–13. On wilderness and its connection with barbarism and "Indianization," see Canup, *Out of the Wilderness*, esp. chaps. 2, 4. Canup's book is profitably read alongside Carroll, *Puritanism and the Wilderness*, and Simmons, "Cultural Bias."

24. Danforth, *Brief Recognition*, 19; Increase Mather, *Times of Men*, 15 (see also Mather, *Heavens Alarm*); Wakeman, *Sound Repentance*, 32; Noyes, *New-England's Duty*, 49.

25. Rosenmeier, "'New-England's Perfection'"; also Hughes, *American Quest*.

26. Whiting, *Way of Israel's Welfare*, 20; Hooker, *Righteousness Rained from Heaven*, i; Danforth, *Brief Recognition*, 6, 14. James Allen's formulation was perhaps the tersest of all: "evil men make evil days" (Allen, *New-Englands Choicest Blessing*, 6). There seems, at times, no limit to the powerful and destructive force of sin. Years earlier, William Hooke had gone so far as to propose that New-England's sins might even be responsible for destruction and civil strife in *Old* England! See Hooke, *New-England's Teares*, 15–19.

When encountering the New-England jeremiad in its many instantiations, one comes quickly to realize that separating the sins from their consequences can be difficult. Take just one example: worldliness can be viewed as a sin in itself, or as the fruit, the consequence, of the more fundamental sin of pride. Either explanation implicates sin, to be sure.

27. Davenport, *Gods Call*, 22, 25; Higginson, Introduction to Noyes, *New-England's Duty*, iv; Stoughton, *New-Englands True Interest*, 14. The passages along these lines are voluminous: see also Allen, *New-Englands Choicest Blessing*, 6; Adams, *Gods Eye*, 11.

28. See Torrey, *Exhortation unto Reformation*; the author laments "a spirit of profaneness, a spirit of pride, a spirit of sensuality, a spirit of gainsaying and rebellion, a spirit of libertinism, a spirit of carnality, formality, hypocrisy, and spiritual idolatry in the worship of God" (8); also *Necessity of Reformation*, 2–9.

29. Oakes, *New-England Pleaded with*, 36, 39; Shepard, *Wine for Gospel Wantons*, 6; Mather, *Day of Trouble*, 23–24; Walley and Thatcher, "To the Reader," in Arnold, *David Serving His Generation*, ii. Arnold adds that "a private spirit is an un-Christlike, un-Christian spirit" (2). Increase Mather's brother Eleazar was especially concerned with the ways a spirit of contention threatened structures of authority in the colony: see his posthumously published *Serious Exhortation*, 10. See also Wilson and Whiting, "Christian Reader," introduction to Higginson, *Cause of God*, i; Davenport, *Gods Call*, 4; Walley, *Balm in Gilead*, 8–10; and *Necessity of Reformation*, 5, 8.

30. "Thomas Shepard's Election Sermon," 362.

31. Stoughton, *New-Englands True Interest*, 20; Oakes, *New-England Pleaded with*, 32–33; Mather, "To the Reader," in Torrey, *Exhortation unto Reformation*. Worldliness is also condemned in Mather, *Day of Trouble*, 23; Mather, *Heavens Alarm*, 11–12; Torrey, *Plea for the Life*, 11–12; Higginson, *Cause of God*, 10; Whiting, *Way of Israel's Welfare*, 6–8; Wakeman, *Sound Repentance*, 27; and *Necessity of Reformation*, 7.

32. Danforth, *Brief Recognition*, 10, 12; Oakes, *New-England Pleaded with*, 27, also 29; Walley, *Balm in Gilead*, 8. Noyes also used the temperature metaphor, drawn from Revelation 3:16, criticizing New-England for having grown lukewarm in its religious profession (*New-England's Duty*, 67–68). See also Fitch, *Holy Connexion*, i; *Necessity of Reformation*, 2.

33. Hubbard, *Happiness of a People*, 55; Oakes, *New-England Pleaded with*, 36. See also Mather, *Day of Trouble*, 8, 22–23; Rowlandson, *Possibility of God's Forsaking*, 18–20; Wakeman, *Sound Repentance*, 8–29. Hubbard's discussion of pride may have been a veiled swipe at his rival, Increase Mather: see Nelsen, "King Philip's War."

34. Slotkin and Folsom, "Introduction," in *So Dreadfull a Judgment*, 8–9. The phrases "first works" and "first love" appear in Danforth, *Brief Recognition*, 5, 9; Mather, *Day of Trouble*, 29; Torrey, *Exhortation unto Reformation*, 15; Whiting, *Way of Israel's Welfare*, 22.

For the remaining three quotations, see Mather, *Discourse Concerning the Danger*, in *Call from Heaven*, 109; Mather, "To the Reader," in Torrey, *Exhortation unto Reformation*; and Allen, *New-Englands Choicest Blessing*, 11. Allen did follow this quotation with the observation that, following such religious decline, "then the Lord hath raised a new spirit of reformation" (3). See also Arnold, *David Serving His Generation*, 8; Allen, *New-Englands Choicest Blessing*, 2–3; Hooker, *Righteousness Rained from Heaven*, 18; Walley, *Balm in Gilead*, 13.

35. Noyes, *New-England's Duty*, 45; Stoughton, *New-Englands True Interest*, 27; Wakeman, *Sound Repentance*, 29. See also Hooker, *Righteousness Rained from Heaven*, 17; and Oakes, *New-England Pleaded with*, 24. Bruegemann lays out the imagery of planting and uprooting at the heart of Jeremiah's message (especially Jeremiah 1:10) in *Old Testament Theology*, chap. 2; the "true vine" imagery also appears in

John 15:1. See also Whiting, *Way of Israel's Welfare*, 33; Hubbard, *Happiness of a People*, 49–50.

36. Bozeman, *To Live Ancient Lives*, 306; Mather, *Discourse*, 76–77.

37. Oakes, *New-England Pleaded with*, 17, 21–22. For a recent account of Winthrop's role in the founding of Massachusetts Bay and its importance not only to second-generation New-England but to the American tradition more generally, see Holland, *Bonds of Affection*, chaps. 1–2.

38. Generational concerns are voiced in a number of jeremiads. Samuel Hooker compares New-England with Israel after the death of Joshua. "[T]here arose another generation that knew not Jehovah, and then how soon did their prosperity and welfare fail also" (*Righteousness Rained from Heaven*, 15–16; for the Scriptural reference, see Numbers 17:6); see also Hubbard, *Happiness of a People*, 49–50; Allen, *New-Englands Choicest Blessing*, 10–11; Stoughton, *New-Englands True Interest*, 8–9; Torrey, *Exhortation unto Reformation*, Epistle dedicatory; and Arnold, *David Serving His Generation*. More generally, see Miller, *New-England Mind: Colony to Providence*, chap. 1.

39. Oakes, *New-England Pleaded with*, 22–23; *Necessity of Reformation*, Epistle Dedicatory; Higginson, *Cause of God*, 11; Arnold, *David Serving His Generation*, 8. See also Hubbard, *Happiness of a People*, 50; Torrey, *Exhortation unto Reformation*; Noyes, *New-England's Duty*, Epistle dedicatory, also 45–47; Oxenbridge, *New-England Freemen Warned*, 21–22; Stoughton, *New-Englands True Interest*, 16.

40. Mather, *Serious Exhortation*, 9.

41. Buchanan, "Puritan Philosophy of History," 342.

42. Increase Mather, *Day of Trouble*, 29; Torrey, *Exhortation unto Reformation*, 7; 32.

43. Fitch, *Holy Connexion*, 16, 12–13; Mitchell, *Nehemiah on the Wall*, 30; Hubbard, *Happiness of a People*, 12–21; Allen, *New-Englands Choicest Blessing*, 10. See also Arnold, *David Serving His Generation*, 7; Mather, *Day of Trouble*, 22, 28–30; Higginson, *Cause of God*, 22; Stoughton, *New-Englands True Interest*, 37–38; Torrey, *Exhortation unto Reformation*, 38; and Walley, *Balm in Gilead*, 17–18. On the example for the younger generation, see especially Oxenbridge, *New-England Freemen Warned*, 43–44.

44. Arnold, *David Serving His Generation*, 9; Hubbard, *Happiness of a People*, 25–28; *Necessity of Reformation*, Epistle Dedicatory. See also Allen, *New-Englands Choicest Blessing*, 9; Walley, *Balm in Gilead*, 13–15; Noyes, *New-England's Duty*, 81–84; Higginson, *Cause of God*, 18–23; Oxenbridge, *New-England Freemen Warned*, 35–38; and Wakeman, *Sound Repentance*, 38, 40–41. Puritans viewed government as charged with serving the people, preserving the peace, and protecting the country, "but their governments must also establish orthodox religion and suppress rank heresy and immorality. Any other concept of government would threaten the covenant and, for that reason, defeat the common good" (Stout, *New-England Soul*, 71).

45. Mitchell, *Nehemiah on the Wall*, 18.

46. Davenport, *Gods Call*, 18–20; Whiting, *Way of Israel's Welfare*, 27; Mather, *Heaven's Alarm*, 16; Rowlandson, *Possibility of God's Forsaking*, 20; Increase Mather, *Day of Trouble*, 24; Eleazar Mather, *Serious Exhortation*, 14–17; Arnold, *David Serving His Generation*, 12; Stoughton, *New-Englands True Interest*, 26; and Increase Mather, *Pray for the Rising Generation*, 16–19, 13, 25. The quotation is from Hall, *Last American Puritan*, 108.

47. Danforth, *Brief Recognition*, 16, 22.

48. Of the roughly three dozen sermons on which I have drawn most extensively in this chapter, only a handful take New Testament passages for their texts. Partly, of course, this fact is due to the extreme paucity of explicit political content in the New compared to the Old Testaments, and thus their inaptness for explicitly political occasions. But if the *intention* of such text selections was not to highlight parallels with the

Israelites among the gathered New-Englanders, the *effect* certainly did reinforce these parallels.

49. Bishop, in Wakeman, *Sound Repentance*; Hubbard, *Happiness of a People*, 6; Noyes, *New-England's Duty*, 45–47.

50. Higginson, *Cause of God*, 4, 10; Wakeman, *Sound Repentance*, 18. Urian Oakes even used the term "New-England-Israel" (Oakes, *New-England Pleaded with*, 17, 23). See also Hooker, *Righteousness Rained from Heaven*, 15–16; Walley, *Balm in Gilead*, 8; and Noyes, *New-England's Duty*, 44–49, for comparisons, short of specific parallels.

51. "Chosen Peoples: Why Ethnic Groups Survive," in Smith, *Myths and Memories*, 131, 132.

52. *American Jeremiad*, 6, 8, 31, 55; Bercovitch, *Puritan Origins*, 100. See also Bercovitch, "Historiography," 270–72.

53. See Increase Mather, *Day of Trouble*, 27; Danforth, *Brief Recognition*, 22; Davenport, *Gods Call*, 20–21; Mitchell, *Nehemiah on the Wall*, 32; Torrey, *Man's Extremity*, 1–2.

54. Miller, *New England Mind: Colony to Province*, 22.

55. Stoughton, *New-England's True Interest*, 32; Bishop, "Christian Reader," in Wakeman, *Sound Repentance*; Wakeman, *Sound Repentance*, 14, 15; see also 18–19, 36; Whiting, *Way of Israel's Welfare*, 36; Hooker, *Righteousness Rained from Heaven*, 16–17; and Oakes, *New-England Pleaded with*, 11–12.

56. B.W., "To the Courteous Reader," in Rowlandson, *Possibility of Gods Forsaking*; Eleazar Mather, *Serious Exhortation*, 6, also 28; Miller, "Declension in a Bible Commonwealth," 48. On the conditional nature of the covenant, or the threat of failure that often overshadowed promises of success, see Stout, *New-England Soul*, 72; Bozeman, *To Live Ancient Lives*, 337.

57. Andrew Delbanco claims that "Winthrop's ideal of 1630 was in shambles before the decade was out" ("Looking Homeward, Going Home," 377). To Louise Breen, "the people of Puritan Massachusetts were deeply and consistently divided, no less in 1638 than in 1692, over where the colony's social and religious boundaries should be drawn and how their society should relate to the wider transatlantic world" (*Transgressing the Bounds*, 9). Robert Pope sees "declension" as just a different way of describing the maturation of a sect-type movement into a churchlike one, while James Henretta offers a morphological account of the growth of New-England settlements emphasizing land and population: see Pope, "New-England versus the New-England Mind," and Henretta, "Morphology of New-England Society."

On the other hand, T. H. Breen and Stephen Foster emphasize the relative social peace during the early years, while Michael P. Winship stresses the practical bases of unity among the Boston church, as reasons for thinking that some sort of unity *did* characterize the early years of settlement. See Breen and Foster, "The Puritans' Greatest Achievement," and Winship, "'The Most Glorious Church'"; also Wagner, "Jeremiad and Social Reality." On the jeremiad as "ritual response," see Elliot, "New-England Puritan Literature," 255–57.

58. Arch, *Authorizing the Past*, 109; Minter, "Puritan Jeremiad," 50.

59. See Lovejoy, *Glorious Revolution*. Mather saw the 1691 charter as inadequately endorsing his vision of the role that clergy and church membership ought to play in New-England, but also understood that it was the best deal that New-Englanders were likely to get, and he urged its acceptance (see Hall, *Last American Puritan*, chap. 7); Bercovitch, *Puritan Origins*, 143; see also Bercovitch, "Typology of America's Mission."

Debates over the process of "Americanization" continue, but are less germane to the issues under consideration here. See McConville, *King's Three Faces*, esp. chap. 10; and Butler, *Becoming America*.

60. Mather, *Magnalia Christi Americana*, "To the Reader," 85, 86, 95, 97. Note Mather's language in this final passage, its evocation of the "old" spirit of "New" England.

61. John Webb, *Duty of a Degenerate People*, 5–6; Prince, *Earthquakes*, 11. See also Andrews, "Literature of the Earthquake."

62. Sewall, *Nineveh's Repentance and Deliverance*, 13, 17; also 18, 29–33; Wales, *Dangers of Our National Prosperity*. These are just a few examples of an enormous literature; see Dickson, "Jeremiads." Many others are anthologized in Sandoz, *Political Sermons*, as well as in Cherry, *God's New Israel*.

63. Street, *American States*, 31; Keteltas, *God Arising*, 19. Melvin B. Endy Jr. emphasizes the *political* nature of preachers' justification of the Revolution, arguing that clergy who supported the revolution did so based on their view of the Revolution as a just war of resistance to tyranny. A more expansive treatment of the religiously infused interpretations of the New-England clergy is found in Sassi, *Republic of Righteousness*.

64. Stiles, *United States Elevated*, 7; Langdon, *Republic of the Israelites*, 30. After recounting the many blessings that God has bestowed on the young nation, especially overseeing its successful struggle for independence, Langdon concludes that "we cannot but acknowledge that God has graciously patronized our cause, and taken us under his special care, as he did his ancient covenant people" (32). See Gribbin, "The Covenant Transformed," 302.

65. Morgan, "Puritan Ethic," 3–43; see also Winship, "Were There Any Puritans in New-England?"

66. Noll, *America's God*, 31; and Lambert, *Founding Fathers*, which distinguishes between Puritan Fathers and Founding Fathers.

67. Hammer, "Puritans as Founders," 166.

Chapter 3

1. Henry Ward Beecher, "Against a Compromise of Principle," in *Patriotic Addresses*, 231–33; Boardman, *Thanksgiving in War*, 5–6; Cheever, *Responsibility of the Church*, 14.

2. Taft, *Washington During the Civil War*, entry for 4 January 1861. Available online at http://memory.loc.gov/cgi-bin/query/r?ammem/mtaft:@field(DOCID+lit(mtaftmtaft1div6)); accessed 11 May 2007.

3. Guion, *Sermon*, 9; Beecher, "Peace, Be Still," 276; Bellows, "Crisis," 295; Van Dyke, "Character and Influence"; Guion, *Sermon*, 9–11; Chase, *Discourse*, 10–11; Cummins, *The African*. John S. C. Abbott opined that "slavery is the source of most of our troubles" (*Address*, 3). See also Mines, *Duty*, 10–11; Hutton, *True Refuge*, 8–9; and Wadsworth, *Our Own Sins*, 12–14.

On slavery abetting polarization and extremism, see Vinton, "Fanaticism Rebuked"; William Adams, "Prayer for Rulers," 326–27.

4. Hervey, *Liberty*, 6–15; Beecher, "Peace, Be Still"; Vinton, "Fanaticism Rebuked"; Brown, *Sermon*, 11; Dorr, *American Vine*, 16–17; Read, *National Fast*, 13–15; McGill, *Sinful but Not Forsaken*, 6–11; Wadsworth, *Our Own Sins*, 7–8. See also Adams, "Prayer for Rulers," 325–27; Chase, *Discourse*, 9; Chew, *God's Judgments*, 7; Hutton, *True Refuge*, 11–13; Swope, *National Calamities*, 12–13; and Handy, *Our National Sins*, 8, 17–18.

5. Swope, *National Calamities*, 12; Abbott, *Address*, 12; Read, *National Fast*, 16; Mines, *Duty*, 5–6.

6. Breckinridge, *Discourse*, 2; also Read, *National Fast*, 17; Brown, *Sermon*, 13–14; Chew, *God's Judgments*, 12–13; Mines, *Duty*, 15–18; Wadsworth, *Our Own Sins*, 16–19.

7. Breckinridge, *Discourse*, 16; Gannon, *Rebel Bishop*. Abbott opposed any concessions to the slave states, and invoked providence in the case of widespread secession: "God will undoubtedly overrule this even for the furtherance of freedom and Christianity" (*Address*, 14). Bellows also pronounced the Southern states free to leave ("Crisis," 304).

8. Dorr, *American Vine*, 10; Hutton, *True Refuge*, 6; McGill, *Sinful but Not Forsaken*, 18–19. See also Mines, *Duty*, 3–4; and Swope, *National Calamities*, 8–9; Brown, *Sermon*, 8–10.

9. "To J. J. Pettis, 4 January 1861."

10. Our understanding of these topics has been helped immeasurably in recent years by the appearance of two important works: Harry S. Stout's *Upon the Altar of the Nation*, which pays special attention to the language of the jeremiad as it figured into American political discourse during the mid-nineteenth century, and Mark Noll's *The Civil War as a Theological Crisis*, which places the war into broader social and theological contexts. Stout's book has advanced a number of provocative claims—that a failure to engage in just-war thinking prior to the war's outbreak led to carnage on a scale previously unimaginable; that American civil religion is the product of a self-conscious blood sacrifice overseen by Lincoln, Grant, Sherman, and other Union leaders—to which any scholar in years to come will have to attend. Noll's volume on the Civil War provides a concise version of the much more elaborate synthesis he sketched in *America's God*.

11. See Howe, *What Hath God Wrought*, esp. chaps. 7, 10, 15, 19.

12. Rose, *Voice of the Marketplace*, 28. On the growing disjuncture between religious and political culture in the nineteenth century, see Hanley, *Beyond a Christian Commonwealth*. Hanley's claim that American Protestants evinced an opposition to Enlightenment rationalism (18) seems to me a careless use of the term "Enlightenment," since Americans' pragmatic views were firmly grounded in Scottish Enlightenment "common sense" philosophy. I fully concur, though, with Hanley's larger argument, that "Protestant dissent developed in the wake of an evangelical thrust that undeniably tapped the democratic impulse of the Republic. . . . As social processes evolving in tandem, democratic culture and mainstream Protestantism forged a complex, volatile relationship that resists easy analysis" (29–30).

On nineteenth-century religious developments more generally, see Smith, *Revivalism and Social Reform*, esp. chaps. 10–13; Hatch, *Democratization of American Christianity*; Cole, *Social Ideas*; Bodo, *Protestant Clergy*; and Young, *Bearing Witness Against Sin*. Most recently, and magisterially, on all of these topics, see Howe, *What Hath God Wrought*, esp chaps. 5, 8.

13. Noll, "The Bible and Slavery" and *Civil War as a Theological Crisis*.

14. Genovese, "Religion in the Collapse," 74–75. See also Howe, *Political Culture*; Schlesinger, *Age of Jackson*; Wood, *Radicalism*. With regard to the political disputes, I am referring to the Missouri Compromise (1820); the Webster-Hayne debates (1830); the Wilmot Proviso (1846); Henry Clay's Compromise of 1850, and the Fugitive Slave Act enacted in the same year; Stephen Douglas's Kansas-Nebraska Act (1854); and the Supreme Court's *Dred Scott* decision (1857).

15. Tuveson, *Redeemer Nation*, 187; Hatch, *Sacred Cause of Liberty*; Blight, *Frederick Douglass' Civil War*, 104; Hughes, *Myths America Lives By*.

On the "Christian republican synthesis," see Noll, *Civil War as Crisis*, chap. 2; *America's God*, 52–250; and *God and Mammon*. Finally, see Forbes, "Slavery and Evangelical Enlightenment," 68.

16. Glaude, *Exodus!*; Butler, *Awash in a Sea of Faith*, chap. 5; Raboteau, *Slave Religion*, esp. chaps. 2, 5; and Albrecht, "Theological Response," 21–34.

17. Cited in David Morgan, *Protestants and Pictures*, 24. The definitive work on religious media during this time period is Nord, *Faith in Reading*. Such materials aimed not only at individual piety and salvation; evangelical Protestants played important roles in the early temperance movement and other movements for social reform, which were often connected to the postmillennial impulse so common during those years. One scholar has claimed that "[p]robably the most successful years of postmillennialism in the concept of national mission were those between 1815 and the Civil War" (Maclear, "Republic and the Millennium," 194). On the "communications revolution," see Howe, *What Hath God Wrought*, 5.

18. That their monopoly was never as certain as they would have liked, and that dissidents continually challenged both the margins and the center of that monopoly, does not invalidate the fact that New-England clergy held real social and cultural power.

19. See Fredrickson, "Coming of the Lord"; Paludan, "Religion"; Hanley, *Beyond a Christian Commonwealth*; and Aamodt, *Righteous Armies*, 53. Bercovitch emphasizes the coincidence between American expansionism and jeremiadic rhetoric as well as the middle-class nature of the jeremiad (passim, esp. 141ff); while Hanley (*Beyond a Christian Commonwealth*) highlights the disjuncture and the "critical republican vision" of Protestant dissent.

20. Palmer, "National Responsibility Before God," 178. See also Palmer's 1860 Thanksgiving sermon, reprinted in Palmer and Leacock, *Rights of the South Defended*, 1–2; Hodgman, *Great Republic Judged*, which asserts that "nations, as well as individuals, are punished for their crimes" (76): Beecher, "Peace, Be Still"; Clapp, *God's Purposes*, 4; Thornwell, "Our National Sins"; Leacock, "Thanksgiving sermon," 14; Paddock, *God's Presence*, 5; Canfield, *American Crisis*, 4–5; and William Adams, *Christian Patriotism*, 4.

21. Cheever, *Fire and Hammer*, 7; Palmer, "Thanksgiving Sermon," 3; Haven, "Letter to the London Watchman" (1862), in *National Sermons*, 306; Hodgman, *Great Republic Judged*, 76; Haven, "The Beginning of the End" (1859), in *National Sermons*, 164. Early in his career, Abraham Lincoln acknowledged the intractability of slavery as a national issue by admitting that "When Southern people tell us that they are no more responsible for the origin of slavery than we are, I acknowledge the fact.... I surely will not blame them for not doing what I should not know what to do as to the existing institution" ("Speech in Peoria" [1854], *Collected Works*, II: 255). See also Abbott, *Address*, 14; Ames, *Dead Flies*; Boardman, *What Christianity Demands*, 8; 13; Carey, *The War*, 13; Chase, *Discourse*, 11–12; Abbott, *Address*, 5–6; and Beecher, "Peace, Be Still," 279. If slavery was the primary national sin, then the Emancipation Proclamation began a process of national repentance and redemption (see Carey, *The War*, and Hodgman, *Great Republic Judged*).

22. Genovese, "Religion in the Collapse," 74. Such a claim is certainly overstated—condemnation of slavery as sinful did not automatically lead to a call for *immediate* emancipation—but does point out the way that perceptions of such high stakes can frustrate attempts to negotiate compromises. See also Cummins, *The African*; van Dyke, "Character and Influence"; Raphall, "Bible View of Slavery"; and Wightman, *Glory of God*, 9. More generally, see Noll, *Civil War as Crisis*; and Genovese, "*Slavery Ordained of God*."

23. Duffield, *Our National Sins*; Brainerd, *Patriotism Aiding Piety*. See also Beecher, "Peace, Be Still," and, more generally, Hanley, *Beyond a Christian Commonwealth*, chap. 3.

24. Henry Boardman, *What Christianity Demands*, 18; Dabney, "Christian's Best Motive," 89; see also Palmer, "National Responsibility Before God" [delivered 13 June 1861] 190. On drunkenness, see Barnes, *Throne of Iniquity*; also Cleaveland, *Discourse*, and Hutton, *True Refuge*, 12–13.

The critique of Americans as greedy had regional and national dimensions. There is, of course, a generic condemnation of materialism and worldliness: Philip Shaw Paludan notes the "protest from both North and South that the nation was losing its soul in the search for wealth" ("Religion and the American Civil War," 21). But Southerners often saw Northerners as *particularly* avaricious, given the market capitalism that predominated in the nation's northern cities, and claimed that their own region was characterized by interlocking personal loyalties and mutual responsibility (e.g., the responsibility of the master to care for his slaves). Such a worldview has been explicated with great care by Eugene D. Genovese, in such works as *Roll Jordan Roll*; and more recently by Elizabeth Fox-Genovese and Eugene D. Genovese, *Mind of the Master Class*, esp. chap. 21. See also Dawson, "Puritan and the Cavalier."

25. Boardman, *Thanksgiving in War*, 19; Carey, *The War*, 22; Freeman, *God in Our National Affairs*, 7; Gannett, "Repentance amidst Deliverance"; Palmer, "National Responsibility Before God," 190. See also Clapp, *God's Purposes*, 11–12; Ames, *Dead Flies*; Paddock, *God's Presence*, 10–11; and Sturtevant, "Lessons of Our National Conflict."

On the camps, see Woodworth, *While God Is Marching On*. See also Beecher, "The Camp, Its Dangers and Duties" (1861), in *Patriotic Addresses*. On the salutary effects of war, see Carey, *The War*; Boardman, *Thanksgiving in War*; Brewer, *Wrath of Man*; and Dwinell, *Hope*.

26. Dwinell, *Hope*, 11–12.

27. Boardman, *What Christianity Demands*, 14; Mines, *Duty*, 4–5; Douglass, "The Fourth of July and the Negro" [speech, Rochester, 4 July 1852], *Life and Writings*, II: 183, 186; Parker, *Sermon*, 11 (also Guion, *Sermon*, 20); and Douglass, *Life and Writings*, III: 77–78. Lincoln himself had earlier drawn a stark contrast between Jefferson and Stephen Douglas in his 1859 Columbus speech, *Collected Works*, III: 410.

28. Beecher, "The Battle Set in Array" (1861), 167; Dwinell, *Hope*, 11; Elliot, *Sinfulness of American Slavery*, I: 254–55; Douglass, "Capt. John Brown not Insane" (1859), *Life and Writings*, II: 458; and Haven, "The Martyr" (1859), in *National Sermons*. See also *America and Her Slave-System*, 8–9; Hodgman, *Great Republic Judged*, 261.

It goes without saying that such sentiments were not universal. Despite the overwhelming pressures to venerate the nation's founders, some found ways to dissent. Locating the roots of the nation's troubles in a lack of recognition of God in the Constitution often involved criticism of the influence of Jeffersonianism, which Benjamin Palmer called "the free-thinking and infidel spirit which swept like a pestilence over Europe in the seventeenth and eighteenth centuries..." (Palmer, "National Responsibility Before God," 183). Disclaiming any notion of personally attacking the third president, Horace Bushnell nonetheless located two streams of thought in the American founding, Puritanism and Jeffersonianism, arguing that "[p]roximately our whole difference is an issue forced by slavery; but if we go back to the deepest root of the trouble, we shall find that it comes from trying to maintain a government without moral ideas." See Bushnell, *Reverses Needed*, 13; also Vinton, "Fanaticism Rebuked," 250.

29. Thornwell, "Our National Sins," 28ff; Palmer, "Thanksgiving Sermon," 8; and Palmer, "National Responsibility Before God," 192. In its boastfulness, its partisanship, its lack of respect for the rule of law, and its slavish devotion to material interests, Palmer argued, the North had apostatized from the commitment to republican self-government that lay at the basis of the national experiment ("National Responsibility Before God," 193; see also Aamodt, *Righteous Armies*, 54–60). Decline of this sort would be punished, Palmer predicted, by the eventual victory of the Confederate armies.

See also Elliot, "Ezra's Dilemma," 249–51; Bushnell, *Reverses Needed*, 10–14. On Southern attachment to the Founders, see Rubin, *Shattered Nation*, esp. chaps. 1–2.

30. Furness, *Discourse*, 19; Beecher, "Battle Set in Array," 171, 174; Douglass, *Life and Writings*, II: 185–6, III: 248; Haven, "The Death of Freedom" (1854), in *National Sermons*, 35; "The World War" (1864), in *National Sermons*, 439ff; also Bellows, "Crisis of Our National Disease," 295; *America and Its Slave-System*, 8; Lincoln, "To Henry L. Pierce and others" [6 April 1859], *Collected Works*, II: 376; also *Collected Works*, III: 88, 91, 254.

31. See, generally, the Lincoln-Douglas debates (*Collected Works*, III); Allen Guelzo, *Lincoln's Emancipation Proclamation*. For a more generous reading of Lincoln's anti-slavery politics, see Striner, *Father Abraham*. For Lincoln's famous comparison of the Constitution and the Declaration—the "apple of gold" passage—see his "Fragment," [January 1861?] in *Collected Works*, IV:169.

Questions of constitutional interpretation led to one of the more dramatic events in the history of American abolitionism, when Frederick Douglass, under the increasing influence of Gerrit Smith and Lysander Spooner, pronounced in the 23 May 1851 *North Star* that he no longer regarded the Constitution as a proslavery document (*Life and Writings*, II: 155–56). The implications of this shift away from Garrisonianism may be seen by contrasting Douglass's comments on the U.S. founders prior to this point (*Life and Writings*, I: 207, 276; II: 133–37) with perhaps his most famous address, "The Fourth of July and the Negro" (*Collected Works*, II: 185ff). Without understating the improvements that could still be made in the document, Albert Barnes called the U.S. Constitution the "noblest and best that the world has seen" (*Conditions of Peace*, 12).

32. Beecher, "Battle Set in Array," 167.

33. Haven, "Death of Freedom" (1854); in *National Sermons*, 38; Beecher, "Battle Set in Array," 166–67; Higginson, *Massachusetts in Mourning*, 10. The notable quotation in which Lincoln charged "Stephen [Douglas], Franklin [Pierce], Roger [Taney], and James [Buchanan]" with conspiring to nationalize slavery appears in Lincoln's "House Divided" speech (*Collected Works*, II: 465–66); and the Lincoln-Douglas debates of 1858 (*Collected Works*, III: 20). The eventual abolition of the Atlantic slave trade in 1808, foreshadowed in the Constitution, as well as the congressional restriction of slavery in the Northwest Territories (1787), reinforced this interpretation of founding intentions. See Moorhead, *American Apocalypse*, 30–35.

On the slave power conspiracy, see Parker, *Sermon*; and Furness, *Discourse*. For secondary scholarship, see Blight, *Frederick Douglass's Civil War*, 39–43. David Brion Davis, *Slave Power Conspiracy*, views the slave power narrative through the lens of Richard Hofstader's thesis about the paranoid style in American politics. (Of course Southerners saw just the opposite: a growing capture of the national government by the forces of abolition. See Jefferson Davis's letters.) George Fredrickson points out that denunciations of the slave power did not in the least entail support for emancipation ("Coming of the Lord," 116).

34. Beecher, "Shall We Compromise?" (1850), in *Patriotic Addresses*, 170–71; "American Slavery" (1850), in *Patriotic Addresses*, 180; Haven, "The Death of Freedom" (1854), in *National Sermons*, 42, 44. Adams, "Prayer for Rulers," 326–27; Lincoln, in the Lincoln-Douglas debates (*Collected Works*, III: 18, 87, 117, 276) and the Cooper Union speech (*Collected Works*, III: 526ff). In an 1850 sermon, Henry Ward Beecher had expressed his belief "that the compromises of the Constitution looked to the destruction of Slavery and not its establishment" (*Patriotic Addresses*, 171).

35. Lincoln, "Speech at Hartford, Connecticut" [5 March 1860], *Collected Works*, IV: 3–4, 9; see also Moorhead, *American Apocalypse*, 83.

36. Haven "The State Struck Down" (1856), in *National Sermons*, 71; see also "Death of Freedom" (1854), in *National Sermons*, 51. For Haven, of course, such penitential abasement would include an end to slavery, and thus was *prima facie* unacceptable to one side in the dispute, as well as to Northern audiences who valued Union

over emancipation; see, e.g., *American Society for Promoting National Unity*, 6. The Society's leadership reads like a who's who of antebellum American dignitaries: headed by Samuel F. B. Morse, its vice presidents included Martin van Buren, John Tyler, Millard Fillmore, Franklin Pierce, and James Buchanan. Other prominent Americans listed on the organization's masthead included John Crittenden, William Meade, Stephen Elliot, Leonidas Polk, Stephen Douglas, and James Henly Thornwell. Honorary memberships were held by Edward Everett and Benjamin Palmer.

Henry Ward Beecher stressed the importance of acknowledging individual responsibility for the nation's sins ("Peace, Be Still," 270, 271); see also William Adams, *Christianity and Civil Government*; and Boardman, *What Christianity Demands*, 19.

37. Vinton, "Fanaticism Rebuked," 250–51; Bushnell, *Reverses Needed*, 26; Tucker, "God's Providence in War," 236; and Elliot, "Ezra's Dilemma," 257. See also Woodworth, *While God Is Marching On*, chaps. 13–14; Stout, *Upon the Altar*.

38. Clerical figures often proved more direct in their calls for straightforward abolition, and less concerned than political leaders with the details or economic, social, or political ramifications. See, for example, Elliot, *Sinfulness of American Slavery*, I: chaps. 1–2; Hosmer, *Higher Law*; Cheever, *Guilt of Slavery*; idem, *Responsibility of the Church*; Abbott, *Address*; and Haven, *National Sermons*. This was no doubt an occupational luxury, as well, since Northern clergy would not be responsible for solving the enormous economic, political, and social questions attendant upon abolition. On the District of Columbia slavery question, see Bushnell, *Discourse*, 15–16. (As a congressman, Abraham Lincoln introduced legislation providing for compensated emancipation within the District of Columbia. It went nowhere.)

Frederick Douglass, "The End of All Compromises with Slavery—Now and Forever" (1854), *Life and Writings*, II: 282–83; Lincoln, for his part, rebuked Ohio Republicans who wanted to insert language opposing the Fugitive Slave Act into the party's platform ("To Salmon P. Chase," *Collected Works*, III: 384–86). The justification of restricting the spread, but not the existence of, slavery, culminated in Lincoln's Cooper Union speech of 1860 (*Collected Works*, III: 522).

39. Jefferson, *Notes on Virginia*, Query 18; Cheever, *Responsibility of the Church*, 13; Douglass, *Life and Writings*, II: 412–13 (also II: 190, III: 64); William Hosmer, *Higher Law*; Haven, "State Struck Down" (1856), in *National Sermons*, 71–72; "Caste the Cornerstone" (1854, 1858), in *National Sermons*, 126ff, 142–48; Beecher, "Nation's Duty to Slavery" (1859), in *Patriotic Addresses*, 217; American and Foreign Anti-Slavery Society, *Address*, 10–12.

40. See *American Society for Promoting National Unity*; Wightman, *Glory of God*, 13; Cummins, *The African*; Tucker, "God's Providence in War," 229–30. Providence could be invoked against secessionists as well, to justify a singular American nation:

> Providence has marked out this country as the heritage of one nation.... We are made one nation by [geography and] our descent, our language, our history, our traditions, our diversified climate and production, our mutual dependence and our reciprocal interests. Our capacity for self-development and self-protection, our just position among the nations, our charters, our schools, our religion, all require that we shall be one nation. (Boardman, *Thanksgiving in War*, 23, 24)

41. This was Stephen Douglas's position; and, in large part, Lincoln's; although, unlike Douglas, Lincoln did not see criticism of the *Dred Scott* ruling as tantamount to disobedience of law. See also William Adams, "Prayer for Rulers," 329–31.

42. Liggett, *Our National Reverses*, 253; Douglass, "How to End the War" (1861), *Life and Writings*, III: 94; and indeed much of the entire third volume of Douglass's *Life and Writings*.

43. Beecher, "Success of American Democracy" (1862), in *Patriotic Addresses*, 355; "National Injustice and Penalty" (1862), in *Patriotic Addresses*, 375, 378, 381.

44. "The restoration of the Rebel States to the Union must rest upon the principle of civil and political equality of both races; and it must be sealed by a general amnesty" ("To James S. Wadsworth" [January 1864?], *Collected Works*, VII: 102; see also Lincoln, "Reply to Committee Notifying Lincoln of his Renomination" [9 June 1864], *Collected Works*, VII: 380; Canfield, *American Crisis*, 22–23; Douglass, "How to End the War" (1861), *Life and Writings*, III; 94; "The Mission of the War" (1864), *Life and Writings*, III: 388, 391; Barnes, *Conditions of Peace*; Hodgman, *Great Republic Judged*, chap. 7. On the career of Lincoln's antislavery politics, see Striner, *Father Abraham*.

45. Moorhead, *American Apocalypse*, 43.

46. William Adams, *Christian Patriotism*, 7, 11.

47. Maclear, "Republic and the Millennium," 185, 194.

48. Hutton, *True Refuge*, 6; Hodgman, *Great Republic Judged*, 271. Recall Increase Mather's purgative imagery (evoking Malachi) from *Day of Trouble*. See also Clapp, *God's Purposes*, 6; Wightman, *Glory of God*, 5–6; Breckinridge, *Discourse*, 3; Boardman, *Thanksgiving in War*, 23–24; Barnes, *Conditions of Peace*, 9; and Adams, *Christian Patriotism*, 10–11.

49. Ames, *Dead Flies*, 15; also Dorr, *American Vine*: "Never, in the annals of the world, was there an instance of a nation rising so rapidly to perfect maturity and strength. And for all this, we were indebted, under God, to the piety and wisdom of our forefathers...for to him they looked for guidance and assistance, and he was their guide and helper" (12).

50. Paludan, "Religion and the American Civil War," 24. George Fredrickson sees the Protestant pulpit as the "single most important source of Northern patriotic exhortation" (Fredrickson, "The Coming of the Lord," 118; also Woodworth, *While God Is Marching On*, chap. 6). There is a strong echo here of the dynamic Harry Stout has pointed out with regard to New-England sermons:

> Those sermons that addressed internal problems like leadership turnover, materialism, instability, and contention invoked the rhetoric of failure and impending doom for New-England's native-born generation. Other sermons directed against external enemies celebrated the superior piety and unconquerable faith of the same generation (*New-England Soul*, 85).

The difference in emphasis between such sermons can explain both the promise of the American experience *and* the bitter trials through which it was currently passing. As we shall shortly see, such a narrative was complicated by a simultaneous, and equally strongly held, narrative of *Southern* chosenness, which challenged even while it was parasitic upon Northern versions of the narrative (Woodworth, *While God Is Marching On*, chap. 7; Charles Reagan Wilson, *Baptized in Blood*).

See Moorhead, *American Apocalypse*, x; Edmund Wilson, *Patriotic Gore*, 94; Blight, "Frederick Douglass and the American Apocalypse," 316. On Douglass's apocalyptic millennialism, see Blight, *Frederick Douglass's Civil War*, 73–79, 101–02.

51. Aamodt, *Righteous Armies*, 76–88; Woodworth, *While God Is Marching On*, chap. 2; on the ebb and flow of battlefield success, see Paludan, "Religion and the American Civil War," 27; Aamodt, *Righteous Armies*, chap. 6, esp 120–27; Paddock, *God's Presence*, 21–24; Doggett, *Nation's Ebenezer*, 7; Carey, *The War*, 9; Canfield, *American Crisis*, 26; and *Diary of Caroline Seabury*, 70.

See also Gannett, "Repentance amidst Deliverance," 15; Tucker, "God's Providence in War," 229, 233–34.

52. "The Day Dawns" (1862), in *National Sermons*, 269, 287; "The State a Christian Brotherhood" (1863), in *National Sermons*, 319, 357; "Why Grant Will Succeed" (1864), in *National Sermons*, 395; "Three Summers of War" (1864), in *National*

Sermons, 413; "The World War" (1864), in *National Sermons*, 460; "The Wonderful Year" (1865), in *National Sermons*, 497.

53. Bushnell, *Discourse*, 3; Stowe, *Uncle Tom's Cabin*, 625. Indeed, such ideas about divine judgment spanned a variety of media; Alexander Lawson suggested, in visual form, that the burning of Washington, D.C., during the War of 1812 was due to the sin of slavery. "Although Christian writers identified many reasons for eliminating slavery, the ultimate justification for emancipation or abolition always came down to the same issue: America must renounce slavery in order to escape divine punishment" (Aamodt, *Righteous Armies*, 22; also 15–17, chap. 2).

54. "The Death of Freedom" (1854), in *National Sermons*, 52 (see also "The Day Dawns" [1862], in *National Sermons*, 275, 288–89); "The Church and the Negro" (1863), in *National Sermons*, 365; also 385; "The Crisis Hour" (1864), in *National Sermons*, 423.

55. Elliot, "Ezra's Dilemma," 260; Tucker, "God's Providence in War," 230.

56. Quint, *National Sin*, 4. See also Bercovitch, *American Jeremiad*, 6–10; and Clebsch, *Christian Interpretations*, 7–9.

57. *National Sermons*, 423, 434. Also Boardman, *Thanksgiving Sermon*, 19.

58. Walker's *Appeal*, 5, 75–76, 22, 78. See Glaude, *Exodus!*, 42.

59. Maria Stuart, "Address," 63. See also Glaude, *Exodus!*, chap. 1, especially 56ff; 44; more generally, chap. 3. For African-Americans, argues Glaude, the Exodus narrative "provided a hermeneutic lens to account for their condition and to articulate a faith that God was active in history" (29).

More generally, see Howard-Pitney, "Jeremiads," 47; and Morone, *Hellfire Nation*, chap. 4.

60. Pennington, *Text Book*, 78.

61. "The Fourth of July and the Negro" [Rochester, 4 July 1852], *Life and Writings*, II: 185.

62. Douglass, "The Blood of the Slave on the Skirts of the Northern People" (1848), *Life and Writings*, I: 346–47 (Blight notes that "[t]he notion of God's retributive justice was a powerful force in his mind and, therefore, in his social analysis" [*Frederick Douglass' Civil War*, 23]); "Lecture on Slavery, No. 2" (1850), *Life and Writings*, II: 148 (see also "The Claims of the Negro Ethnologically Considered" (1854), *Life and Writings*, II: 308–9); "The Dred Scott Decision" (1857), *Life and Writings*, II: 412–13; "The Reasons for our Troubles" (1862), *Life and Writings*, III: 197 (see also "Valedictory" [1863], *Life and Writings*, III: 376); Douglass, "Speech on Emancipation Day."

According to David Blight, Douglass consistently argued that "[a] chosen but guilty people had to repent, suffer, and reform, or lose its destiny altogether." See Blight, *Frederick Douglass' Civil War*, 7–10, 240. According to Blight, "Douglass embraced virtually every aspect of America's mythology of mission—he believed that the very idea of a republic was being tested in the Civil War, he believed the world was watching, and he staked his future on the outcome" (112).

63. See Turner, "On the Anniversary," and Crummell, "Destined Superiority."

64. Palmer, "National Responsibility before God," 177; Elliot, "Ezra's Dilemma," 249, 256; more generally, Howard-Pitney, *African American Jeremiad*, chaps. 1–2.

65. Wilson, *Baptized in Blood*, 1; chaps. 1–2.

66. See, e.g., Stringfellow, *Scriptural and Statistical Views*; see also Eugene D. Genovese, "King Solomon's Dilemma"; Genovese, *Consuming Fire*, 38–48; Stout, *Upon the Altar*.

67. Genovese, *Consuming Fire*, 71; Wilson, *Baptized in Blood*, chap. 4; also Rubin, *Shattered Nation*, chaps. 5–7.

68. Wilson, *Baptized in Blood*, chap. 4, 5; Stowell, "'We Have Sinned'"; idem, "Stonewall Jackson," and Wight, "Churches and the Confederate Cause."

69. Beecher, *Oration*, 13, 17; Stowe, "The Chimney-Corner," 114–15.

70. "First Inaugural Address," *Collected Works*, IV: 270.

71. Guelzo, *Lincoln's Emancipation Proclamation*, 153; see also idem, *Abraham Lincoln*; Donald, *Lincoln*, 374–75; Wolf, *Almost Chosen People*, 17.

72. Noll, *Civil War as Crisis*, 89.

73. Lincoln, *Collected Works*, V: 403–404.

74. "Second Inaugural Address," *Collected Works*, VIII: 332–333.

75. Noll, *America's God*, 434; "Second Inaugural" [4 March 1865], *Collected Works*, VIII: 333.

76. Kazin, *God and the American Writer*, 139. This tentative nature of Lincoln's thought must lead us to view with some skepticism Lincoln's authorship of the noted "Proclamation Appointing a National Fast Day," which resembles nothing so much as the stem-winders delivered by New-England divines in the heyday of the jeremiad [20 March 1863]; *Collected Works*, VI: 155–157. I make this claim more fully in my "Religion and the Presidency of Abraham Lincoln"; See also Stout, *Upon the Altar of the Nation*, 426; also 145–46.

77. See Booth, *Personal Forgiveness*, 5–7; George Freeman, *God in Our National Affairs*, 13–17; and, most clearly, Laurie, *Three Discourses*, who reported "the opinion of many that the heart now forever laid to rest was too tender for the stern work of punishing evil-doers" (24).

78. "The Fourth of July and the Negro" (1852), *Life and Writings*, II: 190. I elaborate this distinction between foundational principles and foundational practices in chapter 5.

79. See Douglas's remarks during his third debate with Lincoln, at Jonesboro, in Lincoln, *Collected Works*, III: 112–113.

80. Clebsch, *Christian Interpretations*, 12–15; Stout, *Upon the Altar*, xxi, 459; Tuveson, *Redeemer Nation*, 209–14.

Chapter 4

1. Jerry Falwell, *Listen, America!*, 119; Pat Robertson, *Ten Offenses*, 204.

2. Speech available online at http://www.commonwealthclub.org/archive/20thcentury/92–05quayle-speech.html; accessed 11 May 2007.

3. Gaines M. Foster, *Moral Reconstruction*, 223.

4. On these developments, see Hamburger, *Separation*, chap. 11.

5. Billy Sunday's sermons are widely anthologized; perhaps the most accessible version of the "Booze Sermon" is online at http://www.billysunday.org/sermons/booze.php3.

6. Strong, *Our Country*; Putney, *Muscular Christianity*, 24–25, 45. Brooks Adams put this concern into larger historical context in his *Law of Civilization and Decay*.

7. Herrick and Herrick, *Life of William Jennings Bryan*, 398–99.

8. See Michael Kazin, *Godly Hero*.

9. Carpenter, *Revive Us Again*, 116. On the post-Scopes withdrawal from politics, see Christian Smith, *Secular Revolution*, 25–28; and Sweet, "Modernization of Protestant Religion." On fundamentalist educational and communications efforts, see Hadden, "Religious Broadcasting"; Ammerman, "North American Protestant Fundamentalism," 29–34; Carpenter, *Revive Us Again*, chaps. 1–3.

10. Falwell, *The Fundamentalist Phenomenon*, 144. Roughly similar accounts of the defensive nature of this reentry into politics appear in Dobson, "Bible, Politics, and Democracy," and Reed, *Politically Incorrect*, 16–18. See also Fowler, *New Engagement*; idem, *Enduring Liberalism*.

Not all, of course, who endorse the Christian Right jeremiad are fundamentalists. My point, rather, is that the Christian Right as a social movement (and a mainstream political narrative) emerges against the larger background of developments in American fundamentalism and the relationship between evangelicalism and American culture. On these definitional questions, see Marsden, *Fundamentalism and American Culture*.

11. Findlay, "Religion and Politics," 90; Henry, *Twilight*, 172. Richard John Neuhaus draws on Seymour Martin Lipset's notion of "aggressive defense": "Their defense is against what they perceive as governmental actions dictated by 'secular humanists' in control of American public life"; see "What the Fundamentalists Want," in *Piety and Politics*, 16.

12. Jenkins, *Decade of Nightmares*, 175–76; 155–56. Carter's speech is online at http://www.pbs.org/wgbh/amex/carter/filmmore/ps_crisis.html (accessed 14 May 2007); in what is commonly known as the "malaise" speech, Carter in fact did not use the word in his remarks to the nation. The description of Falwell is from Harding, *Book of Jerry Falwell*, 272.

13. Lienesch, *Redeeming America*, 8–9; Coleman, "Conservative Protestantism," 37–39; and Hopson and Smith, "Changing Fortunes," 4–6.

14. *Politically Incorrect*, 192. Premature reports of the Christian Right's demise appear in D'Antonio, *Fall from Grace*, and Bruce, *Rise and Fall*.

15. Watson, *Christian Coalition*, chap. 2.

16. See Hertzke, *Freeing God's Children*; William Martin, "Christian Right"; Mead, "God's Country?"; Hopson and Smith, "Changing Fortunes," 10.

17. Christian Smith, *Christian America?* It is less clear, however, whether Smith ought so confidently to claim that "[t]he vast majority of ordinary American evangelicals are not particularly interested in cultural warfare; they do not share many of the assumptions and proclivities that make such warring attractive" (194) based on 200 interviews. See also Shibley, "Contemporary Evangelicals." For just a few of the many works on these topics, see the following: Green et al., *The Values Campaign?*; Wilcox and Larson, *Onward Christian Soldiers?*; Muirhead et al., "Religion in the 2004 Presidential Election"; Rozell and Wilcox, *God at the Grass Roots* and *God at the Grass Roots, 1996*.

On the recent voting behavior of evangelicals, see the essays collected in Campbell, *A Matter of Faith?* and Layman, "Religion and Political Behavior." More recently, friction within the evangelical-fundamentalist political alliance on environmental issues like global warming has led many evangelicals to consider global warming real, scientifically validated, and a matter for human concern. The fundamentalist community, to speak broadly, remains far more suspicious of both the science and the politics behind global warming concerns. These suspicions are consistent with a general fundamentalist suspicion of elite institutions such as secular higher education, the federal bureaucracy, and the media.

18. Colson, "Common Cultural Task," 3, 31. It is possible that Evangelicals and Catholics Together represents a harbinger of things to come: see Bendyna et al., "Catholics and the Christian Right," 321–22, which reports Catholic sympathies with Christian Right issue positions but skepticism of Christian Right leaders. Paul Johnson also notes how the abortion debate has unified people of differing religious traditions ("God and the Americans," 43–44). Walter Dean Burnham locates the roots of the Roman Catholic/evangelical Protestant alliance in opposition to *Roe v. Wade*; see "The Reagan Heritage," 5.

There are important definitional debates regarding the precise use of such terms as evangelical, fundamentalist, charismatic, Pentecostal, and so on, but these are not immediately germane to the larger argument of this chapter. Those interested in such distinctions should see the following: Marsden, *Fundamentalism in American Culture*; Woodberry and Smith, "Fundamentalism et al."; Ammerman, "North American

Protestant Fundamentalism"; and the essays collected in Part I of Neuhaus and Cromartie, *Piety and Politics*. Sensitive ethnographic accounts of fundamentalist communities are rare but can vividly illustrate the contours of fundamentalism; two worth consulting are Harding, *Book of Jerry Falwell*; and Ault, *Spirit and Flesh*.

19. Dobson, "The Bible, Politics, and Democracy," 3. The precise content of the phrase "Judeo-Christian" is not always clear: see Silk, "Notes on the Judeo-Christian Tradition."

20. Senator Robert Byrd, "The Plight of our Nation." This view was shared by Senator Zell Miller (D-Ga.), in a Senate speech on February 2004, available at http:// www.pubtheo.com/page.asp?pid=1322 (accessed 11 May 2007). See also Colson and Neuhaus, *Evangelicals and Catholics Together*, 3; Neuhaus, *Naked Public Square*, 140; Novak, *Catholic Ethic*, 205; idem, "Truth and Liberty"; Bork, *Slouching Toward Gomorrah*, 2–3.

21. Weigel, "Talking the Talk," 88–89. In the view of Allen Hertzke, "In perhaps no other area of society [than sexuality] has the idea of fixed moral laws been so quickly undermined" ("Theory of Moral Ecology," 646). The full story of the loosening of sexual mores, of course, reaches back far beyond the 1960s—see Rochelle Gurstein, *Repeal of Reticence*—but that decade was crucial, for obvious reasons, in the history of American sexuality. See also Falwell, *Listen, America!* 200 (Falwell listed pornography just behind abortion and homosexuality in the list of five major national political sins: 253–54), and Reed, *Politically Incorrect*, 39.

22. Falwell, *America Can Be Saved!* 118; Falwell, *Listen, America!* 123 (later in the same volume, Falwell offered his view that contemporary feminism is driven by a small number of women who never accepted their God-given roles: 150); Henry, "Making Political Decisions," 107–08; Weigel, "Faith, Freedom, Responsibility," 62–63; Reed, *Politically Incorrect*, chap. 6; idem, "What do Religious Conservatives Really Want?" 2, 5, 9. See also McLellan, *Christians in the Political Arena*, 49–50.

23. Reed, *Politically Incorrect*, 39; Reed, "What do Religious Conservatives Really Want?" 7–8; Falwell, "God's Plan"; Robertson, *Turning Tide*, chap. 7, 183–88; Bennett, *Index*. Christian Smith notes the irony of widespread evangelical belief that the family is in crisis alongside a reluctance among evangelicals to do much about it (*Christian America?*, chap. 5).

24. Falwell, *Listen, America!* 181, 183; Falwell, *Fundamentalist Phenomenon*, 203; *Lawrence v. Texas*; Zell Miller speech; Henry, *Twilight*, 40; McLellan, *Christians in the Political Arena*, 49–56. Alan Wolfe notes the limits of American tolerance on issues relating to homosexuality: see *One Nation After All*; and Jenkins, *Decade of Nightmares*, 119–25.

25. Johnson, "God and the Americans," 43; Falwell, *If I Should Die*; Henry, *Twilight*, 40; Weigel, "Faith, Freedom, Responsibility," 64; Robertson, *America's Dates with Destiny*, chap. 19 (see also Watson, *Christian Coalition*, 22–25). Falwell listed abortion at the top of his list of five major sins with political consequences for the nation: see *Listen, America!* 179; 253–54; also *Fundamentalist Phenomenon*, 188; and "Agenda for the 1980s," 112.

See also Reed, *Politically Incorrect*, 10; idem, in *Disciples and Democracy*, 2; Schaeffer, *Christian Manifesto*, 69–70; Colson with Vaughn, *Kingdoms in Conflict*, 45; McLellan, *Christians in the Political Arena*, 42–47.

26. Reagan, *Abortion*; Colson and Neuhaus, *Evangelicals and Catholics Together*, xxv.

27. See *Abington v. Schempp*, which removed school-sponsored prayer; one year earlier, in *Engel v. Vitale*, the Court had ruled school-sponsored Bible reading to be unconstitutional (I explore the *Schempp* decision more fully in chapter 6). See also Falwell, *America Can Be Saved!* 24; Falwell, *Listen, America!* 205 (also McLellan, *Christians in the Political Arena*, 28–37; Colson, *Kingdoms in Conflict*, 44); Neuhaus, *Naked Public Square*, 102; Neuhaus, "What the Fundamentalists Want," 16–18; and Dobson, "Bible, Politics, and Democracy," 3–4.

28. Byrd, "Plight of our Nation"; Zell Miller, speech; Robertson, *Ten Offenses*, 22; see also Garry, "Cultural Hostility to Religion"; Reed, "What do Religious Conservatives Really Want?," 4–6; also Reed, *Politically Incorrect*, chap. 3.

29. Eastland, "In Defense," 43–44; Colson and Neuhaus, *Evangelicals and Catholics Together*, xxiv; Byrd, "Plight of our Nation," S6994, S6998; Robertson, *Turning Tide*, 9–10 and chap. 9; Garry, "Cultural Hostility to Religion." This critique is not limited to "conservative" critics, but was also famously made in Carter, *The Culture of Disbelief*.

30. Bork, *Slouching Toward Gomorrah*, 105–10. Also Frohnen, *New Communitarians*, 39; Robertson, *Turning Tide*, 20–21, and chap. 4.

31. Miller speech; Falwell, *Listen, America!* 25; Robertson, *Turning Tide*, 136 and chap. 5 (see also the discussion of media violence in Hertzke, "Theory of Moral Ecology," 638–41). See Toplin, *Radical Conservatism*. In an otherwise rather overheated volume, Toplin's chap. 7 on "media wars" is helpful.

32. Wilcox, *Onward Christian Soldiers*, 34–36; Jenkins, *Decade of Nightmares*, 84–85. Whether or not Carter actually *was* soft on communism is unclear, but debatable; certainly Carter had far more military experience than Reagan (that is to say, he had served). But perceptions become reality, and Carter's presidential style certainly *appeared* indecisive. See Jenkins, *Decade of Nightmares*, chaps. 6–7; McLellan, *Christians in the Political Arena*, 61–64.

33. Himmelfarb, *One Nation*, 20; Schaeffer, *Christian Manifesto*, chap.1; Frohnen, *Virtue*, 17; Henry, *Twilight*, 40; Robertson, *Ten Offenses*, 67.

34. Frohnen, *New Communitarians*, 46; Bork, *Slouching Toward Gomorrah*, 57, 61; Wolfe, *Moral Freedom*; Elshtain, *Who Are We?* 4; Frohnen, *Virtue*, 17.

35. Henry, *Twilight*, 170; Popenoe, "Family Condition of America," 90, 83; Hammond, *Religion and Personal Autonomy*, 12; see also Himmelfarb, *One Nation*, chap. 6; Neuhaus, *Naked Public Square*, 75; Bennett, *Death of Outrage*, 9, 129.

36. *America Can Be Saved!* 21–22; *Listen, America!* 30–34 (see also Robertson, *America's Dates with Destiny*, chap. 1–3; idem, *Ten Offenses*, 2–7); Byrd, "Plight of our Nation," S6997; S6994.

37. Johnson, "Almost-Chosen People," 6 (also 9–12); Robertson, *America's Dates with Destiny*, 20. See also McLellan, *Christians in the Political Arena*, 104–06; Miller, speech (see also the Summer 2006 *WallBuilders* newsletter); Bennett, "Religious Belief," 366; Eastland, "In Defense," 39; and Johnson, "God and the Americans." Johnson continues by arguing that the young American republic was "religious not necessarily in its forms but in its bones" (31). An especially intriguing interpretation of Jefferson's Christian sympathies may be found in Holland, *Bonds of Affection*. Prominent Americans who did not live during the founding era, such as Abraham Lincoln or Daniel Webster (or prominent foreigners like Tocqueville, who contributed in important ways to American self-understandings), often receive a kind of "honorary" founder status for their role in rearticulating national purpose at key moments in the national life. See Elshtain, "Religion and American Democracy."

38. This Protestant hegemony was supported and strengthened by long-standing American anti-Catholicism. See Hamburger, *Separation of Church and State*; and McGreevy, *Catholicism and American Freedom*, 15, 213; Neuhaus, *Naked Public Square*, xii.

39. Himmelfarb, *One Nation*, 15, 18. William Bennett claims that "[between the 1960s and 1990s], American society has experienced substantial social regression" (*De-Valuing of America*, "Preface to the Updated Edition," n.p.). See also Hammond, *Religion and Personal Autonomy*, 135. Hammond links an increasing concern for "personal autonomy" with a recent "Third disestablishment" that removed even the vague public religiosity of the mid-twentieth century and made "[b]ehavior…once widely regarded

as deviant…now promulgated as a preferred, or at least legitimate, option" (12); Robertson, *Ten Offenses*, 149; Reed, "What do Religious Conservatives Really Want?," 3; McLellan, *Christians in the Political Arena*, 59; Robertson, *Turning Tide*, 21–22.

40. Frohnen, *New Communitarians*, 229, also 15; Neuhaus, "From Providence to Privacy," 61, 63; Colson and Neuhaus, *Evangelicals and Catholics Together*, xxiii. See also Frohnen, "Commitment and Obligation," 169–70; and McClay, "Mr. Emerson's Tombstone"; Colson and Neuhaus, *Evangelicals and Catholics Together*, xxiii.

41. Reed, *Politically Incorrect*, 77, 78; Byrd, "Plight of our Nation," S6999.

42. *Listen, America!* 249; Robertson, *Turning Tide*, 112–13.

43. Falwell, *America Can Be Saved!* 118; idem, *Listen, America!* 253–54.

44. Weigel, "Faith, Freedom, Responsibility," 50; Perkins, "Justice Sunday."

45. Henry, *Twilight of a Great Civilization*, 175; Reed, *Politically Incorrect*, 33–34.

46. Reed, *Politically Incorrect*, 36–37.

47. McLellan, *Christians in the Political Arena*, 103–04; Falwell, *Fundamentalist Phenomenon*, 58; Johnson, "God and the Americans," 26 (Johnson notes that many of the first American settlers saw themselves as akin to the ancient Israelites); Robertson, *Ten Offenses*, chap. 1; Falwell, *America Can Be Saved!* 21–24; see also Watson, *Christian Coalition*, 96–100; and Falwell, *Listen, America!* 49.

48. *Listen, America!* 16. And as with any overarching claim, there are always exceptions, figures who reject at least a stronger reading of such providentialism. Edward Dobson, a close associate of Jerry Falwell, wrote that "[a]s fundamentalists, we believe that God was sovereignly involved in the founding of this nation but that he was no more sovereignly involved in its affairs than he is in the affairs of any other nation (*Bible, Politics, and Democracy*, 11). Yet this is the same Edward Dobson who just a few years earlier wrote the following passage, with Falwell: "One cannot help but observe that Columbus's discovery of America came less than twenty-five years before the beginning of the Reformation in Europe. It was as if God had preserved a great 'Island in the Sea' as a place of refuge for persecuted believers from continental Europe" (*Fundamentalist Phenomenon*, 58).

See Falwell, *Listen, America!* 29; also McLellan, *Christians in the Political Arena*, 103–06; *WallBuilders*, Summer 2006. As Pat Robertson puts it, "In Vietnam, for the first time in America's history, our armed forces were defeated in a major war, a war whose beginning coincided with the Supreme Court's decision to ban God from our schools" (*Turning Tide*, 296).

49. Quotations taken from Bush, "President's Remarks" (14 September 2001) and "Address to a Joint Session" (20 September 2001). See also Bostdorff, "George W. Bush's Post-September 11 Rhetoric."

50. Bush, "Second Inaugural Address."

51. Lincoln, "To Henry L. Pierce and others" [6 April 1859], *Collected Works*, III: 376.

52. I return to this distinction between Lincoln and the Christian Right in chapter 6, where I use their rhetoric to illustrate progressive and traditionalist jeremiads, respectively.

53. I am, of course, oversimplifying a complex topic here; for helpful discussions see O'Neill, *Originalism*, and Whittington, *Constitutional Interpretation*.

54. See the work of Michael McConnell, e.g., "Accommodation of Religion." On constitutional interpretation, contrast the approach of Justice Scalia with that exemplified by Justice Thurgood Marshall. For a concise statement of objections to the "living constitution" argument, see Rehnquist, "Notion of a Living Constitution."

55. Crapanzano, *Serving the Word*. I thank Bill Olmsted for bringing this work to my attention.

56. Watson, *Christian Coalition*, chap. 7.

57. Foner, *Story of American Freedom*; Richards, *Identity*; Morone, *Hellfire Nation*.

58. Reed, *Politically Incorrect*, chap. 16; Cromartie, *Disciples and Democracy*, 1.

Chapter 5

1. Danforth, *Brief recognition*, 10; Arch, *Authorizing the Past*, 109; Minter, "Puritan Jeremiad," 50. So effective were these Jeremiahs, in fact, that they persuaded countless scholars that declension was in fact happening in New-England; in recent years, scholars have come to see a more complex picture of social development. See Henretta, "Morphology"; Greene, *Pursuits of Happiness*. Morone (*Hellfire Nation*) locates anxieties over sexuality and the government of the family as fundamental to American moralism since the earliest days in New-England.

2. Jenkins, *Decade of Nightmares*. It may also be worth noting that the early 1960s represents the high point of Robert Putnam's measurement of social capital; see *Bowling Alone*.

3. Moore, *So Help Me God*, 199.

4. Falwell, *America Can Be Saved!* 23.

5. Contrast, for example, Reed's account with that found in Diana C. Eck, *New Religious America*. For a comparable account, less explicitly focused on the present but which would take issue with monolithic claims about Christian hegemony in the American past, see Schmidt, *Restless Souls*. Contrast, too, Mohr, *Long Arc of Justice*; and Richards, *Case for Gay Rights*.

6. Allan Hertzke's account of the Pat Robertson and Jesse Jackson presidential campaigns of 1988 views each of them as a populist crusade, and provides an illuminating window on the ways in which such populism often coexists uneasily with American pluralism. See Hertzke, *Echoes of Discontent*. See also Smith, *Christian America?*; Hunter, *Evangelicalism*; and Watson, *Christian Coalition*, chap. 7.

7. Such openings in New-England were generally forced on reluctant New-England elites by English rulers during the Restoration. Those making proposals regarding the freeing of slaves generally made them as measures of military necessity aimed at ensuring political independence for the Confederacy over the longer term, and not as attacks on the basics of Confederate society. See Levine, *Confederate Emancipation*, 153.

8. Bellah et al., *Habits of the Heart*; Putnam, *Bowling Alone*; Etzioni, *Spirit of Community*.

9. For a similar argument directed particularly at Bellah and communitarians, see Bernard Yack, "Liberalism and Its Communitarian Critics"; Arneil, *Diverse Communities*.

10. Higginson, *Massachusetts in Mourning*, 10–11.

11. "The Fourth of July and the Negro" [Rochester, 4 July 1852], *Life and Writings*, II: 185; "The Slaveholders' Rebellion" [Himrods Corners, N.Y., 4 July 1862], *Life and Writings*, III: 248.

12. "First Debate with Stephen A. Douglas at Ottawa, Illinois" [21 August 1858], *Collected Works*, III: 18. Frederick Douglass also argued that the founders expected the "speedy downfall of slavery": see "The Present and Future of the Colored Race in America" [Church of the Puritans, New York City, May 1863], *Life and Writings*, III: 354. Most recently on the debates, see Guelzo, *Lincoln and Douglas*.

13. "To Henry L. Pierce and others" [6 April 1859], *Collected Works*, III: 376. The connections between Lincoln and Jefferson are skillfully probed in Holland, *Bonds of Affection*, chaps. 5–7.

14. See, e.g., Striner, *Father Abraham*, chap. 4. This idea of honoring the founders' intentions is quite different from the school of "originalism" or "original intent"

jurisprudence, which as we saw in chapter 4 interprets such intentions in ways to mini-mize variation between past and present.

15. Wolin, "Contract and Birthright," 183.

16. Franklin D. Roosevelt, "State of the Union Address" and "Acceptance Speech." For a recent assessment of the Economic Bill of Rights and its importance to contem-porary American politics, see Sunstein, *Second Bill of Rights*.

17. Richards, *The Case for Gay Rights*, 42.

18. White, *Content of the Form*, chap. 1.

19. Crites, "Narrative Quality of Experience"; Gutterman, *Prophetic Politics*; also Glaude, *Exodus!*

20. Hauerwas, *Community of Character*, 9.

21. See Bruce Lincoln, *Holy Terrors*. Commenting on Jerry Falwell's post–Septem-ber 11 remarks, Lincoln offered the following analysis: in Falwell's view, "There is a good, faithful Christian America that has been brought to mortal peril by the actions and views of another part of the nation that is secular and immoral. Secular America was the problem, to which Christian America...was the solution" (38).

22. Cronon, "Place for Stories," 1350.

23. Cronon, "Place for Stories," 1350; Kort, *Narrative Elements*, 62; Tudor, *Politi-cal Myth*, 123; Putnam, *Bowling Alone*. See also Toolan, *Narrative*, 3.

24. See Blight, "'For Something Beyond the Battlefield'"; also Blum, *Reforging the White Republic*, and Blight, *Race and Reunion*.

25. See Coutu, "Narrative." The moral decline–divine punishment narrative repre-sents a particularly salient version of cultural politics in the American tradition; for the best recent treatment of this phenomenon, see Leege et al., *Politics of Cultural Difference*.

26. Hunter, *Culture Wars*.

27. "To Caleb Russell and Sallie A. Fenton" [5 January 1863], *Collected Works*, VI: 40; Lincoln, *Collected Works*, VII: 512.

Chapter 6

1. Machiavelli, *Discourse*, Preface to Book II; Stephen Foster, *Their Solitary Way*, 126.

2. *School District of Abington Township, Pennsylvania, et al. v. Schempp et al.*, 224.

3. *Schempp* at 213, 222.

4. *Schempp* at 234, 237, 241.

5. *Schempp* at 309, 312; see also *Cantwell v. Connecticut*.

6. Franklin, "Pennsylvanians Lead School Prayer Revolt."

7. http://archives.cnn.com/2001/US/09/14/Falwell.apology/

8. Brooks, "On Creating a Usable Past," 339.

9. Neuhaus, *Naked Public Square*, 102. See also Neuhaus, "What the Fundamen-talists Want," 16–18; and Dobson, "Bible, Politics, and Democracy," 3–4.

10. See, e.g., Balmer, *Thy Kingdom Come*.

11. David Carr refers to "the quintessential element of narrative, the crisis or turn-ing point," as "the stuff of communal life"; see *Time, Narrative, and History*, 159. More generally on the role of the sixties in subsequent American political narratives, see Jenkins, *Decade of Nightmares*.

12. Hall, *Last American Puritan*, 55–58.

13. "[T]he past which is the object of nostalgia must in some fashion be a per-sonally experienced past rather than one drawn solely...from chronicles, almanacs, history books, memorial tablets, or, for that matter, legend"; see Fred Davis, *Yearning for Yesterday*, 8; also Wildschut et al., "Nostalgia," 976. See also Sedikides et al., "Nos-talgia: Conceptual Issues," 202; Lowenthal, *Past Is a Foreign Country*, 11. Lowenthal's

wording—nostalgia "attracts or afflicts"—nicely highlights the combination of long-ing and regret that lie at the heart of nostalgia.

14. Sedikides et al., "Nostalgia: Conceptual Issues," 203–08; Lowenthal, *Past Is a Foreign Country*, 208; Dudden, "Nostalgia and the American," 517; emphasis in origi-nal. See also Davis, *Yearning for Yesterday*, 16; Leboe and Ansons, "On Misattributing," 596.

15. Wildschut et al., "Nostalgia," 988. Nostalgia returns us to a place of signif-icance in our lives, "a world as it was once established in a place" (Casey, "World of Nostalgia"); Lowenthal, *Past Is a Foreign Country*, 41–46, 335; Sedikides et al., "Nostalgia: Conceptual Issues," 206; Leboe and Ansons, "On Misattributing," 607.

16. Falwell, *Listen, America!* 205; on Moore, see the account online at http://pewforum.org/news/display.php?NewID=2868 (accessed 22 May 2007).

17. Davis, *Yearning for Yesterday*, 105.

18. See Quayle's speech; also Gertrude Himmelfarb, *One Nation*.

19. Warner, "De-Europeanization of American Christianity," 248–49.

20. Reed, *Politically Incorrect*, 36–37.

21. Hesiod, *Works and Days*; Juvenal, *Satire 6*; Ovid, *Metamorphoses*; see also, in the Chinese Confucian tradition, the presentation of the Sage Kings Yao, Shun, and Yu, in the *Mencius*; Baldry, "Who Invented the Golden Age?" To be more precise, Hesiod referred to a golden *race*, not a golden *age*; for the golden age, see Ovid, *Metamorphoses*, I: "That first age was an age of gold: no law and no compulsion then were needed; all kept faith; the righteous way was freely willed" (6).

22. Lowenthal, *Past Is a Foreign Country*, 25. See also Anthony D. Smith, *Myths and Memories*, 260–65; Smith, *Chosen Peoples*, 190.

23. Johnson, "Almost-Chosen People," 6 (also 9–12); Eastland, "In Defense of Religious America," 39; Bennett, "Religious Belief," 366. See also Byrd, "Plight of our Nation," S6994: "[E]arly American documents reflect aspirations, which are, at their core, based on a belief in a Supreme Being and on the existence of a human soul."

See also Johnson, "God and the Americans," 31: Johnson continues by arguing that the young American republic was "religious not necessarily in its forms but in its bones" (31); also Elshtain, "Religion and American Democracy."

24. See Hamburger, *Separation of Church and State*.

25. For details of these incidents, see the following: Winthrop, *Journal*; Godbeer, "'Cry of Sodom'"; Archer, *Fissures in the Rock*, chaps. 6, 7; David D. Hall, *Worlds of Wonder*; Arch, *Authorizing the Past*, 115–17; and Pestana, *Quakers and Baptists*.

26. Breen, *Transgressing the Bounds*, 6; Arch, *Authorizing the Past*, 115–16. On Williams and Hutchinson, see my *Conscience and Community*, chap. 2.

27. Miller, *New-England Mind: The Seventeenth Century*, 474.

28. Miller, *New-England Mind: The Seventeenth Century*, 474; 22.

29. Morone, *Hellfire Nation*; Jenkins, *Decade of Nightmares*.

30. Coontz, *Way We Never Were*, 9; also chaps. 2, 15–17.

31. Wolin, "Contract and Birthright."

32. Greenfeld, *Nationalism*, 458–60.

33. Nash, *Rights of Nature*.

34. King, "Beyond Vietnam."

35. Dienstag, *Dancing in Chains*, 3.

Chapter 7

1. Pat Buchanan, "Speech to the 1992 Republican National Convention"; O'Reilly, *Culture Warrior*, Preface; Moyers, "This is Your Story."

2. Buchanan, "Speech to the 1992 Republican National Convention."

3. O'Reilly, *Culture Warrior*, Introduction.

4. Moyers, "This Is Your Story."

5. Moyers, "Keynote Address to Call to Renewal." For a sympathetic profile and analysis of Call to Renewal, see Gutterman's *Prophetic Politics*, chap. 5.

6. Hunter, *Culture Wars*, 42, 44–45.

7. Hunter, *Culture Wars*, 50. The speeches by Buchanan and Moyer certainly bear out this observation. See also Hunter's remarks at Pew Forum, "Is There a Culture War?" That forum was later published as Hunter and Wolfe, *Is There a Culture War?*

8. Wuthnow, *Restructuring of American Religion*, chaps. 5–7. This finding has been repeatedly verified over the past two decades. See also Hunter, *Culture Wars*, chap. 3. On American Islam, see Safi, "Progressive Islam in America."

9. The literature on this topic is voluminous, and much of it gets into technical questions of measurement and methodology that are beyond my focus here. For just a few examples, see Davis and Robinson, "Religious Orthodoxy in American Society"; Miller and Hoffmann, "The Growing Divisiveness"; and especially Fiorina, *Culture War?*

See Wolfe, *One Nation After All*. Hunter's publication, just three years after *Culture Wars*, of a book entitled *Before the Shooting Begins* did little to allay the charge that Hunter's martial and combat metaphors overstated his case. See also Hunter, *Culture Wars*, 43, 59–61, 159–60.

10. Leege et al., *Politics of Cultural Differences*, 5, also chap. 3; Layman, *Great Divide*, x. See also the papers published in Campbell, *A Matter of Faith?*

11. This aspect of Buchanan's critique is especially clear in his book *State of Emergency*.

12. See Carr, *Time, Narrative, and History*, 157; Layman, *Great Divide*, chaps. 3–5.

13. E.g., Richards, *Case for Gay Rights*.

14. On the importance of the turning point, see Carr, *Time, Narrative, and History*, 159.

Chapter 8

1. Bellah, *Broken Covenant*, 142, 151.

2. Smith, *Chosen Peoples*, 24–25. This understanding of national identity echoes Smith's definition of a nation: "a named human population sharing an historical territory, common myths and historical memories, a mass, public culture, and common economic and common legal rights and duties for all members"; see his *Myths and Memories*, 11.

See Billig, *Banal Nationalism*, 77; Friedrich and Brzezinski, *Totalitarian Dictatorship and Autocracy*, 99.

3. McKenna, *Puritan Origins of American Patriotism*, 7; Greenfeld, *Nationalism*, 402; Lambert, *Founding Fathers*.

4. See McKenna, *Puritan Origins*, 86–87; Noll, *America's God*. Matthew S. Holland has recently sketched out an enduring American commitment to "civic charity," the foundations of which were laid by the New-England founders and which found some of its greatest articulators in John Winthrop, Thomas Jefferson, and Abraham Lincoln; see Holland, *Bonds of Affection*. See also Jewett, *Mission and Menace*.

5. McKenna, *Puritan Origins*, 6.

6. Hutchinson and Lehmann, *Many Are Chosen*. The contributors to this volume explore such varied "chosen" nations and peoples as Great Britain, France, Germany, South Africa, the United States, African-Americans, Israel, Sweden, and Switzerland. See Anthony D. Smith, *Chosen Peoples*; see also his "Ethnic Election and National

Destiny," and Guyatt, *Providence*, Introduction. On America more particularly, see Tuveson, *Redeemer Nation*; Hatch, *Sacred Cause of Liberty*; Hughes, *Myths America Lives By*; and McKenna, *Puritan Origins*.

7. McKenna, *Puritan Origins*; Guyatt, *Providence*; Jewett, *Mission and Menace*.

8. Bellah, *Broken Covenant*, chap. 2; Jewett and Lawrence, *Captain America and the Crusade*, 8–9; also chaps. 4, 5. This book represents an updating and elaboration of Jewett's earlier book *The Captain America Complex*.

9. Bercovitch, "Typology of America's Mission."

10. Walter Russell Mead, "God's Country?"

11. William Pfaff, "Manifest Destiny," 54.

12. Niebuhr and Heimert, *A Nation So Conceived*, 126, 128.

13. See, e.g., Wall, "Editorial"; Bellah, *Broken Covenant*, chap. 2; see also Moorhead, "American Israel."

14. Buchanan, *State of Emergency*; Huntington, *Who Are We?*; Dobbs has used his television program *Lou Dobbs Tonight* (CNN) to keep the immigration issue before viewers for much of the first decade of the twenty-first century.

15. Text of letter taken from http://goodeblessamerica.com/ (accessed 8 February 2007).

16. The RSC's Web site described the group as dedicated to "a limited and Constitutional role for the federal government, a strong national defense, the protection of individual and property rights, and the preservation of traditional family values." See Republican Study Committee, "About RSC."

17. Especially since one of the top ten RSC priorities for 2006 involved religious freedom and religion in the public square; for Goode's disavowal of religious tests, see his "Save Judeo-Christian Values."

18. Swarns, "Congressman Criticizes Election of Muslim." See, more generally, Strum and Tarantolo, *Muslims in the United States*.

19. Goode, "Save Judeo-Christian Values." Pat Buchanan uses the language of invasion in discussing immigration, though he focuses on Mexico and not the Middle East; see Buchanan, *State of Emergency*.

20. Schlesinger, *Dis-Uniting of America*; Huntington, *Who Are We?*

21. Huntington, *Who Are We?*, xvii.

22. Buchanan, "The Dark Side of Diversity."

23. Hunter and Franz, "Religious Pluralism and Civil Society," 258; see also Renshon, "America at a Crossroads," 7.

24. *American Jeremiad*, 176, 159; see also 6, 8, 31, 55; Bercovitch, *Puritan Origins*, 100. See also Bercovitch, "Historiography," 270–72.

25. Bercovitch, *American Jeremiad*, xii–xiv, 6, 31.

26. Bercovitch, *American Jeremiad*, 31. The darker interpretation of the jeremiad owes much to the work of Perry Miller, especially *The New England Mind: From Colony to Province*.

27. Miller, *New England Mind: Colony to Province*, 22.

28. Glaude, *Exodus!* 49–53.

29. See Warner, "De-Europeanization of American Christianity," esp. 247–48.

30. Schmidt, *Restless Souls*; Eck, *New Religious America*; Kurien, "Mr. President," esp. 131ff; see also the essays collected in Tweed, *Retelling U. S. Religious History*.

31. See Lasch, *True and Only Heaven*.

32. See the essays in Prothero, *Nation of Religions*; also Leonard et al., *Immigrant Faiths*.

33. Higham, *Hanging Together*, esp. chaps. 5–7; Hollinger, *Postethnic America*.

34. Whitman, *Democratic Vistas*, 425.

Bibliography

This bibliography is divided into primary and secondary sources. Such a division roughly denotes the distinction between jeremiads themselves (the primary building blocks of the account in part I and much of chapter 7) on the one hand, and scholarship about the jeremiad on the other. The categories are not always airtight, of course, and readers who fail to locate a reference in one list should consult the other.

Primary Sources

Abbott, John S. C. *An Address upon Our National Affairs, Delivered in Cheshire, Conn., on the National Fast, January 4th, 1861*. New York: Abbey & Abbott, 1861.

Adams, Brooks. *The Law of Civilization and Decay: An Essay on History*. New York: Macmillan, 1895.

Adams, William. *Christian Patriotism*. New York: Anson D. F. Randolph, 1863.

Adams, William. *Christianity and Civil Government: A Discourse Delivered on Sabbath Evening November 10, 1850*. New York: Charles Scribner, 1851.

Adams, William. *Gods Eye on the Contrite*. Boston, 1685.

Adams, William. "Prayer for Rulers, or, Duty of Christian Patriots" (1861). In *Fast Day Sermons*.

Allen, James. *New-Englands Choicest Blessing and the mercy most to be desired by all that wish well to this people: Cleared in a sermon preached before the Court of Election at Boston on May 28, 1679*. Boston, 1679.

America and her Slave-System; or, The morals and manners of the Americans as exemplified by their conduct to their fellow-beings of the coloured race, both bond and free. London: Simpkin, Marshall, 1845.

American and Foreign Anti-Slavery Society. *An Address to the Anti-Slavery Christians of the United States*. New York, 1852.

American Society for Promoting National Unity. New York: John F. Trow, 1861.

Ames, Charles G. *Dead Flies in Precious Ointment: A Discourse on Morals in America: Delivered in the Unitarian Church, Albany, NY, Sunday, July 3, 1864*. Albany: J. Munsell, 1864.

"Annual Meeting of the Massachusetts Anti-Slavery Society" [from *The Liberator* 13 February 1857]. In Nelson, *Documents of Upheaval*.

Arnold, Samuel. *David Serving His Generation, or, A discourse wherein is shewed that the great care and endeavour of every Christian ought to be that he may be serviceable unto God and to the present generation : delivered in a sermon preached to the General Court of the colony of New-Plimouth in New-England on the 3d. day of June 1674, being the day of election there*. Cambridge, Mass., 1674.

B.W. "To the Courteous Reader, especially the Inhabitants of the Town of Weathersfield, and Lancaster, in New-England." In Rowlandson, *Possibility*.

Barnes, Albert. *The Conditions of Peace. A Thanksgiving Discourse delivered in the First Presbyterian Church, Philadelphia, November 27, 1862*. Philadelphia: Henry B. Ashmead, 1863.

Barnes, Albert. *The Throne of Iniquity, or, Sustaining Evil by Law: a Discourse in behalf of a Law prohibiting the Traffic in Intoxicating Drinks*. New York: American Temperance Union, 1852.

Beecher, Henry Ward. "The Battle Set in Array" (1861). In Cherry, *God's New Israel*.

Beecher, Henry Ward. *Oration at the Raising of the "Old Flag" at Sumter; and Sermon on the Death of Abraham Lincoln, President of the United States*. Manchester, England: Alexander Ireland and Co., 1865.

Beecher, Henry Ward. *Patriotic Addresses in America and England from 1850 to 1885*. New York: Fords, Howard & Hulbert, 1891.

Beecher, Henry Ward. "Peace, Be Still" (1861). In *Fast Day Sermons*.

Bellah, Robert N., Richard Madsen, William M. Sullivan, and Ann Swidler. *Habits of the Heart: Individualism and Commitment in American Life*. New York: Harper and Row, 1985.

Bellows, Rev. Henry W. "The Crisis of Our National Disease." In *Fast Day Sermons*.

Bennett, William J. *The Death of Outrage: Bill Clinton and the Assault on American Ideals*. New York: Free Press, 1998.

Bennett, William J. *The De-Valuing of America: The Fight for Our Culture and Our Children*. Colorado Springs, Colo.: Focus on the Family, 1994.

Bennett, William J. *The Index of Leading Cultural Indicators: American Society at the End of the 20th Century*. Rev. ed. New York: Doubleday, 1999.

Bennett, William J. "Religious Belief and the Constitutional Order." In Neuhaus and Cromartie, *Piety and Politics*.

Bishop, John. "Christian Reader." In Wakeman, *Sound Repentance*.

Boardman, Henry A. *Thanksgiving in War, A Sermon preached in the Tenth Presbyterian Church, on the 28th Day of November, 1861*. Philadelphia: C. Sherman & Son, 1861.

Boardman, Henry. *What Christianity Demands of us at the Present Crisis: A Sermon Preached on Thanksgiving Day, November 29, 1860*. Philadelphia: J. B. Lippincott, 1860.

Booth, Robert Russell. *Personal Forgiveness and Public Justice. A Sermon preached in the Mercer St. Presbyterian Church, New York, 23, 1865*. New York: Anson D. F. Randolph, 1865.

Bork, Robert. *Slouching Toward Gomorrah: Modern Liberalism and American Decline*. New York: Regan/HarperCollins, 1996.

Brainerd, Thomas. *Patriotism Aiding Piety: A Sermon Preached in the Third Presbyterian Church, Philadelphia, April 30, 1863*. Philadelphia: W.F. Geddes, 1863.

Breckinridge, Dr. Robert J. *Discourse of Dr. Breckinridge, Delivered on the Day of National Humiliation, January 4, 1861, at Lexington, Ky*. Baltimore: John W. Woods, 1861.

Brewer, D. R. *The Wrath of Man Compelled to Praise God: A Sermon Preached in St. Paul's Church, Yonkers, N.Y., on Sunday Evening, May 4th, 1862*. New York: Anson D. F. Randolph, 1862.

Brown, B. Peyton. *A Sermon Preached at Mt. Tabor Methodist E. Church, January 4, 1861, Being the National Fast Day*. Baltimore: Wm. Innes, 1861.

Buchanan, Patrick J. "The Dark Side of Diversity." May 1, 2007. http://buchanan. org/blog/?p=731

Buchanan, Patrick J. *The Death of the West: How Dying Populations and Immigrant Invasions Imperil Our Country and Civilization*. New York: St. Martins, 2002.

Buchanan, Patrick J. "Speech to the 1992 Republican National Convention, Houston, Texas." http://www.buchanan.org/pa-92-0817-rnc.html

Buchanan, Patrick J. *State of Emergency: The Third World Invasion and Conquest of America*. New York: Thomas Dunne, 2006.

Bush, George W. "Address to a Joint Session of Congress and the American People" (20 September 2001). http://www.whitehouse.gov/news/releases/2001/09/20010920-8.html

Bush, George W. "President's Remarks at National Day of Prayer and Remembrance" (14 September 2001). http://www.whitehouse.gov/news/releases/2001/09/20010914-2.html

Bush, George W. Second Inaugural Address. 20 January 2005. http://www.whitehouse.gov/news/releases/2005/01/20050120-1.html

Bushnell, Horace. *A Discourse on the Slavery Question, Delivered in the North Church, Hartford, Thursday Evening, Jan. 10, 1839*. Hartford, Conn.: Case, Tiffany, 1839.

Bushnell, Horace. *Reverses Needed. A Discourse Delivered on the Sunday after the Disaster of Bull Run, in the North Church, Hartford*. Hartford, Conn.: L. E. Hunt, 1861.

Byrd, Robert. "The Plight of Our Nation," *Congressional Record—Senate*, 106th Congress, July 17, 2000.

Canfield, Sherman B. *The American Crisis: A Discourse Delivered on the Day of National Thanksgiving, November 24th, 1864*. Syracuse, N.Y.: Journal Book and Job Office, 1865.

Carey, George W., and Bruce Frohnen, eds. *Community and Tradition: Conservative Perspectives on the American Experience*. Lanham, Md.: Rowman & Littlefield, 1998.

Carey, Isaac E. *The War an Occasion for Thanksgiving: A Discourse for Thanksgiving, Preached at Keokuk, Iowa, November 28, 1861*. Keokuk, Iowa: Daily Gate City Print, 1861.

Carter, Jimmy. "The Crisis of Confidence Speech." http://www.pbs.org/wgbh/amex/carter/filmmore/ps_crisis.html

Chase, Carlton. *A Discourse, Delivered in Trinity Church. Claremont, January 4. 1861, Being the Day Appointed by the President of the United States, for General Fasting and Prayer on Account of the Distracted State of the Country*. Claremont, N.H.: George G. and Lemuel N. Ide, 1861.

Cheever, George B. *Fire and Hammer of God's Word Against the Sin of Slavery*. New York: American Abolition Society, 1858.

Cheever, George B. *The Guilt of Slavery and the Crime of Slaveholding, Demonstrated from the Hebrew and Greek Scriptures*. Boston: John P. Jewett, 1860.

Cheever, George B. *Responsibility of the Church and Ministry Respecting the Sin of Slavery*. Boston: J. P. Jewett, 1858.

Cherry, Conrad, ed. *God's New Israel: Religious Interpretations of American Destiny*. Rev. ed. Chapel Hill: University of North Carolina Press, 1998.

Chesebrough, David B., ed. *"God Ordained This War": Sermons on the Sectional Crisis, 1830–1865*. Columbia: University of South Carolina Press, 1991.

Chew, John. *God's Judgments Teaching Righteousness: A Sermon Delivered on the National Fast Day, January 4, 1861, in St. Matthew's Parish, Prince George's County, Md.* Washington, D.C.: R. A. Waters, 1861.

Clapp, A. Huntington. *God's Purpose in the War: A Sermon preached in the Beneficent Congregational Church, Providence, R.I., May 12, 1861*. Providence, R.I.: Knowles, Anthony, 1861.

Cleaveland, E. L. *A Discourse on the Existing State of Morals in the City of New Haven, Delivered Before the New Haven Washington Temperance Union, in the Court Street Church, Sabbath Evening, Oct. 21st, 1850*. New Haven, Conn.: J. H. Benham, 1850.

Colson, Charles W. "The Common Cultural Task: The Culture War from a Protestant Perspective." In Colson and Neuhaus, *Evangelicals and Catholics*.

Colson, Charles, and Richard John Neuhaus, ed. *Evangelicals and Catholics Together: Toward a Common Mission*. Dallas, Tex.: Word Publishing, 1995.

Colson, Charles, with Ellen Santilli Vaughn. *Kingdoms in Conflict*. Grand Rapids, Mich.: Zondervan/William Morrow, 1987.

Cromartie, Michael, ed. *Disciples and Democracy: Religious Conservatives and the Future of American Politics*. Washington, D.C., and Grand Rapids, Mich.: Ethics and Public Policy Center, and Eerdmans, 1994.

Crummell, Alexander. "The Destined Superiority of the Negro" (1877). In Pinn, *Moral Evil and Redemptive Suffering*.

Cummins, George. *The African a Trust from God to the American: A Sermon Delivered on the Day of National Humiliation, Fasting and Prayer, in St. Peter's Church, Baltimore*. Baltimore: John D. Toy, 1861.

Dabney, Robert L. "The Christian's Best Motive for Patriotism" (1860). In *Fast Day Sermons*.

Danforth, Samuel. *A Brief Recognition of New England's Errand into the Wilderness*. Cambridge, Mass., 1670.

Davenport, John. *Gods Call to His People to Turn unto Him, Together with His Promise to Turn unto Them*. Cambridge, Mass., 1669.

Davis, Jefferson. "To J. J. Pettis, 4 January 1861." In *Jefferson Davis: The Essential Writings*, ed. William J. Cooper Jr. New York: Modern Library, 2003.

Dobson, Edward. "The Bible, Politics, and Democracy." In Neuhaus. *Bible, Politics*.

Doggett, D. S. *A Nation's Ebenezer: A Discourse Delivered in the Broad St. Methodist Church Richmond, Virginia, Thursday, September 18, 1862: The Day of Public Thanksgiving, Appointed by the President of the Confederate States*. Richmond, Va.: Enquirer, 1862.

Dorr, Benjamin. *The American Vine: A Sermon Preached in Christ's Church, Philadelphia, Friday, January 4, 1861. On Occasion of the National Fast*. Philadelphia: Collins, 1861.

Douglass, Frederick. *The Life and Writings of Frederick Douglass*. Ed. Philip S. Foner. 4 vols. New York: International Publishers, 1950.

Douglass, Frederick. "Speech on Emancipation Day." September 1883, Reel 15, Douglass papers, Library of Congress.

Duffield, George, Sr., *Our National Sins to be Repented of and the Grounds of Hope for the Preservation of our Federal Constitution and Union: A Discourse Delivered January 4, 1861, on the Day of Fasting, Humiliation, and Prayer Appointed by the President of the United States*. Detroit, Mich.: Free Press Mammoth Book and Job Printing House, 1861.

Dwinell, Israel E. *Hope for Our Country: A Sermon Preached, in the South Church, Salem, October 19, 1862*. Salem, Mass.: Charles W. Swasey, 1862.

Eastland, Terry. "In Defense of Religious America." *Commentary* 71 (June 1981): 39–45.

Elliot, Charles. *Sinfulness of American Slavery, Proved from Its Evil Sources, Its Injustice, Its Wrongs, Its Contrariety to Many Scriptural Commands, Prohibitions, and Principles, and to the Christian Spirit, and from Its Evil Effects, Together With Observations On Emancipation And The Duties Of American Citizens In Regard To Slavery*. 2 vols. New York, 1850.

Elliot, Stephen. "Ezra's Dilemma" (1863). In Chesebrough, *"God Ordained this War."*

Elshtain, Jean Bethke. "Religion and American Democracy." In *Religion, Politics, and the American Experience: Reflections on Religion and American Public Life*, ed. Edith L. Blumhofer. Tuscaloosa and London: University of Alabama Press, 2002.

Elshtain, Jean Bethke. *Who Are We? Critical Reflections and Hopeful Possibilities*. Grand Rapids, Mich.: Eerdmans, 2000.

Etzioni, Amitai. *The Spirit of Community: The Reinvention of American Society*. New York: Simon & Schuster, 1994.

Falwell, Jerry. "An Agenda for the 1980s." In Neuhaus and Cromartie, *Piety and Politics*.

Falwell, Jerry. *America Can Be Saved!* Murfreesboro, Tenn.: Sword of the Lord Publishers, 1979.

Falwell, Jerry, ed. *The Fundamentalist Phenomenon: The Resurgence of Conservative Christianity*. With Ed Dobson and Ed Hinson. Garden City, N.Y.: Doubleday, 1981.

Falwell, Jerry. "God's Plan to Save a Nation" (1996). http://trbc.org/new/sermons.php?url=960721.html

Falwell, Jerry. *If I Should Die Before I Wake*. Nashville, Tenn.: Thomas Nelson, 1986.

Falwell, Jerry. *Listen, America!* Garden City, N.Y.: Doubleday, 1980.

Fast Day Sermons, or The Pulpit on the State of the Country. New York: Rudd & Carleton, 1861.

Fitch, John. *An Holy Connexion; Or a True Agreement Between Jehovahs Being a Wall of Fire to His People, and the Glory in the Midst Thereof, Or a Word in Season to Stir up to a Solemn Acknowledgement of the Gracious Protection of God over his People, and Especially to a Holy Care that the Presence of God May Yet Be Continued with Us. As it was Delivered in a Sermon Preached at Hartford on Conecticut in NE May 14, 1674, Being the Day of Election There*. Cambridge, Mass., 1674.

Foxe, John. *Actes and Monuments of these Latter and Perillous Days, Touching Matters of the Church*. London, 1563.

Freeman, George E. *God in Our National Affairs. A Sermon Delivered in Trinity Chapel, Neponset, Sabbath Morning, April 16, 1865*. Boston: Alfred Mudge and Son, 1865.

Frohnen, Bruce. "Commitment and Obligation." In Carey and Frohnen, *Community and Tradition*.

Frohnen, Bruce. *The New Communitarians and the Crisis of Modern Liberalism*. Lawrence: University Press of Kansas, 1996.

Frohnen, Bruce. *Virtue and the Promise of Conservatism: The Legacy of Burke and Tocqueville*. Lawrence: University of Kansas Press, 1993.

Furness, Rev. W. H. *A Discourse Delivered on the Occasion of the National Fast, September 26th, 1861, in the First Congregational Unitarian Church in Philadelphia*. Philadelphia: T. B. Pugh, 1861.

Gannett, Ezra S. "Repentance amidst Deliverance." In *Two Discourses Preached in Arlington-Street Church, July 12 and July 19, 1863*. Boston: Crosby and Nichols, 1863.

Garrison, William Lloyd. "Appalling Developments" [from *The Liberator*, December 8, 1837]. In Nelson, *Documents of Upheaval*.

Garrison, William Lloyd. "Fourth of July in Providence" [from *The Liberator*, July 28, 1837]. In Nelson, *Documents of Upheaval*.

Garry, Patrick M. "The Cultural Hostility to Religion." *Modern Age: A Quarterly Review* 47 (2005): 121–31.

Goode, Virgil. Letter to John Cruickshank (2006). http://goodeblessamerica.com/

Goode, Virgil. "Save Judeo-Christian Values." *USA Today*, January 2, 2007. http://www.usatoday.com/printedition/news/20070102/oppose02.art.htm

Guion, Thomas T. *A Sermon, Preached on the Day of the National Fast, January 4th, A. D. 1861, in St. John's Church, Brooklyn, N.Y.* Brooklyn, N.Y.: I. Van Anden's Print, 1861.

Gurstein, Rochelle. *The Repeal of Reticence: A History of America's Cultural and Legal Struggles over Free Speech, Obscenity, Sexual Liberation, and Modern Art*. New York: Hill & Wang, 1996.

Hammond, Phillip E. *Religion and Personal Autonomy: The Third Disestablishment in America*. Columbia: University of South Carolina Press, 1992.

Handy, Isaac. *Our National Sins. A Sermon Delivered in the First Presbyterian Church, Portsmouth, Va., January 4, 1861*. Portsmouth, Va., 1861.

Haven, Gilbert. *National Sermons. Sermons, Speeches, and Letters on Slavery and its War: From the Passage of the Fugitive Slave Bill to the Election of President Grant*. Boston: Lee and Shepard, 1869.

Henry, Carl F. H. "Making Political Decisions: An Evangelical Perspective." In Neuhaus and Cromartie, *Piety and Politics*.

Henry, Carl F. H. *Twilight of a Great Civilization: The Drift Toward Neo-paganism*. Westchester, Ill.: Crossway Books, 1988.

Hertzke, Allen D. "The Theory of Moral Ecology." *Review of Politics* 60 (1998): 629–59.

Hervey, George Winfield. *Liberty, as a Cloak of Maliciousness, a Discourse Delivered Before a Meeting of the Orthodox and Baptist Congregations in Canton, Mass., on the day of the National Fast, Jan. 4th, 1861*. New York: Sheldon and Co., 1861.

Hesiod. *Hesiod's Works and Days: A Translation and Commentary for the Social Sciences*. Translated and edited by David Tandy and Walter C. Neale. Berkeley: University of California Press, 1997.

Higginson, John. *The Cause of God and His People in New-England*. Cambridge, Mass.: Samuel Green, 1663.

Higginson, John. "Epistle Dedicatory to the Earl of Bellomont." In Noyes, *New-England's Duty*.

Higginson, Thomas Wentworth. *Massachusetts in Mourning: A Sermon, Preached in Worcester, on Sunday, June 4, 1854*. Boston: James Munroe and Company, 1854.

Himmelfarb, Gertrude. *One Nation, Two Cultures*. New York: Knopf, 1999.

Hodgman, Rev. S. A. *The Great Republic Judged, but not Destroyed; or, The Beginning and End of Slavery and the Justice of God Displayed in the Doom of Slaveholders*. 2nd ed. New York, 1865.

Holy Bible. Geneva edition.

Hooke, William. *New Englands Teares, for Old Englands Feares*. London: John Rothwell and Henry Overton, 1641.

Hooker, Samuel. *Righteousness Rained from Heaven, or a Serious and Seasonable Discourse Exciting All to an Earnest Enquiry after, and Continued Waiting for the Effusions of the Spirit, unto a Communication and Increase of Righteousness: That Faith, Holiness and Obedience May Yet Abound among Us, and the Wilderness Become a Fruitful Field, As it Was Delivered in a Sermon Preached at Hartford on Connecticut in New-England, May 10, 1677, Being the Day of Election There*. Cambridge, Mass.: Samuel Green, 1677.

Hooker, Thomas. *Thomas Hooker: Writings in England and Holland, 1626–1633*. Ed. George H. Williams, Norman Pettit, Winfried Herget, and Sargent Bush Jr. Cambridge, Mass.: Harvard University Press, 1975.

Hosmer, William. *The Higher Law, in its Relations to Civil Government: with Particular Reference to Slavery, and the Fugitive Slave Law*. Auburn, N.Y.: Derby & Miller, 1852.

Hubbard, William. *The Happiness of a People in the Wisdome of Their Rulers Directing and in the Obedience of Their Brethren Attending Unto What Israel Ought To Do, Recommended in A Sermon Before the Honourable Governour and Council, and the Respected Deputies of the Massachusets Colony in New England. Preached at Boston, May 3rd, 1676, Being the Day of Election There*. Boston: John Foster, 1676.

Hutton, Orlando. *The True Refuge in National Trouble. A Sermon, Preached January 4th, 1861*. Baltimore: W. M. Innes, 1861.

Jefferson, Thomas. *Notes on the State of Virginia*. In *Writings*, ed. Merrill D. Peterson. New York: Library of America, 1984.

Johnson, Paul. "The Almost-Chosen People: Why America Is Different." In Neuhaus, *Unsecular America*.

Johnson, Paul. "God and the Americans," *Commentary*, January 1995: 25–45.

Juvenal. *Satires*. Ed. Susanna Morton Braund. Cambridge, U.K.: Cambridge University Press, 1996.

Keteltas, Abraham. *God Arising and Pleading His People's Cause; or The American War in Favor of Liberty, Against the Measures and Arms of Great Britain, Shewn to Be the Cause of God: In a Sermon Preached October 5th, 1777, at an Evening Lecture, in the Presbyterian Church in Newbury-Port*. Newburyport, Mass.: John Mycall, 1777.

King, Martin Luther, Jr. "Beyond Vietnam" (1967). http://www.stanford.edu/group/ King/publications/speeches/Beyond_Vietnam.pdf

King, Martin Luther, Jr. *Where Do We Go from Here: Chaos or Community?* Boston: Beacon Press, 1968.

Langdon, Samuel. *The Republic of the Israelites an Example to the American States. A Sermon, Preached at Concord, in the State of New Hampshire; Before the Honorable General Court at the Annual Election, June 5, 1788*. Exeter, N.H.: Lamson and Ranlet, 1788.

Laurie, Thomas. *Three Discourses, Preached in the South Evangelical Church, West Roxbury, Mass., April 13th, 19th, and 23d, 1865*. Dedham, Mass.: John Cox, Jr., 1865.

Leacock, W. T. "Thanksgiving sermon" (1860). In Palmer and Leacock, *Rights of the South*.

Liggett, James D. "Our National Reverses" (1862). In *Sermons in American History: Selected Issues in the American Pulpit, 1630–1697*, ed. DeWitte Holland. Nashville, Tenn.: Abington Press, 1971.

Lincoln, Abraham. *The Collected Works of Abraham Lincoln*. Ed. Roy P. Basler. 8 vols. New Brunswick, N.J.: Rutgers University Press, 1953.

McClay, Wilfred. "Mr. Emerson's Tombstone." In Carey and Frohnen, *Community and Tradition*.

McGill, Alexander T. *Sinful but not Forsaken: A sermon, preached in the Presbyterian Church, Fifth Avenue and Nineteenth Street, New York, on the Day of National Fasting, January 4, 1861*. New York: Anson D. F. Randolph, 1861.

McLellan, Vern. *Christians in the Political Arena: Positive Strategies for Concerned Twentieth Century Patriots!* Charlotte, N.C.: Associates Press, 1984.

Machiavelli, Niccolo. *Discourses upon Livy*. Translated and edited by Harvey Mansfield and Nathan Tarcov Chicago: University of Chicago Press, 1996.

Mather, Cotton. *Magnalia Christi Americana*. London, 1702.

Mather, Cotton. *Things for a Distressed People to Think Upon. Election Sermon*. Boston, 1696.

Mather, Eleazer. *A Serious Exhortation to the Present and Succeeding Generations in New-England*. Cambridge, Mass., 1671.

Mather, Increase. *A Brief History of the Warr with the Indians in New-England (from June 24, 1675. When the First English-man Was Murdered by the Indians, to August 12, 1676. When Philip, Aliàs Metacomet, the Principal Author and Beginner of the Warr, Was Slain); Wherein the Grounds, Beginning, and Progress of the Warr, Is Summarily Expressed; Together with a Serious Exhortation to the Inhabitants of That Land*. Boston, 1676.

Mather, Increase. *The Day of Trouble Is Near. Two Sermons Wherein Is Shewed, What Are the Signs of a Day of Trouble Being Near. And Particularly, What Reason There Is for New-England to Expect a Day of Trouble. Also What Is to Be Done, That We May Escape*

These Things Which Shall Come to Pass. Preached the 11th Day of the 12th Moneth, 1673. Cambridge, Mass., 1674.

Mather, Increase. "A Discourse Concerning the Danger of Apostacy." In *A Call from Heaven to the Present and Succeeding Generations or, A discourse wherein is shewed I. that children of godly parents are under special advantages and encouragements to seek the Lord, II. the exceeding danger of apostasie especially as to those that are the children and posterity of such as have been eminent for God in their generation, III. that young men ought to remember God their Creator.* Boston, 1679.

Mather, Increase. *An Earnest Exhortation to the Inhabitants of New-England, To Hearken to the Voice of God in His Late and Present Dispensations As Ever They Desire to Escape Another Judgement, Seven Times Greater Then Any Thing Which as Yet Hath Been.* Boston, 1676.

Mather, Increase. *Heavens Alarm to the World. Or a Sermon Wherein is Shewed, That Fearful Sights and Signs in Heaven are the Presages of great Calamities at Hand.* Boston, 1681.

Mather, Increase. *Pray for the Rising Generation. Or a Sermon Wherein Godly Parents are Encouraged to Pray and Believe for their Children. Preached the third Day of the fifth Moneth 1678, which day was set apart by the second Church in Boston in New-England, humbly to seek unto God by Fasting and Prayer, for a Spirit of Converting Grace, to be poured out upon the Children and Rising Generation in New-England.* Boston, 1679.

Mather, Increase. *The Times of Men Are in the Hands of God. Or a Sermon Occasioned by That Awful Providence Which Happened in Boston in New England, The 4th Day of the 3rd Moneth 1675 (When Part of a Vessel Was Blown Up in the Harbor, and. Nine Men Hurt, and Three Mortally Wounded) Wherein is Shewed How We Should Sanctifie the Dreadfull Name of God Under Such Awful Dispensation.* Boston, 1675.

Mather, Increase. "To the Reader." In Samuel Torrey, *An Exhortation unto Reformation, Amplified, By a Discourse concerning the Parts and Progress of that Work, according to the Word of God. Delivered in a Sermon Preached in the Audience of the General Assembly of the Massachusetts Colony, at Boston in New-England, May 23,1677, Being the Day of Election There.* Cambridge, Mass., 1674.

Mencius. Transl. David Hinton. New York: Basic, 1998.

Miller, Zell. Speech, February 2004: http://www.pubtheo.com/page.asp?pid=1322

Mines, John Flavel. *Duty, Our Highest Right. A Sermon Preached in Grace Church, Bath, Me., on the Occasion of the National Fast, January 4, 1861.* Bath, Me.: Daily Times, 1861.

Mitchel, Jonathan. *Nehemiah on the Wall in Troublesom[e] Times; or, a Serious and Seasonable Improvement of that Great Example of Magistratical Piety and Prudence, Self-denial and Tenderness, Fearlessness and Fidelity, unto Instruction and Encouragement of Present and Succeeding Rulers in our Israel.* Cambridge, Mass., 1671.

Moore, Roy. *So Help Me God: The Ten Commandments, Judicial Tyranny, and the Battle for Religious Freedom.* Nashville, Tenn.: Broadman & Holman, 2005.

Moyers, Bill. "Keynote Address to Call to Renewal" (2004). http://www.sojo.net/index.cfm?action=magazine.article&issue=soj0408&article=040810x.

Moyers, Bill. "This Is Your Story: The Progressive Story of America. Pass It On" (2003). Online at http://www.commondreams.org/views03/0610-11.htm

The Necessity of Reformation. Boston: John Foster, 1679.

Nelson, Truman, ed. *Documents of Upheaval: Selections from William Lloyd Garrison's The Liberator, 1831–1865,* New York: Hill & Wang, 1966.

Neuhaus, Richard John, ed. *The Bible, Politics, and Democracy.* Grand Rapids, Mich.: Eerdmans, 1987.

Neuhaus, Richard John. "From Providence to Privacy: Religion and the Redefinition of America." In Neuhaus, *Unsecular America.*

Neuhaus, Richard John. *The Naked Public Square: Religion and Democracy in America.* Grand Rapids, Mich.: Eerdmans, 1984.

Neuhaus, Richard John, ed. *Unsecular America.* Grand Rapids, Mich.: Eerdmans, 1986.

Neuhaus, Richard John. "What the Fundamentalists Want." In Neuhaus and Cromartie, *Piety and Politics.*

Neuhaus, Richard John, and Michael Cromartie, eds. *Piety and Politics: Evangelicals and Fundamentalists Confront the World.* Washington, D.C.: Ethics and Public Policy Center, 1987.

Novak, Michael. *The Catholic Ethic and the Spirit of Capitalism.* New York: Free Press, 1993.

Novak, Michael. "Truth and Liberty: The Present Crisis in Our Culture." *Review of Politics* 59 (1997): 5–23.

Noyes, Nicholas. *New-England's Duty and Interest to be an Habitation of Justice and a Mountain of Holiness. Election Sermon.* Boston: B. Green and J. Allen, 1698.

Oakes, Urian. *New-England Pleaded with, And Pressed to Consider the Things which Concerne Her Peace. An Election Sermon, 1673.* Cambridge, Mass., 1673.

O'Reilly, Bill. *Culture Warrior.* New York: Broadway, 2006.

Ovid. *The Metamorphoses of Ovid.* Transl. Allen Mandelbaum. New York: Harcourt, 1993.

Oxenbridge, John. *New-England Freemen Warned and Warmed to be Free Indeed, Having an eye to God in their Elections.* Cambridge, Mass., 1673.

Paddock, Wilbur F. *God's Presence and Purpose in Our War: A Thanksgiving Discourse, Delivered in St. Andrew's Church, Philadelphia, Thursday, November 26, 1863.* Philadelphia: Caxton Press, 1864.

Palmer, Benjamin. "National Responsibility Before God" (1861). In Cherry, *God's New Israel.*

Palmer, Benjamin. "Thanksgiving sermon" (1860). In Palmer and Leacock, *Rights of the South.*

Palmer, Benjamin, and W. T. Leacock, *The Rights of the South Defended in the Pulpits.* Mobile, Ala.: J. Y. Thompson, 1860.

Parker, Theodore. *A Sermon of the Dangers Which Threaten the Rights of Man in America: Preached at the Music Hall, on Sunday, July 2, 1854.* Boston: Benjamin B. Mussey, 1854.

Pennington, James W. C. *A Text Book of the Origin and History . . . of the Colored People* (1841). In Pinn, *Moral Evil and Redemptive Suffering.*

Perkins, Tony. "Justice Sunday: Stop the Filibuster Against People of Faith" (2005). http://www.frc.org/get.cfm?i=LH05D02

Pew Forum. "Is There a Culture War?" (2006) http://pewforum.org/events/?EventID=112

Pinn, Anthony B., ed. *Moral Evil and Redemptive Suffering: A History of Theodicy in African-American Religious Thought.* Gainesville: University Press of Florida, 2002.

Popenoe, David. "The Family Condition of America: Cultural Change and Public Policy." In *Values and Public Policy*, ed. Henry J. Aaron, Thomas E. Mann, Timothy Taylor. Washington, D.C.: Brookings Institution, 1994.

Prince, Thomas. *Earthquakes the Works of God, and Tokens of his Just Displeasure. Two Sermons, on Psal. xviii. 7. At the Particular Fast in Boston, Nov. 2. and the General Thanksgiving Nov. 9. Occasioned By the Late Dreadful Earthquake.* Boston: D. Henchman, 1727.

Putnam, Robert. *Bowling Alone: The Collapse and Revival of American Community.* New York: Simon & Schuster, 2001.

Quayle, Dan. Speech to the Commonwealth Club of California. http://www.commonwealthclub.org/archive/20thcentury/92-05quayle-speech.html

Quint, Alonzo H. *National Sin Must Be Expiated By National Calamity*. In *Three Sermons Preached in the North Congregational Church, New Bedford, Mass., Fast day, April 13, and Sunday, April 16, 1865*. New Bedford, Mass.: Mercury Job Press, 1865.

Raphall, J. J. "Bible View of Slavery" (1861). In *Fast Day Sermons*.

Read, C. H. *National Fast. A Discourse Delivered on the Day of Fasting, Humiliation and Prayer, appointed by the President of the United States, January 4, 1861*. Richmond, Va.: Ritchie, Dunnavant, 1861.

Reagan, Ronald. *Abortion and the Conscience of the Nation*. Nashville, Tenn.: T. Nelson, 1984.

Reed, Ralph. *Politically Incorrect: The Emerging Faith Factor in American Politics*. Dallas, Tex.: Word Publishing, 1994.

Reed, Ralph. "What do Religious Conservatives Really Want?" In Cromartie, *Disciples and Democracy*.

Republican Study Committee. "About RSC." http://www.house.gov/hensarling/rsc/rsc_bio.shtml

Rifkin, Jeremy. *The End of Work: The Decline of the Global Labor Force and the Dawn of the Post-Market Era*. New York: Tarcher, 1994.

Ritzer, George. *The McDonaldization of Society*. Thousand Oaks, Calif.: Sage, 2004.

Robertson, Pat. *America's Dates with Destiny*. Nashville, Tenn.: Thomas Nelson, 1986.

Robertson, Pat. *The Ten Offenses*. Nashville, Tenn.: Integrity, 2004.

Robertson, Pat. *The Turning Tide: The Fall of Liberalism and the Rise of Common Sense*. Dallas, Tex.: Word Publishing, 1993.

Roosevelt, Franklin D. "Acceptance Speech for the Renomination for the Presidency, 1936." http://www.presidency.ucsb.edu/ws/print.php?pid=15314

Roosevelt, Franklin D. "State of the Union Address." In *The Public Papers & Addresses of Franklin D. Roosevelt*, ed. Samuel Rosenman. New York: Harper and Brothers, 1950.

Rousseau, Jean-Jacques. *The Government of Poland*. Transl. Willmoore Kendall. Indianapolis: Hackett, 1985.

Rousseau, Jean-Jacques. *On the Social Contract*. Transl. Maurice Cranston. London: Penguin, 1968.

Rowlandson, Joseph. *The Possibility of Gods Forsaking a People, That Have Been Visibly Near & Dear to Him Together with the Misery of a People Thus Forsaken, Set Forth in a Sermon, Preached at Weathersfield, Nov. 21, 1678. Being a Day of Fast and Humiliation*. Cambridge, Mass., 1682.

Sandoz, Ellis, ed. *Political Sermons of the Founding Era, 1730–1805*. 2 vols. Indianapolis: Liberty Press, 1998.

Schaeffer, Francis A. *A Christian Manifesto*. Westchester, Ill.: Crossway Books, 1981.

Seabury, Caroline. *The Diary of Caroline Seabury, 1854–1863*. Ed. and introd. Suzanne L. Bunkers. Madison: University of Wisconsin Press, 1991.

Sewall, Joseph. *Nineveh's Repentance and Deliverance. A Sermon Preach'd before His Excellency the Governour The Honourable Council and Representatives of the Province of the Massachusetts-Bay in New-England, on a Day of Fasting and Prayer in the Council Chamber, Dec. 3, 1740*. Boston: D. Henchman, 1740.

Shepard, Thomas. "Thomas Shepard's Election Sermon, in 1638." *New England Historical and Genealogical Register* 24 (1870): 361–66.

Shepard, Thomas. *Wine for Gospel Wantons; or, Cautions Against Spiritual Drunkenness, Being the Brief Notes of a Sermon Preached at Cambridge in New-England, upon a Day of Publick Fasting and Prayer Throughout the Colony, June 25. 1645*. Cambridge, Mass., 1668.

Slotkin, Richard, and James K. Folsom. *So Dreadfull a Judgment: Puritan Responses to King Philip's War, 1676–1677*. Middletown, Conn.: Wesleyan University Press, 1978.

Stewart, Maria. "An Address Delivered at the African Masonic Hall" (1833). In *Maria W. Stewart: America's First Black Woman Political Writer*. Ed. and introd. by Marilyn Richardson. Bloomington and Indianapolis: Indiana University Press, 1987.

Stiles, Ezra. *The United States Elevated to Glory and Honour: A Sermon Preached before Governor Trumbull and the General Assembly convened at Hartford, May 8, 1783*. New Haven, Conn., 1783.

Stoughton, William. *New-Englands True Interest; Not to Lie*. Cambridge, Mass.: S.G. and M.T., 1670.

Stowe, Harriet Beecher. "The Chimney-Corner." *Atlantic Monthly*, January 1865.

Stowe, Harriet Beecher. *Uncle Tom's Cabin*. Boston: John Jewett, 1852.

Street, Nicholas. *The American States Acting Over the Part of the Children of Israel in the Wilderness and Thereby Impeding their Entrance into Canaan's Rest: or, The Human Heart Discovering Itself Under Trials. A Sermon Preached at East-Haven, April 1777, and Occasionally at Branford*. New Haven, Conn. 1777.

Stringfellow, Thornton. *Scriptural and Statistical Views in Favor of Slavery*. Richmond, Va.: J. W. Randolph, 1856.

Strong, Josiah. *Our Country; Its Possible Future and Its Present Crisis*. New York: Baker and Taylor/American Home Missionary Society, 1885.

Sturtevant, J. M. "The Lessons of Our National Conflict." *The New Englander*, October 1861.

Sunday, Billy. " 'Booze' Sermon." http://www.billysunday.org/sermons/booze.php3

Swope, Cornelius E. *National Calamities the Fruit of National Sins*. Pittsburgh: Barr and Myers, 1861.

Taft, Horatio Nelson, *Washington During the Civil War: The Diary of Horatio Nelson Taft, 1861–1865*. http://memory.loc.gov/ammem/tafthtml

Thornwell, Rev. J. H., Jr. "Our National Sins" (1861). In *Fast Day Sermons*.

Torrey, Samuel. *An Exhortation unto Reformation, Amplified, By a Discourse concerning the Parts and Progress of that Work, according to the Word of God. Delivered in a Sermon Preached in the Audience of the General Assembly of the Massachusets Colony, at Boston in New-England, Being the Day of Election There*. Cambridge, Mass., 1674.

Torrey, Samuel. *Man's Extremity God's Opportunity. Election Sermon, 1695*. Boston, 1695.

Torrey, Samuel. *A Plea for the Life of Dying Religion, from the Word of the Lord, An Election Sermon at Boston, May 16th, 1688*. Boston, 1683.

Tucker, J. W. "God's Providence in War" (1862). In Chesebrough, *"God Ordained this War."*

Turner, Henry McNeal. "On the Anniversary of Emancipation" (1866). In Pinn, *Moral Evil and Redemptive Suffering*.

van Dyke, Rev. Henry J. "The Character and Influence of Abolitionism" (1860). In *Fast Day Sermons*.

Vinton, Francis. "Irreligion, Corruption and Fanaticism Rebuked" (1861). In *Fast Day Sermons*.

Wadsworth, Charles. *Our Own Sins. A Sermon Preached in the Arch Street Church, on the Day of Humiliation and Prayer, Appointed by the President of the United States, Friday, January 4, 1861*. Philadelphia: King and Baird, 1861.

Wakeman, Samuel. *Sound Repentance the Right Way to Escape Deserved Ruine: A Solid and Awakening Discourse, Exhorting the People of God to Comply with his Counsel, by a Hearty Practical Turning from Sin to Himself and His Service Thereby to Prevent Their Being Made Desolate by His Departing from Them. As it was Delivered in a Sermon Preached at Hartford on Conecticut in New-England, May 14th 1685. Being the Day of Election there*. Boston, 1685.

Wales, Samuel. *The Dangers of Our National Prosperity; and the Ways to Avoid Them. A Sermon, Preached before the General Assembly of the State of Connecticut, at Hartford, May 12, 1785*. Hartford, Conn.: Barlow & Babcock, 1785.

Walker, David. *David Walker's Appeal to the Coloured Citizens of the World*, ed. Peter P. Hinks. University Park, Penn.: Penn State University Press, 2000.

Walley, Edmund. *Balm in Gilead to Heal Sion's Wounds. Election Sermon, Plymouth, 1669*. Cambridge, Mass., 1669.

Walley, Thomas, and Thomas Thatcher. "To the Reader." In Samuel Arnold, *David Serving His Generation, or a Discourse Wherein is Shewed that the Great Care and Endeavour of Every Christian Ought to Be, That He May Be Serviceable unto God and to the Present Generation, Delivered in a Sermon Preached to the General Court of the Colony of New-Plimouth in New-England on the 3rd Day of June 1674, Being the Day of Election There*. Cambridge, Mass., 1674.

Webb, John. *The Duty of a Degenerate People to Pray for the Reviving of God's Work. Sermon preach'd June 18, 1734, being a Day of Prayer, with Fasting, observed by the New North Church in Boston*. Boston, 1734.

Weigel, George. "Faith, Freedom, Responsibility: Evangelicals and Catholics in the Public Square." In Colson and Neuhaus, *Evangelicals and Catholics*.

Weigel, George. "Talking the Talk: Christian Conviction and Democratic Etiquette." In Cromartie, *Disciples and Democracy*.

Whiting, John. "To the Christian Reader." In Hooker, *Righteousness Rained from Heaven*.

Whiting, John. *The Way of Israel's Welfare; or an Exhortation to Be with God, that He May Be with Us*. Boston, 1686.

Wightman, John T. *The Glory of God, the Defense of the South, A Discourse delivered in the Methodist Episcopal Church, South, Yorkville, S.C., July 28, 1861, the Day of National Thanksgiving for the Victory at Manassas*. Portland, Maine: B. Thurston and Co., 1871.

Wilson, John, and Samuel Whiting. "Christian Reader." Introduction to Higginson, *Cause of God*.

Winthrop, John. *The Journal of John Winthrop, 1630–1649*, ed. Richard Dunn, James Savage, and Laetitia Yaendle. Cambridge, Mass: Harvard University Press, 1996.

Winthrop, John. "Model of Christian Charity" (1630). In *The Winthrop Papers*, vol. II, 1623–1630. Boston: Massachusetts Historical Society, 1931.

Secondary Sources

Aamodt, Terrie Dopp. *Righteous Armies, Holy Cause: Apocalyptic Imagery and the Civil War*. Macon, Ga.: Mercer University Press, 2002.

Albrecht, Robert C. "The Theological Response of the Transcendentalists to the Civil War." *New England Quarterly* 38 (1965): 21–34.

Ammerman, Nancy T. "North American Protestant Fundamentalism." In *Fundamentalisms Observed*, ed. Martin E. Marty and R. Scott Appleby. Chicago: University of Chicago Press, 1991.

Andrews, William D. "The Literature of the 1727 New England Earthquake." *Early American Literature* 7 (1973): 281–94.

Arch, Stephen Carl. *Authorizing the Past: The Rhetoric of History in Seventeenth-Century New England*. DeKalb: Northern Illinois University Press, 1994.

Archer, Richard. *Fissures in the Rock: New England in the Seventeenth Century*. Hanover: University of New Hampshire Press/University Press of New England, 2001.

Arneil, Barbara. *Diverse Communities: The Problem with Social Capital*. Cambridge, U.K.: Cambridge University Press, 2006.

Ault, James M., Jr. *Spirit and Flesh: Life in a Fundamentalist Baptist Church*. New York: Vintage, 2004.

Axtell, James. *Natives and Newcomers: The Cultural Origins of North America*. New York: Oxford University Press, 2001.

Baldry, H. C. "Who Invented the Golden Age?" *The Classical Quarterly*. n.s., 2 (1952): 83–92.

Balmer, Randall. *Thy Kingdom Come: How the Religious Right Distorts the Faith and Threatens America*. New York: Basic, 2007.

Bellah, Robert N. *The Broken Covenant: American Civil Religion in Time of Trial*. 2nd ed. Chicago: University of Chicago Press, 1992.

Bendyna, Mark, John C. Green, Mark J. Rozell, and Clyde Wilcox. "Catholics and the Christian Right: A View from Four States." *Journal for the Scientific Study of Religion* 39 (2000): 321–32.

Bennett, Oliver. *Cultural Pessimism: Narratives of Decline in the Postmodern World*. Edinburgh: Edinburgh University Press, 2001.

Bercovitch, Sacvan. *The American Jeremiad*. Madison: University of Wisconsin Press, 1978.

Bercovitch, Sacvan. "The Historiography of Johnson's *Wonder-Working Providence*." In Vaughan and Bremer, *Puritan New England*.

Bercovitch, Sacvan. *The Puritan Origins of the American Self*. New Haven, Conn.: Yale University Press, 1975.

Bercovitch, Sacvan. "The Typology of America's Mission." *American Quarterly* 30 (1978): 135–55.

Billig, Michael. *Banal Nationalism*. Thousand Oaks, Calif.: Sage, 1995.

Blight, David W. "'For Something Beyond the Battlefield': Frederick Douglass and the Struggle for the Memory of the Civil War." *Journal of American History* 75 (1989): 1156–78.

Blight, David W. "Frederick Douglass and the American Apocalypse." *Civil War History* 31 (1985): 309–28.

Blight, David W. *Frederick Douglass' Civil War: Keeping Faith in Jubilee*. Baton Rouge: Louisiana State University Press, 1989.

Blight, David W. *Race and Reunion: The Civil War in American Memory*. Cambridge, Mass.: Harvard University Press, 2001.

Blum, Edward J. *Reforging the White Republic: Race, Religion, and American Nationalism, 1865–1898*. Baton Rouge: Louisiana State University Press, 2005.

Bodo, John R. *The Protestant Clergy and Public Issues, 1812–1848*. Princeton, N.J.: Princeton University Press, 1954.

Bostdorff, Denise M. "George W. Bush's Post–September 11 Rhetoric of Covenant Renewal: Upholding the Faith of the Greatest Generation." *Quarterly Journal of Speech* 89 (2003): 293–319.

Bozeman, Theodore Dwight. *To Live Ancient Lives: The Primitivist Dimension in Puritanism*. Chapel Hill: University of North Carolina Press, 1988.

Breen, Louise. *Transgressing the Bounds: Subversive Enterprises Among the Puritan Elite in Massachusetts, 1630–1692*. New York: Oxford University Press, 2001.

Breen, T. H. *Character of a Good Ruler: A Study of Puritan Political Ideas in New England, 1630–1730*. New Haven, Conn.: Yale University Press, 1980.

Breen, T. H., and Stephen Foster. "The Puritans' Greatest Achievement: A Study of Social Cohesion in Seventeenth-Century Massachusetts." In Vaughan and Bremer, *Puritan New England*.

Brooks, van Wyck. "On Creating a Usable Past." *The Dial* 64 (1918): 337–41.

Bruce, Steve. *The Rise and Fall of the New Christian Right*. Oxford, U.K.: Clarendon Press, 1988.

Bruegemann, Walter. *Old Testament Theology: The Theology of the Book of Jeremiah.* Cambridge, U.K.: Cambridge University Press, 2007.

Buchanan, John G. "Puritan Philosophy of History from Restoration to Revolution." *Essex Institute Historical Collections* 104 (1968): 329–48.

Burke, Peter. "Tradition and Experience: The Idea of Decline from Bruni to Gibbon." *Daedalus* 105 (1976): 137–52.

Burnham, Walter Dean. "The Reagan Heritage." In *The Election of 1988: Reports and Interpretations,* ed. Gerald M. Pomper, Ross K. Baker, et al. Chatham, N.J.: Chatham House Publishers, 1989.

Butler, Jon. *Awash in a Sea of Faith: Christianizing the American People.* Cambridge, Mass.: Harvard University Press, 1990.

Butler, Jon. *Becoming America: The Revolution Before 1776.* Cambridge, Mass.: Harvard University Press, 2000.

Campbell. David E., ed. *A Matter of Faith? Religion in the 2004 Presidential Election.* Washington, D.C.: Brookings Institution Press, 2007.

Canup, John. *Out of the Wilderness: The Emergence of an American Identity in Colonial New England.* Middletown, Conn.: Wesleyan University Press, 1990.

Carpenter, Joel. *Revive Us Again: The Reawakening of American Fundamentalism.* New York and Oxford: Oxford University Press, 1997.

Carr, David. *Time, Narrative, and History.* Bloomington and Indianapolis: Indiana University Press, 1986.

Carroll, Peter N. *Puritanism and the Wilderness: The Intellectual Significance of the New England Frontier, 1629–1700.* New York: Columbia University Press, 1969.

Carter, Stephen L. *The Culture of Disbelief: How American Law and Politics Trivialize Religious Devotion.* New York: Anchor, 1994.

Casey, Edward S. "The World of Nostalgia." *Man and World* 20 (1987): 361–84.

Clebsch, William A. *Christian Interpretations of the Civil War.* Philadelphia: Fortress Press, 1969.

Cole, Charles, Jr. *The Social Ideas of the Northern Evangelists, 1826–1860.* New York: Octagon, 1966.

Coleman, Simon. "Conservative Protestantism, Politics and Civil Religion in the United States." In *Questioning the Secular State: The Worldwide Resurgence of Religion in Politics,* ed. David Westerlund. New York: St. Martin's Press, 1996.

Collinson, Patrick. *The Elizabethan Puritan Movement.* Berkeley: University of California Press, 1967.

Collinson, Patrick. *The Religion of Protestants: The Church in English Society, 1559–1625.* Oxford, U.K.: Clarendon Press, 1982.

Cook, Sherburne F. "Interracial Warfare and Population Decline among the New England Indians." *Ethnohistory* 20 (1973): 1–24.

Coontz, Stephanie. *The Way We Never Were: American Families and the Nostalgia Trap.* New York: Basic, 1992.

Crites, Stephen. "The Narrative Quality of Experience." In *Why Narrative? Readings in Narrative Theology,* ed. Stanley Hauerwas and L. Gregory Jones. Grand Rapids, MI: Eerdmans, 1989.

Coutu, Richard. "Narrative, Free Space, and Political Leadership in Social Movements." *Journal of Politics* 55 (1993): 57–79.

Crapanzano, Vincent. *Serving the Word: Literalism in America from the Pulpit to the Bench.* New York: New Press, 2001.

Cronon, William. "A Place for Stories: Nature, History, and Narrative." *Journal of American History* 78 (1992): 1347–76.

D'Antonio, Michael. *Fall from Grace: The Failed Crusade of the Christian Right.* New Brunswick, N.J.: Rutgers University Press, 1992.

Davidson, James West. *The Logic of Millennial Thought: Eighteenth-Century New England*. New Haven, Conn.: Yale University Press, 1977.

Davis, David Brion. *The Slave Power Conspiracy and the Paranoid Style*. Baton Rouge: Louisiana State University Press, 1969.

Davis, Fred. *Yearning for Yesterday: A Sociology of Nostalgia*. New York: Free Press, 1979.

Davis, Nancy J., and Robert V. Robinson. "Religious Orthodoxy in American Society: The Myth of a Monolithic Camp." *Journal for the Scientific Study of Religion* 35 (1996): 229–45.

Dawson, Jan C. "The Puritan and the Cavalier: The South's Perception of Contrasting Traditions." *The Journal of Southern History* 44 (1978): 597–614.

Delbanco, Andrew. "Looking Homeward, Going Home: The Lure of England for the Founders of New England." *New England Quarterly* 59 (1986): 358–86.

Dickson, Charles Ellis. "Jeremiads in the New American Republic: The Case of National Fasts in the John Adams Administration." *New England Quarterly* 60 (1987): 187–207.

Dienstag, Joshua. *Dancing in Chains: Narrative and Memory in Political Theory*. Stanford, Calif.: Stanford University Press, 1997.

Donald, David Herbert. *Lincoln*. New York: Simon & Schuster, 1995.

Dudden, Arthur P. "Nostalgia and the American." *Journal of the History of Ideas* 22 (1961): 515–30.

Eck, Diana C. *A New Religious America: How a "Christian Nation" Has Become the World's Most Religiously Diverse Nation*. San Francisco: HarperSanFrancisco, 2002.

Egan, James. "'This is a Lamentation and Shall Be For a Lamentation': Nathaniel Ward and the Rhetoric of the Jeremiad." *Proceedings of the American Philosophical Society* 122 (1978): 400–10.

Elliot, Emory. "New England Puritan Literature." In *The Cambridge History of American Literature: Vol. I, 1590–1820*, ed. Sacvan Bercovitch. Cambridge, U.K.: Cambridge University Press, 1994.

Elliot, Emory. *Power and the Pulpit in Puritan New England*. Princeton, N.J.: Princeton University Press, 1975.

Endy, Melvin B., Jr. "Just War, Holy War, and Millennialism in Revolutionary America." *William and Mary Quarterly*. 3rd ser., 42 (1985): 3–25.

"Falwell Apologizes to Gays, Feminists, Lesbians." (2001). http://archives.cnn.com/2001/US/09/14/Falwell.apology/

Findlay, James F. "Religion and Politics in the Sixties: The Churches and the Civil Rights Act of 1964." *Journal of American History* 77 (1990): 66–92.

Fiorina, Morris P. *Culture War? The Myth of a Polarized America*. New York: Longman, 2004.

Foner, Eric. *The Story of American Freedom*. New York: W. W. Norton, 1999.

Forbes, Robert P. "Slavery and Evangelical Enlightenment." In *Religion and the Antebellum Debate over Slavery*, ed. John R. McKivigan and Michael Snay. Athens: University of Georgia Press, 1998.

Foster, Gaines M. *Moral Reconstruction: Christian Lobbyists and the Federal Legislation of Morality, 1865–1920*. Chapel Hill: University of North Carolina Press, 2002.

Foster, Stephen. *The Long Argument: English Puritanism and the Shaping of New England Culture, 1570–1700*. Chapel Hill: University of North Carolina Press, 1991.

Foster, Stephen. *Their Solitary Way: The Puritan Ethic in the First Century of Settlement in New England*. New Haven, Conn.: Yale University Press, 1971.

Fowler, Robert Booth. *Enduring Liberalism: American Political Thought Since the 1960s*. Lawrence: University Press of Kansas, 1999.

Fowler, Robert Booth. *A New Engagement: Evangelical Political Thought, 1966–1976*. Grand Rapids, Mich.: Eerdmans, 1982.

Fox-Genovese, Elizabeth, and Eugene D. Genovese. *The Mind of the Master Class: History and Faith in Southern Slaveholders' Worldview*. Cambridge, U.K.: Cambridge University Press, 2005.

Franklin, Ben E. "Pennsylvanians Lead School Prayer Revolt; Schools Defying Ban on Prayers." *New York Times*, March 26, 1969, p. 1.

Fredrickson, George M. "The Coming of the Lord: The Northern Protestant Clergy and the Civil War Crisis." In Miller et al., *Religion*.

Friedrich, Carl J., and Zbigniew L. Brzezinski. *Totalitarian Dictatorship and Autocracy*. New York: Praeger, 1961.

Gannon, Michael. *Rebel Bishop: Augustin Verot, Florida's Civil War Prelate*. Milwaukee, Wisc.: Bruce Publishing, 1964.

Genovese, Eugene D. *A Consuming Fire: The Fall of the Confederacy in the Mind of the White Christian South*. Athens: University of Georgia Press, 1998.

Genovese, Eugene D. "King Solomon's Dilemma—And the Confederacy's." *Southern Cultures* (2004): 55–75.

Genovese, Eugene D. "Religion in the Collapse of the American Union." In Miller et al., *Religion*.

Genovese, Eugene D. *Roll Jordan Roll: The World the Slaves Made*. New York: Random House, 1974.

Genovese, Eugene D. *"Slavery Ordained of God": The Southern Slaveholders' View of Biblical History and Modern Politics*. Gettysburg, Penn.: Gettysburg College, 1985.

Geoghegan, Vincent. "A Golden Age: From the Reign of Kronos to the Realm of Freedom." *History of Political Thought* 12 (1991): 189–207.

Gildrie, Richard P. "The Ceremonial Puritan: Days of Humiliation and Thanksgiving." *New England Historical and Genealogical Review* 136 (1982): 3–16.

Glaude, Eddie J. *Exodus! Religion, Race, and Nation in Early Nineteenth-Century Black America*. Chicago: University of Chicago Press, 2000.

Godbeer, Richard. "'The Cry of Sodom': Discourse, Intercourse, and Desire in Colonial New England." *William and Mary Quarterly*, 3rd ser., 52 (1995): 259–86.

Green, John C., Mark J. Rozell, and Clyde Wilcox, eds. *The Values Campaign? The Christian Right and the 2004 Elections*. Washington, D.C.: Georgetown University Press, 2006.

Greene, Jack P. *Pursuits of Happiness: The Social Development of Early Modern British Colonies and the Formation of American Culture*. Chapel Hill: University of North Carolina Press, 1988.

Greenfeld, Liah. *Nationalism: Five Roads to Modernity*. Cambridge, Mass.: Harvard University Press, 1993.

Gribbin, William. "The Covenant Transformed: The Jeremiad Tradition and the War of 1812." *Church History* 40 (1971): 297–305.

Guelzo, Allen. *Abraham Lincoln: Redeemer President*. Grand Rapids, Mich.: Eerdmans, 1999.

Guelzo, Allen. *Lincoln and Douglas: The Debates That Defined America*. New York: Simon & Schuster, 2008.

Guelzo, Allen. *Lincoln's Emancipation Proclamation: The End of Slavery in America*. New York: Simon & Schuster, 2004.

Gutterman, David S. *Prophetic Politics: Christian Social Movements and American Democracy*. Ithaca, N.Y.: Cornell University Press, 2005.

Guyatt, Nicholas. *Providence and the Invention of the United States, 1607–1686*. New York: Cambridge University Press, 2007.

Hadden, Jeffrey K. "Religious Broadcasting and the Rise of the New Christian Right." *Journal for the Scientific Study of Religion* 26 (1987): 1–24.

Hall, David D. *Worlds of Wonder, Days of Judgment: Popular Religious Belief in Early New England*. New York: Alfred A. Knopf, 1989.

Hall, Michael G. *The Last American Puritan: The Life of Increase Mather, 1639–1723*. Middletown, Conn.: Wesleyan University Press, 1988.

Hamburger, Philip. *Separation of Church and State*. Cambridge, Mass.: Harvard University Press, 2002.

Hammer, Dean C. "The Puritans as Founders: The Quest for Identity in Early Whig Rhetoric." *Religion and American Culture* 6 (1996): 161–94.

Hanley, Mark Y. *Beyond a Christian Commonwealth: The Protestant Quarrel with the American Republic, 1830–1860*. Chapel Hill: University of North Carolina Press, 1994.

Harding, Susan Friend. *The Book of Jerry Falwell: Fundamentalist Language and Politics*. Princeton, N.J.: Princeton University Press, 2000.

Hatch, Nathan O. *The Democratization of American Christianity*. New Haven, Conn.: Yale University Press, 1989.

Hatch, Nathan O. *The Sacred Cause of Liberty: Republican Thought and the Millennium in Revolutionary New England*. New Haven, Conn.: Yale University Press, 1977.

Hauerwas, Stanley. *A Community of Character: Toward a Constructive Christian Social Ethic*. Notre Dame, Ind.: University of Notre Dame Press, 1981.

Henretta, James. "The Morphology of New England Society in the Colonial Period." *Journal of Interdisciplinary History* 2 (1971): 379–98.

Herman, Arthur. *The Idea of Decline in Western History*. New York: The Free Press, 1997.

Herrick, Genevieve Forbes, and John Origen Herrick. *The Life of William Jennings Bryan*. Whitefish, Mont.: Kessinger, 2005.

Hertzke, Allen D. *Echoes of Discontent: Jesse Jackson, Pat Robertson, and the Resurgence of Populism*. Washington, D.C.: Congressional Quarterly Press, 1993.

Hertzke, Allen D. *Freeing God's Children: The Unlikely Alliance for Global Human Rights*. Lanham, Md.: Rowman & Littlefield Publishers, 2004.

Higham, John. *Hanging Together: Unity and Diversity in American Culture*. New Haven, Conn.: Yale University Press, 2001.

Holland, Matthew S. *Bonds of Affection: Civic Charity and the Making of America—Winthrop, Jefferson, and Lincoln*. Washington, D.C.: Georgetown University Press, 2007.

Hollinger, David A. *Postethnic America: Beyond Multiculturalism*. New York: Basic, 1995.

Hopson, Ronald E., and Donald R. Smith. "Changing Fortunes: An Analysis of Christian Right Ascendance within American Political Discourse." *Journal for the Scientific Study of Religion* 38 (1999): 1–13.

Howard-Pitney, David. *The African American Jeremiad: Appeals for Justice in America*, rev. ed. Philadelphia: Temple University Press, 2005.

Howard-Pitney, David. "The Jeremiads of Frederick Douglass, Booker T. Washington, and W.E.B. Du Bois and Changing Patterns of Black Messianic Rhetoric, 1841–1920." *Journal of American Ethnic History* 6 (1986): 47–61.

Howe, Daniel Walker. *The Political Culture of the American Whigs*. Chicago: University of Chicago Press, 1979.

Howe, Daniel Walker. *What Hath God Wrought: The Transformation of America, 1815–1848*. New York: Oxford University Press, 2007.

Hudson, Winthrop S. "Fast Days and Civil Religion." In *Theology in Sixteenth- and Seventeenth-Century England. Papers Read at a Clark Library Seminar, February 6, 1971*. Los Angeles: William Andrews Clark Memorial Library, 1971.

Hughes, Richard T., ed. *The American Quest for the Primitive Church*. Urbana: University of Illinois Press, 1988.

Hughes, Richard T. *Myths America Lives By*. Urbana: University of Illinois Press, 2002.

Hunter, James Davison. *Before the Shooting Begins: Searching for Democracy in America's Culture Wars*. New York: Free Press, 1994.

Hunter, James Davison. *Culture Wars: The Struggle to Define America*. New York: Basic Books, 1991.

Hunter, James Davison. *Evangelicalism: The Coming Generation*. Chicago: University of Chicago Press, 1987.

Hunter, James Davison, and Alan Wolfe. *Is There a Culture War? A Dialogue on Values and Public Life*. Washington, D.C.: Brookings Institution Press, 2006.

Hunter, James Davison, and David Franz. "Religious Pluralism and Civil Society." In Prothero, *Nation of Religions*.

Huntington, Samuel P. *Who Are We? The Challenges to America's National Identity*. New York: Simon & Schuster, 2004.

Hutchinson, William R., and Hartmut Lehmann, eds, *Many are Chosen: Divine Election and Western Nationalism* (Harvard Theological Studies 38). Minneapolis, Minn.: Fortress Press, 1994.

Jenkins, Philip. *Decade of Nightmares: The End of the Sixties and the Making of Eighties America*. New York: Oxford University Press, 2006.

Jewett, Robert S. *The Captain America Complex: The Dilemma of Zealous Nationalism*. Philadelphia: Westminster Press, 1973.

Jewett, Robert S. *Mission and Menace: Four Centuries of American Religious Zeal*. Minneapolis, Minn.: Fortress Press, 2008.

Jewett, Robert S., and John Shelton Lawrence. *Captain America and the Crusade Against Evil: The Dilemmas of Zealous Nationalism*. Grand Rapids, Mich.: Eerdmans, 2004.

Kazin, Alfred. *God and the American Writer*. New York: Alfred A. Knopf, 1997.

Kazin, Michael. *A Godly Hero: The Life of William Jennings Bryan*. New York: Knopf, 2006.

Kort, Wesley A. *Narrative Elements and Religious Meaning*. Philadelphia: Fortress Press, 1975.

Kurien, Prema A. "Mr. President, Why Do You Exclude Us From Your Prayers? Hindus Challenge American Pluralism." In Prothero, *Nation of Religions*.

Lambert, Frank J. *The Founding Fathers and the Place of Religion in America*. Princeton, N.J.: Princeton University Press, 2003.

Lasch, Christopher. *The True and Only Heaven: Progress and Its Critics*. New York: Norton, 1991.

Layman, Geoffrey C. *The Great Divide: Religious and Cultural Conflict in American Party Politics*. New York: Columbia University Press, 2001.

Layman, Geoffrey C. "Religion and Political Behavior in the United States: The Impact of Beliefs, Affiliations, and Commitments from 1980 to 1994." *Public Opinion Quarterly* 61 (1997): 288–316.

Leboe, Jason P., and Tamara L. Ansons. "On Misattributing Good Remembering to a Happy Past: An Investigation into the Cognitive Roots of Nostalgia." *Emotion* 6 (2006): 596–610.

Leege, David C., Kenneth D. Wald, Brian S. Krueger, and Paul D. Mueller. *The Politics of Cultural Differences: Social Change and Voter Mobilization Strategies in the Post–New Deal Period*. Princeton, N.J.: Princeton University Press, 2002.

Leonard, Karen I., Alex Stepick, Manuel A. Vasquez, and Jennifer Holdaway, eds. *Immigrant Faiths: Transforming Religious Life in America*. New York: AltaMira/Rowman & Littlefield, 2005.

Lepore, Jill. "Dead Men Tell No Tales: John Sassamon and the Fatal Consequences of Literacy." *American Quarterly* 46 (1994): 479–512.

Lepore, Jill. *The Name of War: King Philip's War and the Origins of American Identity.* New York: Alfred A. Knopf, 1998.

Levine, Bruce. *Confederate Emancipation: Southern Plans to Free and Arm Slaves During the Civil War.* New York: Oxford University Press, 2006.

Lienesch, Michael. *Redeeming America: Piety and Politics in the New Christian Right.* Chapel Hill: University of North Carolina Press, 1993.

Lincoln, Bruce. *Holy Terrors: Thinking about Religion After September 11.* Chicago: University of Chicago Press, 2003.

Lovejoy, David S. *The Glorious Revolution in America.* Middletown, Conn.: Wesleyan University Press/University Press of New England, 1987.

Lowenthal, David. *The Past Is a Foreign Country.* Cambridge, U.K.: Cambridge University Press, 1987.

Maclear, J. F. "The Republic and the Millennium." In *The Religion of the Republic,* ed. Elwyn A. Smith. Philadelphia: Fortress Press, 1971.

McConnell, Michael. "Accommodation of Religion: An Update and a Response to the Critics." 60 *George Washington Law Review* 685 (1992).

McConville, Brendan. *The King's Three Faces: The Rise and Fall of Royal America, 1688–1776.* Chapel Hill: University of North Carolina Press, 2006.

McGreevy, John. *Catholicism and American Freedom: A History.* New York: W. W. Norton, 2003.

McKenna, George. *The Puritan Origins of American Patriotism.* New Haven, Conn.: Yale University Press, 2007.

Marsden, George. *Fundamentalism and American Culture.* 2nd ed. New York: Oxford University Press, 2006.

Martin, William. "The Christian Right and American Foreign Policy." *Foreign Policy* 114 (1999): 66–80.

Mead, Walter Russell. "God's Country?" *Foreign Affairs* 85 (2006): 24–43.

Miller, Alan S., and John P. Hoffmann. "The Growing Divisiveness: Culture Wars or a War of Words?" *Social Forces* 78 (1999): 721–45.

Miller, Perry. "Declension in a Bible Commonwealth." In *Nature's Nation.* Cambridge, Mass.: Belknap Press of Harvard University Press, 1967.

Miller, Perry. *Errand into the Wilderness.* Cambridge, Mass.: Harvard University Press, 1956.

Miller, Perry. *The New England Mind: From Colony to Province.* Cambridge, Mass.: Belknap Press of Harvard University Press, 1953.

Miller, Perry. *The New England Mind: The Seventeenth Century.* Cambridge, Mass.: Harvard University Press, 1939.

Miller, Randall M., Harry S. Stout, and Charles Reagan Wilson, eds. *Religion and the American Civil War.* New York and Oxford: Oxford University Press, 1998.

Minter, David. "The Puritan Jeremiad as a Literary Form." In *The American Puritan Imagination: Essays in Revaluation,* ed. Sacvan Bercovitch. London and New York: Cambridge University Press, 1974.

Mohr, Richard D. *The Long Arc of Justice: Lesbian and Gay Marriage, Equality, and Rights.* New York: Columbia University Press, 2005.

Moorhead, James H. *American Apocalypse: Yankee Protestants and the Civil War, 1860–1869.* New Haven, Conn.: Yale University Press, 1978.

Moorhead, James H. "The American Israel: Protestant Tribalism and Universal Mission." In Hutchinson and Lehmann, *Many Are Chosen.*

Morgan, David. *Protestants and Pictures: Religion, Visual Culture, and the Age of American Mass Production.* New York: Oxford University Press, 1999.

Morgan, Edmund S. "The Puritan Ethic and the American Revolution." *William and Mary Quarterly*, 3rd ser., 24 (1967): 3–43.

Morone, James. *Hellfire Nation: The Politics of Sin in American History*. New Haven and London: Yale University Press, 2003.

Muirhead, Russell, Nancy L. Rosenblum, Daniel Schlozman, and Francis X. Shen. "Religion in the 2004 Presidential Election." In *Divided States of America: The Slash and Burn Politics of the 2004 Presidential Election*. New York: Pearson Longman, 2006.

Murphy, Andrew R. "Augustine and the Rhetoric of Roman Decline." *History of Political Thought* 26: 4 (2005): 586–606. [Reprinted in *Augustine and History*, ed. Kim Paffenroth and John Doody. Lanham, Md.: Lexington Books, 2006.]

Murphy, Andrew R. *Conscience and Community: Revisiting Toleration and Religious Dissent in Early Modern England and America*. University Park: Penn State University Press, 2001.

Murphy, Andrew R. "Environmentalism and the Recurrent Rhetoric of Decline." *Environmental Ethics* 25 (2003): 79–98.

Murphy, Andrew R. "Religion and the Presidency of Abraham Lincoln." In *Religion and the American Presidency*, ed. Gaston Espinosa. New York: Columbia University Press, 2008.

Murphy, John M. "'A Time of Shame and Sorrow': Robert F. Kennedy and the American Jeremiad." *Quarterly Journal of Speech* 79 (1990): 401–14.

Nash, Roderick. *The Rights of Nature: A History of Environmental Ethics*. Madison: University of Wisconsin Press, 1989.

Nelsen, Ann Kusener. "King Philip's War and the Hubbard-Mather Rivalry." *William and Mary Quarterly*, 3rd ser., 27 (1970): 615–29.

Niebuhr, Reinhold, and Alan Heimert, *A Nation So Conceived: Reflections on the History of America from its Early Visions to its Present Power*. New York: Charles Scribner's Sons, 1963.

Noll, Mark A. *America's God: From Jonathan Edwards to Abraham Lincoln*. New York and Oxford: Oxford University Press, 2002.

Noll, Mark A. "The Bible and Slavery." In Miller et al., *Religion*.

Noll, Mark A. *The Civil War as a Theological Crisis*. Chapel Hill: University of North Carolina Press, 2005.

Noll, Mark A, ed. *God and Mammon: Protestants, Money, and the Market, 1790–1860*. Oxford, U.K.: Oxford University Press, 2001.

Nord, David Paul. *Faith in Reading: Religious Publishing and the Birth of Mass Media in America*. Oxford and New York: Oxford University Press, 2004.

O'Neill, Jonathan. *Originalism in American Law and Politics: A Constitutional History*. Baltimore: Johns Hopkins University Press, 2005.

The Oxford English Dictionary. 2nd ed. Prepared by J.A. Simpson and E.S.C. Weiner. 20 vols. Oxford, U.K.: Oxford University Press, 1989.

Paludan, Phillip Shaw. "Religion and the American Civil War." In Miller et al., *Religion*.

Pestana, Carla Gardina. *Quakers and Baptists in Colonial Massachusetts*. New York: Cambridge University Press, 1991.

Pfaff, William. "Manifest Destiny: A New Direction for America." *New York Review of Books*, February 15, 2007, 54–59.

Pope, Robert G. "New England versus the New England Mind: The Myth of Declension." In Vaughan and Bremer, *Puritan New England*.

Pope, Robert G. *The Halfway Covenant: Church Membership in New England*. Princeton, N.J.: Princeton University Press, 1970.

Prothero, Stephen, ed. *A Nation of Religions: The Politics of Pluralism in Multireligious America*, Chapel Hill: University of North Carolina Press, 2006.

Putney, Clifford. *Muscular Christianity: Manhood and Sports in Protestant America, 1880–1920*. Cambridge, Mass.: Harvard University Press, 2001.

Raboteau, Albert J. *Slave Religion: The "Invisible Institution" in the Antebellum South*. Rev. ed. Oxford, U.K.: Oxford University Press, 2004.

Rehnquist, William H. "The Notion of a Living Constitution." 54 *Texas Law Review* (1976): 693–706.

Renshon, Stanley A. "America at a Crossroads: Political Leadership, National Identity, and the Decline of Common Culture." In *One America? Political Leadership, National Identity, and the Dilemmas of Diversity*, ed. Stanley A. Renshon. Washington, D.C.: Georgetown University Press, 2001.

Richards, David A. J. *The Case for Gay Rights: From* Bowers *to* Lawrence *and Beyond*. Lawrence: University Press of Kansas, 2007.

Roberts, William. *Memoirs of the Life and Correspondence of Mrs. Hannah More*. 4 vols. London: R. B. Seeley and W. Burnside, 1834.

Ronda, James P., and Jeanne Ronda. "The Death of John Sassamon: An Exploration in Writing New England Indian History." *American Indian Quarterly* 1 (1974): 91–102.

Rose, Anne C. *Voices of the Marketplace: American Thought and Culture, 1830–1860*. Lanham, Md.: Rowman & Littlefield, 2004.

Rosenmeier, Jesper. " 'New England's Perfection': The Image of Adam and the Image of Christ in the Antinomian Crisis, 1634 to 1638." *William and Mary Quarterly* 27 (1970): 435–59.

Rozell, Mark J., and Clyde Wilcox, eds. *God at the Grass Roots: The Christian Right in the 1994 Elections*. Lanham, Md.: Rowman & Littlefield, 1995.

Rozell, Mark J., and Clyde Wilcox, eds. *God at the Grass Roots, 1996*. Lanham, Md.: Rowman & Littlefield, 1997.

Rubin, Anne Sarah. *A Shattered Nation: The Rise and Fall of the Confederacy, 1861–1868*. Chapel Hill: University of North Carolina Press, 2005.

Safi, Omid. "Progressive Islam in America." In Prothero, *Nation of Religions*.

Sassi, Jonathan D. *A Republic of Righteousness: The Public Christianity of the Post-Revolutionary New England Clergy*. New York: Oxford University Press, 2001.

Schlesinger, Arthur, Jr. *The Age of Jackson*. Boston: Little, Brown, 1945.

Schlesinger, Arthur J., Jr. *The Dis-Uniting of America: Reflections on a Multicultural Society*. New York: Norton, 1998.

Schmidt, Leigh Eric. *Restless Souls: The Making of American Spirituality*. San Francisco: HarperSanFrancisco, 2005.

Sedikides, Constantine, Tim Wildschut, and Denise Baden. "Nostalgia: Conceptual Issues and Existential Functions." In *Handbook of Experimental Existential Psychology*, ed. Jeff Greenberg, Sander L. Koole, and Tom Pyszczynski. New York: Guilford Press, 2004.

Shibley, Mark A. "Contemporary Evangelicals: Born-Again and World-Affirming." *Annals of the American Academy of Political and Social Science* 558 (1998): 67–87.

Silk, Mark. "Notes on the Judeo-Christian Tradition in America." *American Quarterly* 36 (1984): 65–85.

Simmons, William S. "Cultural Bias in the New England Puritans' Perceptions of Indians." *William and Mary Quarterly*, 3rd ser., 38 (1981): 56–72.

Smith, Anthony D. *Chosen Peoples*. Oxford, U.K.: Oxford University Press, 2003.

Smith, Anthony D. "Ethnic Election and National Destiny: Some Religious Origins of Nationalist Ideals." *Nations and Nationalism* 5 (1999): 331–55.

Smith, Anthony D. *Myths and Memories of the Nation*. Oxford, U.K.: Oxford University Press, 1999.

Smith, Christian. *Christian America? What Evangelicals Really Want*. Berkeley: University of California Press, 2000.

Smith, Christian, ed. *The Secular Revolution: Power, Interests, and Conflict in the Secularization of American Public Life*. Berkeley and Los Angeles: University of California Press, 2003.

Smith, Timothy L. *Revivalism and Social Reform: American Protestantism on the Eve of the Civil War*. Baltimore: Johns Hopkins University Press, 1980.

Spengler, Oswald. *The Decline of the West*. 2 vols. Transl. C. F. Atkinson. New York: Knopf, 1926–1928.

Stout, Harry S. *The New England Soul: Preaching and Religious Culture in Colonial New England*. New York and Oxford: Oxford University Press, 1986.

Stout, Harry S. *Upon the Altar of the Nation: A Moral History of the Civil War*. New York: Viking, 2006.

Stowell, Daniel L. "Stonewall Jackson and the Providence of God." In Miller et al., *Religion*.

Stowell, Daniel L. "'We Have Sinned, and God Has Smitten us!' John H. Caldwell and the Religious Meaning of Confederate Defeat." *The Georgia Historical Quarterly* 78 (1994): 1–38.

Striner, Richard. *Father Abraham: Lincoln's Relentless Struggle to End Slavery*. New York: Oxford University Press, 2006.

Strum, Philippa, and Danielle Tarantolo. *Muslims in the United States: Demography, Beliefs, Institutions*. Washington, D.C.: Woodrow Wilson International Center for Scholars, 2003.

Sunstein, Cass R. *The Second Bill of Rights: FDR's Unfinished Revolution and Why We Need it More than Ever*. New York: Basic, 2004.

Swarns, Rachel L. "Congressman Criticizes Election of Muslim." *New York Times*, 21 December 2006, online at http://www.nytimes.com/2006/12/21/us/21koran.html?ex=1173243600&en=10e04d59d526678a&ei=5070

Sweet, Leonard. "The Modernization of Protestant Religion in America." In *Altered Landscapes: Christianity in America, 1935–1985*, ed. David W. Lotz, Donald W. Shriver, and John F. Wilson. Grand Rapids, Mich.: Eerdmans, 1989.

Toolan, Michael J. *Narrative: A Critical Linguistic Introduction*. London and New York: Routledge, 1988.

Toplin, Robert Brent. *Radical Conservatism: The Right's Political Religion*. Lawrence: University Press of Kansas, 2006.

Tudor, Henry. *Political Myth*. London: Pall Mall, 1972.

Tuveson, Ernest Lee. *Redeemer Nation: The Idea of America's Millenial Role*. Chicago and London: University of Chicago Press, 1968.

Tweed, Thomas A., ed. *Retelling U.S. Religious History*. Berkeley: University of California Press, 1997.

van Seters, John. "Historiography in Ancient Israel." In *A Companion to Western Historical Thought*, ed. Lloyd Kramer and Sarah Maza. Malden, Mass., and Oxford, U.K.: Blackwell, 2002.

Vaughan, Alden T., and Francis J. Bremer, ed. *Puritan New England: Essays in Religion, Society, and Culture*. New York: St. Martin's Press, 1977.

Wagner, Peter. "The Jeremiad and Social Reality in Mid-Seventeenth-Century New England." In *Studies in New England Puritanism*, ed. Winfried Herget. Frankfurt: Verlag Peter Lang, 1983.

Wall, James. "Editorial." *The Christian Century*, December 4, 1996.

Walsham, Alexandra. *Providence in Early Modern England*. Oxford, U.K.: Oxford University Press, 1999.

Warner, R. Steven. "The De-Europeanization of American Christianity." In Prothero, *Nation of Religions*.

Washburn, Wilcomb E. "Governor Berkeley and King Philip's War." *New England Quarterly* 30 (1957): 363–77.

Watson, Justin. *The Christian Coalition: Dreams of Restoration, Demands for Recognition*. New York: St. Martin's, 1997.

White, Hayden. *The Content of the Form: Narrative Discourse and Historical Representation*. Baltimore: Johns Hopkins University Press, 1987.

Whitman, Walt. *Democratic Vistas*. In *Prose Works 1892. Volume II: Collect and Other Prose*, ed. Floyd Stovall. *The Collected Writings of Walt Whitman*. New York: NYU Press, 2007.

Whittington, Keith E. *Constitutional Interpretation: Textual Meaning, Original Intent, and Judicial Review*. Lawrence: University Press of Kansas, 1999.

Wight, Willard E. "The Churches and the Confederate Cause." *Civil War History* 6 (1960): 361–73.

Wilcox, Clyde, and Carin Larson. *Onward Christian Soldiers? The Christian Right in American Politics*. 3rd ed. Boulder, Colo.: Westview Press, 2006.

Wildschut, Tim, Constantine Sedikides, Jamie Arndt, and Clay Routledge. "Nostalgia: Content, Triggers, Functions." *Journal of Personality and Social Psychology* 91 (2006): 975–93.

Wilson, Charles Reagan. *Baptized in Blood: The Religion of the Lost Cause, 1865–1920*. Athens: University of Georgia Press, 1980.

Wilson, Edmund. *Patriotic Gore: Studies in the Literature of the American Civil War*. New York: Oxford University Press, 1962.

Winship, Michael P. "'The Most Glorious Church in the World': The Unity of the Godly in Boston, Massachusetts, in the 1630s." *Journal of British Studies* 39 (2000): 71–98.

Winship, Michael P. *Seers of God: Puritan Providentialism in the Restoration and Early Enlightenment*. Baltimore: Johns Hopkins University Press, 1996.

Winship, Michael P. "Were There Any Puritans in New England?" *New England Quarterly* 74 (2001): 118–38.

Wolf, William J. *The Almost Chosen People: A Study of the Religion of Abraham Lincoln*. Garden City, N.Y.: Doubleday, 1959.

Wolfe, Alan. *Moral Freedom: The Impossible Idea That Defines the Way We Live Now*. New York: Norton, 2001.

Wolfe, Alan. *One Nation After All: What Middle-Class Americans Really Think About God, Country, Family, Racism, Welfare, Immigration, Homosexuality, Work, the Right, the Left, and Each Other*. New York: Viking, 1998.

Wolin, Sheldon. "Contract and Birthright," *Political Theory* 14 (1986): 179–93.

Wood, Gordon S. *The Radicalism of the American Revolution*. New York: Knopf, 1991.

Woodberry, Robert D., and Christian Smith. "Fundamentalism et al.: Conservative Protestants in America." *Annual Review of Sociology* 24 (1998): 25–56.

Woodworth, Steven E. *While God Is Marching On: The Religious World of Civil War Soldiers*. Lawrence: University Press of Kansas, 2001.

Wright, Joanne H. *Origin Stories in Political Thought: Discourses on Gender, Power, and Citizenship*. Toronto: University of Toronto Press, 2004.

Wuthnow, Robert C. *The Restructuring of American Religion*. Princeton, N.J.: Princeton University Press, 1988.

Yack, Bernard. "Liberalism and Its Communitarian Critics: Does Liberal Practice 'Live Down' to Liberal Theory?" In *Community in America: The Challenge of*

Habits of the Heart, ed. C.H. Reynolds and R.V. Norman. Berkeley: University of California Press, 1988.

Young, Michael P. *Bearing Witness Against Sin: The Evangelical Birth of the American Social Movement*. Chicago: University of Chicago Press, 2006.

Supreme Court Decisions

Cantwell v. Connecticut, 310 U. S. 296 (1940).

Engel v. Vitale, 370 U.S. 421 (1962).

Lawrence v. Texas, 39 U.S. 558 (2003).

School District of Abington Township v. Schempp et al., 374 U.S. 203 (1963).

Index

"Judeo-Christian" values, 79, 80, 88–89, 93, 94, 96, 99, 100, 129, 134, 135, 143, 152, 154, 164, 168, 170
Justice Sunday, 100
Juvenal, 133

Kansas-Nebraska Act, 59, 60, 65–66, 69
Katrina (Hurricane), 3, 4, 5, 14
Kazin, Alfred, 74
Kennedy, D. James, 86, 106. See also Center for Reclaiming America for Christ; Coral Ridge Presbyterian Church
Kennedy, Robert, 12
Keteltas, Abraham, 41
King, Martin Luther, Jr., 8–9, 12, 117–118, 119, 121, 129, 138–141, 152, 161, 165, 168, 171
King, Rodney, 77
King Philip's War, 18, 19–20, 23, 25, 34, 39, 79, 175 n. 7
Kiwanis Club, 113
Koran, 162, 163
Koreatown (Los Angeles), 154
Kort, Wesley, 120

Lambert, Frank, 158
Langdon, Samuel, 42, 180 n. 64
Lawrence, John Shelton, 159
Lawrence v. Texas, 90. See also gay/lesbian rights
Lawson, Alexander, 187 n. 53
Layman, Geoffrey, 151, 153
Leboe, Jason, 131
Lee, Robert E., 49
Leege, David, 150–151
Lepore, Jill, 175 n. 7–8
lesbians, 4, 90. See also gay/lesbian rights; gay marriage
liberty, religious, 100, 126, 129, 158
Limbaugh, Rush, 7, 144
Lincoln, Abraham, 45, 47, 48, 50, 59, 60, 61–62, 69, 71–74, 103, 111, 121, 123, 138–139, 141, 182 n. 21
  on the Constitution, 57–58
  Cooper Union speech, 47, 75–76
  Emancipation Proclamation, 58, 72, 73
  First Inaugural, 56, 72, 73, 171
  Gettysburg Address, 165
  on Jefferson and the Declaration of Independence, 57–58

"Meditation on the Divine Will," 73
  as practitioner of progressive jeremiad, 114–116, 117–118, 138
  providentialism of, 72–74, 188 n. 76
  Second Inaugural, 12, 73, 74, 80
literalism, 76, 104–105
living constitution, 104
Locke, John, 102
"long civic generation," 121. See also Putnam, Robert
Los Angeles riots, 77–79
Lost Cause. See jeremiad, Southern
Louisiana Purchase, 49
Lowenthal, David, 134
Luke (gospel), 161
luxury (as sinful), 27–28, 46, 54, 136

Maclear, J. F., 63, 182 n. 17
Madison, James, 96, 115, 126, 127, 158
Malcolm X, 13
Manifest Destiny, 13, 159
marriage. See family, traditional; gay marriage
Mather, Cotton, 5, 25, 40, 41, 158, 159
Mather, Eleazar, 31, 34, 37, 158
Mather, Increase, 17–20, 25, 26, 27, 28, 34, 39, 110, 121, 136, 157, 158, 174 n. 2, 179 n. 59
  Brief History of the Warr with the Indians, 19
  Earnest Exhortation, 19–20, 175 n. 9
  on Halfway Covenant, 130
Mayflower Compact, 96, 101
McClellan, Vern, 101
McGill, Alexander, 48
McKenna, George, 157, 158
McKinley, William, 161
media,
  bias in, 91, 93–94
  violence in, 88, 93–94, 99
  See also Christian Right
Medicaid, 91, 105
Methodists, in early New England, 113
Mexican War, 49, 54
millennialism, 10–11, 62–63, 65, 68, 87
Miller, Perry, 21, 36–37, 137, 167
Miller, Zell, 92, 93–94
Mines, John Flavell, 47
minorities, religious, 100, 168–169, 193 n. 5
Minter, David, 110
Mitchell, Jonathan, 33–34

Wall Builders, 9, 86. *See also* Barton, David
Walley, Thomas, 27, 28
Wallis, Jim, 146
Wampanoags, 19
Washington, George, 9, 14, 47, 56, 62, 96, 115, 158
Watson, Justin, 105, 112
Watergate, 97, 101, 133
Webster, Daniel, 56
welfare state, growth of, 97, 101, 133
Weigel, George, 89, 91
Welles, Gideon, 72
Whigs, 42, 49
Whiting, John, 25
Whitman, Walt, 171
Williams, Roger, 136
Wilson, Charles Reagan, 70
Wilson, John, 136
Wilson, Woodrow, 160
Winship, Michael P., 175 n. 13, 179 n. 57

Winthrop, John, 10, 29, 31, 33, 63, 101, 119, 158, 178 n. 37
Wolfe, Alan, 95, 150, 153
Wolin, Sheldon, 116
Women's Christian Temperance Union, 81
women's rights movement, 49, 145, 154, 168
Woodworth, Steven, 55
worldliness, 18–19, 27–8, 33, 40, 54, 55, 71, 136, 183 n. 24
World War I, 81, 160
World War II, 80, 96, 116, 121, 137, 150, 151
Wuthnow, Robert, 149

YMCA, 82

"zealous nationalism." *See* "Captain America" complex